Blessing

Corporate
Entrepreneurship

Corporate
Entrepreneurship

How to Create a Thriving
Entrepreneurial Spirit
Throughout Your Company

ROBERT D. HISRICH
AND CLAUDINE KEARNEY

New York   Chicago   San Francisco   Lisbon   London
Madrid   Mexico City   Milan   New Delhi   San Juan
Seoul   Singapore   Sydney   Toronto

1 2 3 4 5 6 7 8 9 10   DOC/DOC 1 9 8 7 6 5 4 3 2 1

ISBN   978-0-07176316-5
MHID   0-07-176316-3

e-ISBN   978-0-07-176687-6
e-MHID   0-07-176687-1

McGraw-Hill books are available at special quantity discounts to use as premiums and sales promotions or for use in corporate training programs. To contact a representative, please e-mail us at bulksales@mcgraw-hill.com.

This book is printed on acid-free paper.

Dedication

To Tina Hisrich; Kary and Katy Hisrich; Kelly, Rich, Rachel, and Andrew Nash; Kaiya; and Patricia and Syl Kearney.

May you always think entrepreneurially.

Contents

Preface   ix

Part One
Managing Corporate Entrepreneurship

1 Entrepreneurship and Corporate Entrepreneurship   3

2 Behavioral Aspects of Corporate Entrepreneurship   31

3 Understanding and Managing the
   Entrepreneurial Process   57

4 Identifying, Evaluating, and Selecting the Opportunity 89

Part Two
Organizing Corporate Entrepreneurship

5 Locating the Venture in the Organization   119

6 Organizing the Venture   135

7 Controlling the Venture   159

8 The Internal Politics of Venturing   183

Part Three
Operationalizing Corporate Entrepreneurship

9 Developing the Business Plan   207

10 Selecting, Evaluating, and Compensating
Corporate Entrepreneurs   231

11 Funding the Venture   257

12 Implementing Corporate Venturing in
Your Organization   279

Notes   305

Suggested Readings   309

Index   325

Preface

While starting and operating a new venture in one's own country or globally involves considerable risk and energy to overcome all the obstacles involved, a similar degree of risk and energy is involved in corporate entrepreneurship—entrepreneurship in an existing organization. Corporate entrepreneurship, which has also been called *intrapreneurship* and *corporate venturing*, involves overcoming the inertia, rigidity, rules and regulations, and bureaucratic nature of an existing organization to create something new—a new way of doing things, a new system, and sometimes a new product or service. This becomes increasingly important in a global, hypercompetitive environment.

While entrepreneurship has traditionally been viewed as a private sector phenomenon, corporate and social entrepreneurship have developed in a number of different domains, such as not-for-profits, for-profits, and public sector organizations. Entrepreneurship is a universal concept and can be applied in small and medium-sized enterprises (SMEs), large national and multinational organizations, as well as in social ventures, enterprises, communities, and governments. Entrepreneurship is not limited to a select group of people; any person with the right orientation, drive, and motivation can develop an entrepreneurial perspective and mindset. This perspective and mindset identify a need and transform it from a creative and innovative idea into reality.

In organizations, nations, and markets, entrepreneurs challenge existing assumptions and look to generate value in more innovative and creative ways. Entrepreneurs change the way business is conducted by identifying opportunities and successfully filling them. Organizations need to renew themselves in order to sustain competitiveness. This can take such forms as championing innovative ideas, providing necessary resources or expertise, or institutionalizing the entrepreneurial activity within the organization's systems and processes.

To fully cover this topic of corporate entrepreneurship, the book is divided into three parts and twelve chapters. Part One, "Managing Corporate Entrepreneurship," contains four chapters: "Entrepreneurship and Corporate Entrepreneurship" (Chapter 1), "Behavioral Aspects of Corporate Entrepreneurship" (Chapter 2), "Understanding and Managing the Entrepreneurial Process" (Chapter 3), and "Identifying, Evaluating, and Selecting the Opportunity" (Chapter 4).

Part Two, "Organizing Corporate Entrepreneurship," contains four chapters as well: "Locating the Venture in the Organization" (Chapter 5), "Organizing the Venture" (Chapter 6), "Controlling the Venture" (Chapter 7), and "The Internal Politics of Venturing" (Chapter 8).

Finally Part Three, "Operationalizing Corporate Entrepreneurship," also contains four chapters: "Developing the Business Plan" (Chapter 9), "Selecting, Evaluating, and Compensating Corporate Entrepreneurs" (Chapter 10), "Funding the Venture" (Chapter 11), and "Implementing Corporate Venturing in Your Organization" (Chapter 12).

Many individuals—corporate executives, entrepreneurs, small business managers, professors from all over the world, and the publishing staff—have made this book possible. Our special thanks go to the research assistants Nicole Baum, Vilayphone Douangpangna, and Debra Wheat; Professor Frank Roche, for his advice;

and to our editors and editorial assistants. Our utmost appreciation goes to Carol Pacelli, without whom this book would never have been prepared in a timely manner.

Robert D. Hisrich
Claudine Kearney

Part One

Managing Corporate Entrepreneurship

1

Entrepreneurship and Corporate Entrepreneurship

What is meant by the term corporate entrepreneurship? What are the similarities and differences between private, corporate, and social entrepreneurs/entrepreneurship? How does an entrepreneur differ from a manager? What is the entrepreneurial process in a private, corporate, and social context? To what extent does this context influence the entrepreneurial process?

Scenario: Loctite Corporation

Fritz Henkel and his two partners founded Henkel & Cie in Aachen on September 26, 1876. Since then, this German family of entrepreneurs and their employees built Henkel into a global company, which is headquartered in Düsseldorf, Germany. It has 48,000 employees worldwide and is ranked among the Fortune Global 500. Henkel is a global leader in the consumer and industrial businesses with brands such as Persil, Schwarzkopf, and Loctite.

The Loctite brand is a registered trademark of Henkel and is one of its largest global brands. For 58 years, Loctite Corporation has provided customers with advanced adhesive and sealing solutions. It is committed to innovation with over 5,000 patents. It provides the most extensive range of premium quality acrylics, anaerobics, cyanoacrylates, epoxies, aerosols, silicones, and urethanes. While Loctite's success comes from its consumer products, predominately Super Glue, the company derives the majority of its sales from industrial customers. Loctite's products are used in diverse industrial applications ranging from electronics to cosmetics.

Loctite Corporation (formerly called American Sealants) was originally founded in 1953 by Vernon K. Krieble, a chemistry professor of German descent at Trinity College in Hartford, Connecticut. This entrepreneurial chemistry professor discovered a revolutionary anaerobic adhesive. He developed a cure inhibition system for a unique bonding resin that hardened in the absence of air—an anaerobic sealant. On July 26, 1956, Loctite made its official public debut at a press conference at the University Club in New York. Professor Krieble was succeeded by his son, Robert, after his death in 1964. That same year, Loctite introduced "Super Glue," the first of many products including silicones, epoxies, acrylics, and new Loctite anaerobics. By 1965, Loctite sales reached $2.8 million with a net income of $260,000.

In the mid-1970s, U.S. automakers were producing smaller, lightweight vehicles, and Loctite's new product lines helped stop vibrations in their smaller, higher-revving engines. Additional products were developed in the early 1980s, including a new generation of microanaerobic adhesive that did not activate until the parts were assembled. Founded on the basic technology of the Loctite product, the company wanted to expand its product range. The most significant addition to the Loctite product stable had been Super Glue, developed in the company's labs in Ireland and Connecticut. Research and development produced new acrylics, silicone, and urethanes, and Loctite also expanded its industrial product base through several key corporate acquisitions. Among those acquisitions was Permatex, an automotive line acquired in

1972. Permatex's gasket dressings were a leader in the automotive repair market. Loctite purchased Woodhill Chemical Sales in 1974. Woodhill's product line of adhesives opened up new markets for car and home repairs. In 1974, the two companies were combined into the automotive and consumer division of Loctite. In the 1980s, Loctite introduced a line of microanaerobic adhesives.

The roots of Loctite's Super Glue for wound closure date back to 1970. The idea arose, like many such ideas, from negative perceptions of the product. While Super Glue was considered an excellent, fast-setting glue, it caused concerns because it bonded skin. The idea began to emerge to use this property to develop a wound closure glue to replace sutures in surgery. Stitches have been used in the medical profession for over 2,000 years. Since Loctite had no experience in medical products and no knowledge of this market, the project failed. But in 1988, Professor Alan Roberts of Leeds/Bradford University, who was doing research in adhesives in reconstruction surgery and wound healing, contacted Loctite about a "Super Glue for wound closure." A prototype, which could be sterilized and bond skin to the satisfaction of Professor Roberts and his medical team, was developed. In 2002, the new product obtained FDA approval.

The growth of various Loctite product lines as well as corporate acquisitions helped the company expand into international markets. In many cases, companies were established separately by Loctite agents and were eventually purchased by Loctite. Loctite merged with International Sealant in 1970 and also acquired several of its overseas distributors throughout the 1970s. Robert Krieble led Loctite through acquisitions, reorganizations, a public offering, a merger, and international expansions, before retiring in 1980. At that time, International's sales were $5 million compared to Loctite's $18 million. CEO Kenneth W. Butterworth stated in *The Loctite Story* that the merger of International into Loctite was a significant factor in Loctite's history, making Loctite a solid transnational corporation.

In 1985, Henkel acquired a 25 percent shareholding in the Loctite Corporation. Product diversification led to revenues of $400 million in 1988, only 25 percent of which were derived from the original anaerobic Loctite product line. In 1991, Loctite ranked 477 on the Fortune 500 list of the largest U.S. industrial corporations; the company employed 3,500 people. The company's 10-year annual earning per share growth rate of 22.4 percent was the eighteenth highest among the Fortune 500.

In late 1996, the importance of adhesive and sealant activity in Europe took on greater significance. In 1997, Henkel acquired all the shares of Loctite Corporation, a major supplier of do-it-yourself and household adhesives and the leading specialist in engineering adhesives worldwide. With the integration of Loctite, Henkel became the undisputed world market leader in adhesives and improved its sales structure in the United States and worldwide.

Since 1997, Loctite has remained a primary Henkel brand and a supplier of household adhesives, epoxies, spray adhesives, construction adhesives, and home repair sealants and fillers. In recent years, the company has increased its focus on green and sustainable technologies.

In August 2002, the FDA approved Indermil, Henkel Loctite's tissue adhesive, for the U.S. market. This adhesive for wound closure is currently licensed worldwide. The following month, Henkel opened the Henkel Loctite Technology Center Asia Pacific in Yokohama, Japan, which was built at a cost of 23 million euro. In 2003, Henkel introduced new stick formula Threadlockers, PST Pipe Sealants, and Anti-Seize under the Loctite brand.

Loctite was a global company from the beginning. Distributors were set up in the United Kingdom and throughout Europe in 1956, and products were shipped across the Atlantic Ocean. Since its founding, Loctite has continuously created markets by discovering opportunities where no one knew they existed. Since 1953, based on a product that solved an "unsolvable" problem, Loctite has achieved success through innovation. Today, Loctite is an elite adhesives and sealant producer, firmly rooted in decades of innovation.

www.loctite.com
www.loctiteproducts.com
www.fundinguniverse.com/company-histories/Loctite-Corporation-
  Company-History.html

Introduction

As organizations, industries, and consumers become more dynamic, corporate entrepreneurship becomes more important. While entrepreneurship has traditionally been viewed as a private sector phenomenon, corporate and social entrepreneurship have developed in a number of different domains such as not-for-profits, for-profits, and public sector organizations. Entrepreneurship is a universal concept and can be applied in small and medium-sized enterprises (SMEs), large national and multinational organizations, as well as in social ventures, enterprises, communities, and governments. Entrepreneurship is not limited to a select group of people; any person with the right mindset, drive, and motivation can develop an entrepreneurial perspective. This perspective identifies a need and transforms it from a creative and innovative idea into reality.

In most industries, nations, and markets, entrepreneurs challenge existing assumptions and look to generate value in more innovative and creative ways. Entrepreneurs change the way business is conducted by identifying opportunities and successfully filling them. Organizations need to renew themselves in order to sustain competitiveness. This can take such forms as championing innovative ideas, providing necessary resources or expertise, or institutionalizing the entrepreneurial activity within the organization's systems and processes.

This chapter develops an understanding of the historical perspectives on entrepreneurship by analyzing the concept of private entrepreneurship, corporate entrepreneurship, and social entrepreneurship. The nature of the entrepreneurial process is then explored along with how it applies within established organizations. Entrepreneurship is a unifying framework for successful management practices that can be achieved by combining the key roles of managers and entrepreneurs. The chapter concludes by introducing the overall framework of this book.

An Overview of Entrepreneurship

The term *entrepreneurship* means different things to different individuals. Even though entrepreneurship has come into its own as an area of study, there remain several questions: Who is an entrepreneur? What is entrepreneurship? What is corporate entrepreneurship? What is social entrepreneurship? What is the entrepreneurial process? These frequently asked questions reflect the increased national and international interest in entrepreneurs and entrepreneurship by individuals, groups, academics, students, and government officials. The development of the theory of entrepreneurship parallels to a great extent the development of the term itself. The word *entrepreneur* is French and, literally translated, means "between-taker" or "go-between."

The Entrepreneur and Entrepreneurship

An early definition and example of an entrepreneur as a go-between is Marco Polo, who attempted to establish trade routes to the Far East. In the Middle Ages, the term *entrepreneur* was used to describe both an actor and a person who managed large production projects. For example, a person in charge of architectural works, such as castles, public buildings, and cathedrals, was considered the entrepreneur. In such large production projects, this individual did not take any risks but rather managed the project using the resources provided by the government of the country.

In the seventeenth century, an entrepreneur was a person who entered into a contractual arrangement with the government to perform a service or to supply stipulated products. For example, John Law, a Frenchman, was allowed to establish a royal bank. This monopoly on French trade led to Law's downfall when he attempted to push the company's stock price higher than the value of its assets, leading to the collapse of the company. Richard Cantillon, a noted economist and author in the 1700s, developed one of the early theories of the entrepreneur and is regarded by some as the founder of the term. He described the entrepreneur as a rational decision maker who assumed the risk and provided management for the firm. He viewed the entrepreneur as a risk taker.

In the eighteenth century, the entrepreneur was distinguished from the capital provider. Many of the inventions developed during this time were reactions to the needs of the changing world, as was the case with the inventions of Eli Whitney and Thomas Edison. These inventors were developing new technologies but were unable to finance their inventions themselves. Whereas Whitney financed his cotton gin with expropriated British crown property, Edison raised capital from private sources to develop and experiment in the fields of electricity and chemistry. Both Edison and Whitney were capital users (entrepreneurs), not capital providers.

In the late nineteenth and early twentieth centuries, entrepreneurs were frequently not distinguished from managers and were viewed mostly from an economic perspective. English philosopher John Stuart Mill believed that the key factor in distinguishing a manager from an entrepreneur was the bearing of risk.[1] An example of this type of entrepreneur is Andrew Carnegie, who invented nothing but rather adapted and developed new technology in the creation of products to achieve economic vitality in the steel industry. In the middle of the twentieth century, the notion of an *entrepreneur as an innovator* was established along with a more refined definition. The function of the entrepreneur was to reform the pattern of production by exploiting an invention; developing a new technological method of producing a new or old product;

opening a new source of material supply or a new outlet for products; or organizing a new industry.

The concept of innovation and newness became an integral part of entrepreneurship in the mid-twentieth century. Innovation, the act of introducing something new and relevant, is one of the most difficult tasks for the entrepreneur. It takes not only the ability to create and conceptualize, but also the ability to understand all the forces at work in the environment. The newness can consist of anything from a new product to a new distribution system to a method for developing a new organizational structure. Examples of these entrepreneurs include Edward Harriman, a railroad investor who bought underperforming railroads such as Lake Ontario Southern Railroad and poured money into them to make them more efficient and profitable, and John Pierpont Morgan, who developed his large banking house by reorganizing and financing industries.

Entrepreneurship Today

The term *entrepreneurship* has historically referred to the efforts of an individual who takes on the odds in translating a vision into a successful business enterprise. While some definitions focus on the creation of new organizations, others focus on wealth creation and ownership. This includes other routes to ownership such as franchising, corporate entrepreneurship, management buyouts, and business inheritance. Still others focus on discovering and exploiting opportunities. The concept of an entrepreneur is further refined through the principles and terms from a business, managerial, and personal perspective. In particular, the concept of entrepreneurship from a personal perspective has been thoroughly explored in this century. This is reflected in three behavioral attributes of an entrepreneur: (1) initiative taking, (2) organizing and reorganizing of social and economic mechanisms to turn resources and situations to practical account, and (3) acceptance of risk or failure.

To an economist, an entrepreneur is one who brings resources, labor, vision, materials, and other assets into combinations that increase product or service value and introduce and implement change, innovation, and a new order. To a psychologist, such a person is typically driven by certain forces—the need to attain something, to experiment, to accomplish, or perhaps to escape authority. To one businessperson, an entrepreneur may appear as a threat, an aggressive competitor, whereas to another businessperson the same entrepreneur may be an ally, a supplier, a customer, or a creator of wealth. The entrepreneurial ally finds better ways to utilize resources, reduce waste, and produce jobs for willing candidates.

Entrepreneurship is the dynamic process of creating incremental wealth and stimulating the surrounding environment. The wealth is created by individuals who assume the major risks in terms of equity, time, and career commitment by providing value for a product or service. The product or service can have varying degrees of newness but needs to be infused by the entrepreneur regardless of its degree. Great entrepreneurs of this century include Richard Branson, Michael Dell, Bill Gates, Steven Jobs, and Anita Roddick. The challenge facing organizations today is recognizing the creativity and innovative capability of its internal members and allowing these individuals to have the power to utilize their potential.

While the definitions have slightly different views of the entrepreneur, the descriptions also contain similar notions, such as newness, organizing, creating wealth, and risk taking. Yet these definitions are somewhat restrictive, since entrepreneurs are found in all professions—education, medicine, research, law, architecture, engineering, social work, distribution, and government. To include all types of entrepreneurial behavior, there is a need for an all-inclusive definition: "*Entrepreneurship* is the process of creating something new with value by devoting the necessary time and effort assuming the accompanying financial, psychic, and social risks and uncertainties; and receiving the resulting rewards of monetary and personal satisfaction."[2]

Corporate Entrepreneurship

Corporate entrepreneurship, which is often referred to as intrapreneurship or corporate venturing, is the process by which individuals inside organizations pursue opportunities independent of the resources they currently control; this involves doing new things and departing from the customary to pursue opportunities. The spirit of entrepreneurship within an existing organization results in the creation of a new organization or in the development of renewal and innovation within that organization. Corporate entrepreneurship requires engendering entrepreneurial behaviors within an established organization. It can be viewed as a system that enables individuals to use creative processes for applying and inventing technologies and new ways of doing things. Besides intrapreneurship, corporate entrepreneurship is often referred to as organizational entrepreneurship, intracorporate entrepreneurship, or corporate venturing.

Corporate entrepreneurship involves extending the organization's degree of competence and corresponding opportunity through internally generated new resource combinations. Organizations can foster profit-making innovations by encouraging employees to think like entrepreneurs and then giving them the freedom and flexibility to pursue projects without being inhibited by bureaucratic barriers. Internal generation of innovation influenced by organizational and environmental characteristics requires motivated individuals and groups and an open, conducive environment. Companies such as IBM recognized the value of corporate entrepreneurship in increasing corporate growth. Hewlett-Packard (HP), 3M, Thermo Electron Corporation, and Xerox have also experienced significant success in corporate entrepreneurship. Entrepreneurship can also be indirectly encouraged as in the case of Starlight Telecommunications, which was the successful result from the lack of support by GTE making William O'Brien and Pete Nielsen resign and start this new firm.

A broad definition of corporate entrepreneurship was proposed by Guth and Ginsberg, who stressed that corporate entrepreneurship encompasses two major phenomena: new venture creation within existing organizations and the transformation of organizations through strategic renewal.[3] This renewal usually involves formal or informal activities aimed at creating new businesses or processes in established companies at the corporate, division (business), functional, or project levels. The ultimate aim of the renewal is to improve a company's competitive position and financial performance. Renewal is achieved through the redefinition of an organization's mission through the creative redeployment of resources, leading to new combinations of products and technologies. Corporate entrepreneurship in terms of renewal emphasizes strategy reformulation, reorganization, and organizational change.

Social Entrepreneurship

Definitions of social entrepreneurship are much more limited and diverse than those for corporate entrepreneurship. While the term *entrepreneurship* is mostly associated with private sector activity, in the last 20 years, the value creation aspect of entrepreneurship has been extended to social organizations. Social entrepreneurship has made significant contributions to communities and society in general by adopting business models to offer innovative and creative solutions to complex social issues. Despite increased interest in social entrepreneurship and the credence of the growing impact of social entrepreneurship as evidenced in *Fast Company* magazine's Social Capitalist Awards and the Skoll Foundation's Awards for Social Entrepreneurship, there has been limited research in the area.

One challenge is that the definition of social entrepreneurship has been developed in a number of different domains such as not-for-profits, for-profits, public sector organizations, and a combination of the three. Social entrepreneurship can be broadly defined as innovative activity with a social objective in the for-profit sector, such as social commercial ventures; nonprofit sector; public sector; or even across sectors in terms of hybrid organizations that combine for-profit and nonprofit approaches.

Social entrepreneurship can be more narrowly defined as the application of business expertise and market skills in the for-profit, nonprofit, or public sector when these organizations develop more innovative approaches in business activities. Common across all definitions of social entrepreneurship is that its core objective is to create social value rather than personal and stakeholder wealth.

Even though all of the above definitions of entrepreneurship, corporate entrepreneurship, and social entrepreneurship have slightly different perspectives, they contain similar concepts since entrepreneurship involves creative activity. The core components of entrepreneurship involve the discovery and exploitation of opportunities. In fact, an entrepreneurial event cannot occur without identifying and addressing an opportunity.

Table 1.1 depicts a typology that identifies the similarities and differences between the three types of entrepreneurship and entrepreneurs: private sector, corporate, and social. This table indicates that entrepreneurship and entrepreneurs are characterized as having a preference for creating activity, manifested by some degree of proactiveness and innovativeness. The core components of entrepreneurship include the discovery and exploitation of opportunities.

Entrepreneur versus Manager

There is some confusion about the nature of an entrepreneur versus a manager. Although the entrepreneur is different from the traditional manager, entrepreneurship represents a mode of management. Management involves achieving the objectives of an organization while reducing variability to increase stable processes. It involves accomplishing work through people. To manage effectively means to forecast, plan, organize, coordinate, communicate, lead, facilitate, motivate, and control. Management is the transformation of inputs into outputs through conceptual, human, and technical skills. Managers are required to efficiently and effectively utilize resources to achieve optimum results in line with organizational goals and objectives.

An entrepreneur is future orientated, seeking opportunities and identifying innovations to fill these opportunities. An entrepreneur has a preference for creative activity, manifested by some innovative combination of resources, for achieving financial, economic, or social wealth. Entrepreneurs are creative in obtaining resources, overcoming obstacles, and implementing ideas. While there is considerable overlap between managers and entrepreneurs, the concepts are not the same; entrepreneurs can be managers and managers can be entrepreneurs by consciously combining the various functions of the key roles at the appropriate times as indicated in Table 1.2.

The Entrepreneurial Process

The *entrepreneurial process*, however, involves more than just problem solving. All entrepreneurs—private, corporate, and social— must find, evaluate, and develop an opportunity by overcoming the forces that resist the creation of something new. Understanding how entrepreneurship works requires recognition of the process involved and how to effectively manage that process. It is a process that can occur in different settings but changes due to the diversity that exists among private, corporate, and social contexts.

The entrepreneurial process has four distinct phases: (1) identification and evaluation of the opportunity, (2) development of the business plan, (3) determination and evaluation of resource requirements, and (4) implementation and management of the resulting enterprise. Tables 1.3, 1.4, and 1.5 indicate, respectively, the

TABLE 1.1 Similarities and Differences among Private, Corporate, and Social Entrepreneurs and Entrepreneurship

	Private Entrepreneurs/ Entrepreneurship	Corporate Entrepreneurs/ Entrepreneurship	Social Entrepreneurs/ Entrepreneurship
Objectives	Freedom to discover and exploit profitable opportunities; independent and goal orientated; high need for achievement	Freedom and flexibility to pursue projects without being bogged down in bureaucracy; goal orientated; independently motivated but also influenced by the corporate characteristics	Freedom and resources to serve constituencies; add value to existing services; address social problems and enrich communities and societies; driven by the desire for social justice
Opportunity	Pursues an opportunity, regardless of the resources it controls; relatively unconstrained by situational forces	Pursues opportunities independent of the resources it currently controls; doing new things and departing from the customary to pursue opportunities	Shows a capacity to recognize and take advantage of opportunities to create social value by stimulating social change; develops a social value proposition to challenge equilibrium
Focus	Strong focus on the external environment; competitive environment and technological advancement; primary focus is on financial returns, profit maximization, and independence	Focus on innovative activities and orientations such as development of new products, services, technologies, administrative techniques, strategies, and competitive postures; primary focus is economic returns generated through innovation	Aims to create value for citizens by focusing on serving long-standing needs more effectively through innovation and creativity; aims to exploit social opportunities and enhance social returns, social wealth, social justice

Innovation	Create value through innovation and seizing that opportunity without regard to resources (human and capital); produces resources or endows existing resources with enhanced potential for creating wealth	A system that enables and encourages individuals to use creative processes that enable them to apply and invent technologies that can be planned, deliberate, and purposeful in terms of the level of innovative activity desired; instigation of renewal and innovation within that organization	Creates practical, innovative, and sustainable approaches to social problems for the benefit of society in general; mobilizes ideas and resources required for social transformation
Risk Taking	Risk taking is a primary factor in the entrepreneurial character and function; assumes significant personal and financial risk but attempts to minimize it	Calculated risk taker; recognizes that risks are career related and absorbed by organization as a whole	Recognizes the social value of creating opportunities and key decision making characteristics of innovation, proactivity, and risk taking; accepts an above average degree of risk
Character and Skills	Self-confident; strong business knowledge; independent	Self-confident; strong self belief in ability to manipulate the system; strong technical or product knowledge; good managerial skills	Self-confident; high tolerance for ambiguity; strong political skills

TABLE 1.2   The Role of the Entrepreneurial Manager

The Entrepreneur		The Manager
✓ Discover		✓ Forecaster
✓ Visionary	⟶	✓ Planner
✓ Innovative		✓ Organizer
✓ Creative	**The Entrepreneurial Manager**	✓ Coordinator
✓ Calculated Risk Taker		✓ Communicator
✓ Opportunity Seeker		✓ Facilitator
✓ Resource Leverage		✓ Motivator
✓ Self-Confident	⟵	✓ Leader
✓ Drive and Intrinsic Motivation		✓ Controller

private entrepreneurship process, the corporate entrepreneurship process, and the social entrepreneurship process. Although these phases proceed progressively, no one stage is dealt with in isolation or is totally completed before work begins on other phases. For example, to successfully identify and evaluate an opportunity (phase 1), an entrepreneur must already have in mind the type of desired business (phase 4).

Identification and Evaluation of the Opportunity

Opportunity identification and evaluation is a most difficult task. Entrepreneurship does not always begin with the creative concept for a new product, service, or process. It often begins with the entrepreneur's alertness to identify an opportunity. Whether the opportunity is identified by using input from consumers, business associates, channel members, or technical experts, the entrepreneur needs to carefully screen and evaluate each opportunity. This evaluation of the opportunity is perhaps the most critical element of the entrepreneurial process as it assesses whether the specific product or service has the needed returns compared to the required resources.

TABLE 1.3 The Entrepreneurial Process: Private Context

Identification and Evaluation of the Opportunity	Development of the Business Plan	Determine and Evaluate Resource Requirements	Implementation and Management of the Resulting Enterprise
Opportunity assessment	Title Page	Determine needed resources	Develop management style
Creation and length of opportunity	Table of Contents	Determine existing resources	Understand key variables for success
Real and perceived value of opportunity	Executive Summary	Identify resource gaps and available suppliers	Identify problems and potential problems
Risk and returns of opportunity	Major Sections: 1. Description of Business 2. Description of Industry	Develop access to needed resources	Implement control systems
Opportunity versus personal skills and goals	3. Technology Plan 4. Marketing Plan 5. Financial Plan		Develop growth strategies
Competitive environment	6. Production Plan 7. Organizational Plan		
Develop an opportunity analysis plan	8. Operational Plan 9. Summary		
	Appendices (Exhibits)		

TABLE 1.4 The Entrepreneurial Process: Corporate Context

Identify and Evaluate the Opportunity	Develop the Business Plan	Determine and Evaluate Resource Requirements	Start and Manage the Resulting Enterprise
Opportunity assessment and exploration	Title Page	Determine resources needed and the viability of obtaining those resources	Viability to adapt to the current management style
Longer approval cycles to create the opportunity	Table of Contents		Understand key variables for successful implementation
	Executive Summary	Determine existing resources and their availability	
Real and perceived value of opportunity for the organization; limits on the financial rewards for the corporate entrepreneur	Product/Service Analysis		Identify problems, potential problems, and limitations
	Corporate Fit	Identify resource gaps and the potential of filling those gaps	Adaptation to the existing control systems
Organization assumes the risk rather than career related risk	Market Analysis		
Opportunity versus personal and team skills; internal network for generating ideas	Marketing Plan	Identify available access to needed resources	Opportunity for growth and profitability
	Profitability		
Competitive environment	Plan for Further Action		
Develop an opportunity analysis plan			

TABLE 1.5 The Entrepreneurial Process: Social Context

Identification and Evaluation of the Opportunity	Development of the Business Plan	Determine and Evaluate Resource Requirements	Implementation and Management of the Resulting Enterprise
Opportunity assessment and viability concerning greater diversity and multiplicity of objectives	Title Page	Determine resources needed in the context of the sector and budgetary restrictions and limitations	Develop in the context of existing management style
Creation and length of opportunity takes longer due to bureaucratic inertia and public scrutiny	Table of Contents		Understand key variables for successful implementation and social outcomes
	Executive Summary	Determine existing resources available for this project	
Real and perceived value of opportunity for society, communities, and constituencies	Service/Process Analysis		Identify problems, potential problems, internal restrictions, and limitations
	Social/Community Need/ Constitutional Fit	Identify financial and nonfinancial resource gaps and viable opportunity to fill those gaps	
Risk and reward trade-offs favor avoiding mistakes; lower financial incentives; do not share enterprise profits	Operational Analysis		Adapt to existing control systems while attempting to overcome restrictions
	Implementation Plan	Identify if there are opportunities to access needed resources	
Opportunity in light of political and social objectives versus personal and team skills and goals	Social Value		Opportunities for economic and social growth and development
	Financial Sustainability Plan/ Funding		
Economic and social environment	Plan for Further Action		
Develop an opportunity analysis plan			

Offering a better product, service, or process at a lower price with higher quality, greater availability, and better customer- and after-sales service means nothing if there is not an existing market.

The evaluation process involves looking at the length of the opportunity, its real and perceived value, its risks and returns, its fit with the personal skills and goals of the entrepreneur (or the organization that the corporate entrepreneur or social entrepreneur is part of), and its uniqueness or differential advantage in the environment. All entrepreneurs must believe in the opportunity to such an extent that they will make the necessary sacrifices in order to overcome any potential organizational obstacles to develop and manage the opportunity.

Key issues for the private, corporate, or social entrepreneur include a description of the product, service, or process; an assessment of the opportunity in terms of source, size, and sustainability; an assessment of the entrepreneur and the team; specifications of all the activities and resources needed to translate the opportunity into a viable business venture; and the source of capital to finance the initial venture as well as its growth.

Development of the Business Plan

With the opportunity identified and evaluated, all entrepreneurs need to specify the business concept. The business concept for a new product, service, or process specifies the innovative and creative approach for capitalizing on the opportunity. A good *business plan* needs to be developed to capture the defined opportunity. This is a time-consuming phase of the entrepreneurial process and varies according to the context. For example, the business plan for the entrepreneur start-up is different from the corporate entrepreneur business plan, which also differs from the social entrepreneur business plan (see Tables 1.3, 1.4, and 1.5). A good business plan is essential to capturing the opportunity and determining the required resources, obtaining those resources, and successfully starting and managing the resulting venture.

Determine and Evaluate Resource Requirements

All entrepreneurs need to determine the resources required for addressing the opportunity. This process starts with an appraisal of present financial and nonfinancial resources (e.g., technical skills, team competencies, licenses, patents, customer contacts, and location). Care must be taken not to underestimate the amount and variety of those resources needed. While for the corporate entrepreneur, sponsorship from a senior executive can be the most valuable resource, for the social entrepreneur, government support can be a more significant resource. Some of the most critical entrepreneurial behaviors involve leveraging resources, thus allowing concepts to move toward development without major financial commitments and giving the organization greater flexibility to utilize resources where needed.

Starting and Managing the Resulting Enterprise

After resources are acquired, all entrepreneurs must use them to implement the business plan. For the private entrepreneur, this involves implementing a management style and structure, whereas the corporate entrepreneur and social entrepreneur need to adapt and overcome restrictions or limitations. A control system needs to be implemented in order to quickly identify and resolve any problem areas. Some entrepreneurs thrive during the creation stage but have difficulty managing and growing the venture. In comparison, some corporate and social entrepreneurs have difficulty managing their innovations because of organizational restrictions and limitations.

All entrepreneurs need to be able to tolerate risk, uncertainty, and ambiguity by adapting and adjusting accordingly. Ultimately, their mindset needs to rapidly sense, act, and mobilize even under uncertain conditions. They need to be dynamic, flexible, self-regulating, and engaged in the process of generating multiple decision frameworks focused on sensing and acting on the changes occurring in the environment.

The Entrepreneurial Process for Each Context

While entrepreneurship is a universal concept, successfully applying the entrepreneurial process within private start-ups, established organizations, or social enterprises requires appreciating the uniqueness of each context and adapting the process. The four stages of the entrepreneurial process apply within all contexts as the same stages would be pursued by a corporate entrepreneur or social entrepreneur attempting to introduce a new service or concept. In all instances, opportunities need to be identified and evaluated, innovative concepts need to be planned, resources need to be evaluated, and ideas need to be managed and implemented within the specified time frame.

A Framework for Corporate Entrepreneurship

Within the area of entrepreneurship, corporate entrepreneurship is one of the fastest growing. Many entrepreneurs find it difficult to manage and expand the venture once they have created it. Likewise, many managers find it difficult to allow innovative employees to engage in venturing activities. In order to develop and grow the organization, managers need to be entrepreneurial by building and developing an organization that encourages corporate entrepreneurship behavior and rewards employees for taking creative risks.

Never before has there been such a need for corporate entrepreneurship as organizations face increased competition from globalization and rapid technological advancement. Since customers have access to most product and service substitutes through technological advancement, a firm's competitors can be anywhere in the world. There is a pressing need for organizations to stay competitive by becoming more innovative and engaging in corporate entrepreneurship activities. Leading international corporate entrepreneurship companies include 3M, Lucent Technologies, Nokia, Siemens Nixdorf, DuPont, Thermo Electron Corporation, and Raychem.

This book focuses on the importance of corporate entrepreneurship by discussing how to establish an entrepreneurial spirit in the organization. An integrative framework about corporate entrepreneurship has been developed as indicated in Figure 1.1. The framework has three major components: (1) managing corporate entrepreneurship, (2) organizing corporate entrepreneurship, and (3) operationalizing corporate entrepreneurship.

The starting point is to develop an understanding of managing corporate entrepreneurship. Since entrepreneurship is a universal concept, there are certain commonalities regardless of the context; there are also fundamental differences when attempting to apply it within a large corporation or a social enterprise. Building on this foundation, leaders must develop and build an organizational environment that encourages and motivates employees to identify and recognize opportunities to behave like entrepreneurs. Four key elements for *managing corporate entrepreneurship* include understanding entrepreneurship and corporate entrepreneurship within the different contexts; recognizing the behavioral aspects of corporate entrepreneurship; formatting and managing the venturing process with the structure in place; and effectively managing the opportunity identification, evaluation, and selection process.

The ability to effectively manage the venture requires proper *organization,* which includes proper location of the venture, organization of resources, and controlling and managing the internal politics. Finally, operationalizing corporate entrepreneurship requires a clear understanding and development of the business plan; selecting the right managers and compensating them for their efforts; ensuring adequate funding; and instituting the concept in the organizational structure.

The framework identifies the structure of this book. Part One consists of Chapters 1 through 4 and focuses on the management of corporate entrepreneurship. The chapters identify the similarities and differences among private, corporate, and social entrepreneurship. In addition, the entrepreneurial process is examined

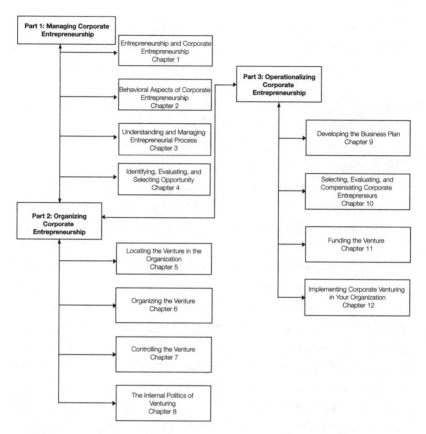

FIGURE 1.1   A Framework of Corporate Entrepreneurship and Guide to This Book's Structure

in light of these distinctions by investigating the unique processes of each type of entrepreneurship. The behaviors associated with corporate entrepreneurship are presented by profiling the motivation, interests, and drive. Elements of behavior are recognized and discussed including identification, facilitation, desire, and motivation. The corporate entrepreneur needs to create a structure, process, and management orientation for the new venture. The aspects of identifying, evaluating, and selecting opportunities are then presented. Motivating individuals and groups to identify, evaluate, and select particular opportunities for developing the organization and improving its profitability is a critical activity for corporate entrepreneurship.

Part Two of the book (Chapters 5 through 8) examines the key elements that must occur together in order to create a corporate venture. Corporate entrepreneurship could involve alterations for specific aspects of the organization or an entire organizational shift. Change is necessary where there are obstacles to corporate entrepreneurship to overcome these barriers. This is followed by a discussion on the local characteristics and particular context of the corporate venture and how these contexts influence the potential for venture success. The venture needs to be organized within and at different levels of the organization. This requires a decentralized structure and low formalization leading to open communication; interpersonal exchanges accompanied by meetings and committees so that the venture process can proceed with the involvement; and support from the necessary participants. The venture is then organized so that it can be successfully managed; this requires a high degree of creativity and a substantial level of teamwork.

Control is needed to ensure that the organization achieves its core goals and objectives efficiently and effectively. There are many forms of control, but ultimately the control system that is implemented should be influenced by the organizational strategy and structure as well as the core business activities. While structures and systems are necessary for the management and control of an organization, these processes must not inhibit flexibility, intuition, innovation, and creativity. The main strategies and roles of management in developing and creating the process of controlling the venture are discussed in this section along with the characteristics of an effective control system. In addition, an approach to developing a management control philosophy that encourages corporate entrepreneurship is explored.

Regardless of changes occurring, an organization has power and politics. The sources of power that are most appropriate for venturing are described in terms of positive and negative politics; tactics, protagonists, and supporters; and the destructive power of politics for a venture in its infancy.

Part Three of the book (Chapters 9 through 12) deals with operations. The Corporate Entrepreneurship Business Plan involves more than a single implementation and needs to be continuous as a living document in order to ensure venture success. This requires monitoring, assessing, and evaluating the external and internal environments to ensure making the right decisions and implementing the appropriate actions.

Next, this part examines ways to engage individuals in corporate entrepreneurship including the processes of selecting, evaluating, and compensating the individuals involved. Whenever a new venture is considered, it needs to have resources, which most likely will involve finance. This will entail a discussion of the various financing alternatives including the Internal Venture Capital Unit. The book concludes with a presentation of various models of corporate entrepreneurship and guidelines for implementing the process in your organization.

Summary

The terms *entrepreneur* and *entrepreneurship* have various meanings to different people and can be viewed in different contexts such as private sector entrepreneurship, corporate entrepreneurship, and social entrepreneurship. In spite of the differences, there are some commonalities such as risk taking, creativity, independence, and rewards.

All entrepreneurs proceed through the entrepreneurial process by identifying, evaluating, and developing opportunities for creating a venture. Each step is essential to eventual success. In established organizations, a corporate imperative is to achieve equilibrium between the role of management and the role of entrepreneur, thus developing entrepreneurial managers.

The challenge for all entrepreneurs is to build organizations for today's work and tomorrow's innovation. Entrepreneurs need to ensure that the organization has sufficient internal diversity in strategies, structures, people, and processes to facilitate different kinds of entrepreneurial behavior. Within existing corporate structures, the corporate entrepreneur needs to be creative, visionary, and flexible and to have the ability to work within the corporate structure. This will create long-term, sustained economic and social wealth as well as the future growth and development of the organization.

2

Behavioral Aspects of Corporate Entrepreneurship

What are the key components in the creative process? What is the difference between innovation and creativity? How can an organization overcome barriers to innovation and creativity? What behaviors promote corporate entrepreneurship activity within an organization?

Scenario: Ericsson

Ericsson has been a recognized leader in the telecommunications industry since 1876. The company is a leading worldwide provider of telecommunications equipment and related services to mobile and fixed network operators globally. It was one of the first companies to establish overseas business operations. Even in the early stages, the founder, Lars Magnus Ericsson, decided to open a production facility in Russia. Technology is the forefront of Ericsson, and today it continues to expand and innovate to be on the cutting edge and make telecom services affordable and available to all. As innovation is most important to Ericsson and is a driver, the company adopts a market-driven innovation strategy focusing on improving available technology with local customization and adaptation to meet consumer specific needs, wants, and expectations.

In 1900, Ericsson employed 1,000 people globally and produced 50,000 telephones; in 1923, the first automatic 500-point switches were put into service; in 1950, LM Ericsson telephone exchange supported the world's first international call; in 1968, the first digital telephone exchange (AXE) was installed; in 1991, AXE lines exceeded 105 million in 11 countries serving 34 million subscribers; in 2000, the company became the world's leading supplier of 3G mobile systems; in 2005, Ericsson won the biggest contracts to date to manage Operator 3's networks in Italy and the United Kingdom; in 2008, a research center was established in Silicon Valley; and in 2009, Verizon and Ericsson collaborated to carry out the first data call on a 4G network. Ericsson has a long history of innovation and the pioneering of next generation technologies for more efficient and higher-quality telecommunications. In 1878, Ericsson introduced telephones with a single trumpet; in 1968, the first digital telephone exchange (AXE) was installed; in 1981, the first mobile system, Nordic Mobile Telephone (NMT), was inaugurated in Saudi Arabia; in 1991, the first GSM (Global System for Mobile Communications) phones were in operation; in 1999, Ericsson pushed for 3G and mobile Internet; in 2003, high-speed broadband (Wideband Code Division Multiple Access, or WCDMA) rollout started globally; in 2007, full-service broadband, with fixed and wireless network converge, was introduced; in 2008, Ericsson pushed for 4G (Long Term Evolution, or LTE), the standard the company helped to form; and in 2009, Ericsson won the IEC InfoVision Award for fiber and backhaul solutions.

Over 1,000 networks in more than 175 countries utilize Ericsson's network equipment, and 40 percent of all mobile calls are made through its systems. Ericsson is the world's principal supplier of mobile networks. In 2010, it employed 88,060 people worldwide. The networks supported over 2 billion subscribers and served over 700 million subscribers, with the United States and China being the company's biggest markets. Ericsson has over 25,000 patents, one of the industry's strongest portfolios. Ericsson is now driving the standardization of the next generation step LTE and Multimedia Telephony (MMTel), which further enhances consumer communication and entertainment experience. Ericsson recognizes the importance of communication in changing the lives of people and the way they work. Innovation is an important component of its culture. It uses innovation to empower people, business, and society. It provides communication networks, telecom services, and multimedia solutions, making it easier to communicate in a dynamic, global environment. This is supported by its global team of researchers that is constantly working on creating breakthrough innovations that will shape the future. Ericsson is a financially strong global innovation leader, investing approximately $5 billion annually in research and development. The research areas of Ericsson include wireless access networks; broadband technologies; multimedia technologies, services, and software; radio access technologies; packet technologies; global services research; and sustainability and electromagnetic frequency.

In October 2001, Sony Ericsson was established through a 50-50 joint venture with Sony Corporation and Telefonaktiebolaget LM Ericsson. For Ericsson, this joint venture provided a vital link to the consumer. The joint venture combines the mobile communications expertise of Ericsson with the consumer electronics and content expertise of Sony Corporation. Sony Ericsson provides a range of mobile devices, including those supporting multimedia applications and other personal communication services.

In 2008, ST-Ericsson was created through a 50-50 joint venture by bringing together ST-NXP Wireless and Ericsson Mobile Platforms, two of the world's leading semiconductor and platform companies. ST-Ericsson is an industry leader in design, development, and creation of cutting-edge mobile platforms and semiconductors across the broad spectrum of wireless technologies.

In July 2010, Ericsson acquired a stake in Nortel and broke into the South Korean market with LG-Ericsson. By combining LG's and Ericsson's research and development competencies, it has strengthened its position and become a unique player in the industry. This has been achieved through wireless, optical, and wire line products. As a result of the combination of innovative ideas and network convergence technologies, LG-Ericsson provides the connectivity that eliminates barriers in the exchange of information, enabling customers to recognize users' potential.

Ericsson has been the leader in driving technology forward from telegraph to telephone all the way to the rollout of 4G. It has contributed significantly to form the industry's standards from NMT and GSM to LTE. It is advancing its vision of being "the prime driver in an all-communicating world" through innovation, technology, and sustainable business solutions. Recognizing that innovation is rapidly changing, its Innovation Centers are focused to create mobile applications that are directly relevant and value adding to the consumer and the society as a whole. It has created a vivid culture of innovation, rapidly transferring from innovation to commercialization.

www.ericsson.com

Introduction

Among all the necessary attributes required for successful entrepreneurship, corporate entrepreneurship, renewal, innovation, and proactivity, the individual entrepreneur or corporate entrepreneur is the most critical. Corporate entrepreneurship and the behavior associated with it are initiated in established organizations for such reasons as profitability, growth, development, venturing, renewal, and innovation. In other words, these organizations support the corporate entrepreneur in order to identify and develop revenue-generating opportunities, expand and grow internationally, and effectively configure resources as a source of competitive advantage.

Management at all levels is crucial to the successful efforts of corporate entrepreneurship. Managerial and employee behavior as well as organizational structure and culture are necessary ingredients for corporate entrepreneurship activity. The corporate entrepreneurship activity requires that creativity and innovative risk taking occur in an organization that enables the organization to renew itself and enhance performance through effective resource utilization. Strong management support and leadership is essential for this to occur.

To effectively facilitate the development of entrepreneurship, organizations need to focus on such key factors as top management support, longer time horizons, resources, rewards, more flexible organizational structures, and a culture that is conducive to corporate entrepreneurship activity. The willingness of top management to facilitate, promote, and support entrepreneurial activity in the organization can take many forms, such as championing innovative ideas, providing necessary resources or expertise, or institutionalizing the corporate entrepreneurship activity within the organization's systems and processes.

The company culture influences behavior within organizations that affects daily operations. The concept of culture describes a range of activities and features that are associated with organizational life. New employees must be effectively integrated into the organization if they are to become useful members of the team. Existing employees must be able to adjust and adapt to structural and cultural changes necessary for growing in a dynamic environment.

Culture also influences a number of aspects of organizational activity including how people interact. From a management perspective, culture occurs organically, naturally, and informally. The bureaucratic structure and rigidity that all too often emerge within organizations may not be appropriate for the achievement of company objectives in a dynamic environment. In some organizations, the dominant culture is hostile to management's intentions. The movement toward a more participative, less hostile culture will fail if it is not supported by appropriate training, encouragement, and tolerance of mistakes. The maintenance of a culture is also challenging as culture does not remain static but evolves over time.

This chapter examines the ways the organization can facilitate corporate entrepreneurial behavior through structural support and cultural change. Innovation and creativity are discussed to provide an understanding of the process, the barriers, and methods for addressing those barriers. Then the key aspects of corporate entrepreneurship are presented along with the individual personality characteristics and differences of corporate entrepreneurs. Following a presentation of the ways in which an organization can develop an entrepreneurial culture, the chapter concludes with a discussion of the transformation needed that will lead to sustainable corporate entrepreneurial behavior and activity.

Innovation and Creativity

Innovation and creativity are vital elements of corporate entrepreneurship. Creativity is the basis for the development of innovative business concepts. It is the application of an individual's ability to discover and develop new ideas, processes, or concepts in novel ways. The resulting innovation indicates the presence or absence of entrepreneurship in an organization. Innovation is a key ingredient in the entrepreneurial process, putting into practice new ideas, a central characteristic of the entrepreneurial endeavor. Innovation harnesses the creative energy and develops those ideas into realistic products, processes, or services. The corporate entrepreneur must be highly creative in moving a concept from idea generation to fruition, overcoming the obstacles in the process.

Innovation in fast-changing environments has been identified as the essence of entrepreneurial behavior. Innovation can take many forms, such as developing new products and services, developing new methods of production, identifying new markets, identifying new sources of supply, and developing new organizational strategies.

While breakthrough innovations are great, most innovations make incremental improvements to existing product lines rather than risk bringing something radically new to market. Breakthrough innovations are rare and include the steam engine, penicillin, the computer, the automobile, and the Internet. Rarely do companies successfully navigate a process that results in breakthrough thinking.

Technological innovations occur more frequently than breakthrough innovations and are, in general, at a lower level of scientific discovery and advancement. Technological innovations offer advancements in the product-market area and should be protected by firms to the extent possible. The personal computer, voice and text messaging, and the jet airplane are examples of technological innovations.

Ordinary innovation is the form of innovation that occurs most frequently. It usually extends a technological innovation into a better product or service with a different and usually greater market appeal. American Express is always looking to extend, modify, and enhance its services. Companies have different strategies of innovation. 3M encourages breakthrough innovation, while Dell, Microsoft, and Starbucks have different strategies. Innovation is clearly evident in Microsoft. Microsoft Office and Windows have become standard for most consumers, with almost 300 million computers sold each year. Yet Microsoft recognizes that business does not stand still and strategically enters new markets to ensure that it does not lose market share and that it continually improves its current products. Companies like General Electric, 3M, and Nokia have been able to continuously innovate and transform themselves to serve new and growing markets by developing innovative products and delivering them effectively. Hewlett-Packard and IBM are committed to corporate entrepreneurship and have taken steps to ensure that they will be leaders in innovation. The link between corporate entrepreneurship, innovation, and creativity occurs through three stages. Stage 1 comprises creativity through idea, activity, ability, and skill; Stage 2 comprises invention through working model and prototype; and Stage 3 comprises innovation through successful commercial introduction of the invention.

The Creative Process

Creativity is originality that is realistic, viable, and marketable. Three key aspects of organizational creativity are knowledge, drive, and ability. *Knowledge* of the course of action is required for opportunity identification, problem solving, and decision making. *Drive* refers to the passion, desire, and motivation to do something new and novel with the courage to proceed as a first mover. This individual has an internal focus of control and is driven by a sense of achievement and self-fulfillment. *Ability* refers to the ways in which an individual seeks to identify a solution to a problem by adopting diverse and creative techniques in order to accurately assess and evaluate the situation and identify the best course of action.

The following five components are the essential aspects of the creative process:

- Identifying, defining, and questioning the problem or challenge
- Incubation
- Identification of potential options
- Selection of the most viable option or combination from the alternatives
- Implementation, testing, and evaluation

The process begins with *defining and questioning a problem or challenge* facing the organization. It is through this identity stage that the individual attempts to find answers to the problem or challenge. Probing requires asking diverse, often controversial questions. At this stage, it is important to look outside the status quo, so it is helpful to include advisors who are removed from the operations of the organization.

The solution takes time and leads to the *incubation* stage, where the individual steps away from the problem. This stage is valuable as it is important to identify where extra help may be needed in order to move forward.

The next stage—the *identification of potential options*—generates possible alternative solutions that respond to the needs of the situation and correct the underlying causes. This leads to *selecting the best option or combination*. The best alternative is one in which the solution fits the overall goals and values of the organization and achieves the desired results using the fewest resources. The individual tries to select the choice with a calculated level of risk and uncertainty. The ultimate success of the chosen alternative depends on whether it can be translated into action. This stage often requires further modification and adjustments to fit the organizational culture.

The final stage—*implementation, testing, and evaluation*—involves the use of managerial, administrative, and persuasive abilities to ensure that the selected alternative is carried out effectively. Once implemented, the concept must be evaluated to identify any deviations since the success of the chosen alternative depends on whether it can be understood and supported by the internal organization.

Personality Attributes of a Creative Individual

Each individual possesses some creative potential. The lack of development, lack of a positive encouraging environment, and poor self-belief often stifle this creativity. Fortunately, creativity is a skill that individuals can develop and improve over time. Attributes of a creative individual include:

- Objective and open-minded
- Recognizes and overcomes obstacles
- Calculated risk-taking

- Intrinsic motivation
- Internal locus of control
- Desire for achievement and recognition
- Driven by growth and development

Creativity Techniques

There are numerous techniques available for the generation of creative ideas and concepts. One such technique is *brainstorming*, where a team of approximately six to twelve members generates a large volume of ideas without criticism and then evaluates each idea. *Brainwriting* is a silent version of brainstorming where the generated ideas are recorded individually on a piece of paper and submitted anonymously to the group. The ideas are exchanged a number of times with each person building on the previously generated ideas. *Focus groups* include individuals providing information in a structured format. *Problem inventory analysis* is a method for generating new ideas and opportunities by focusing on existing problems. The value of these techniques depends on the individual's thinking process, problem-solving ability, and decision making and is further discussed in Chapter 3. The thinking process is usually better if participants have diverse perspectives, backgrounds, experiences, skills, and expertise; this avoids groupthink and enhances out-of-the-box thinking.

The Innovative Process

Innovation successfully implements newness to a given situation. Innovation not only applies to the opening of new markets but also to new ways of serving established and mature segments. It can be the sequence of activities that introduces a new component into a social unit or a product or service. It can occur gradually with small incremental adjustments to current processes or products or happen explosively such as occurred with the Internet, iPhone, and social media. The innovation may not be entirely new or unfamiliar to the organization, but it should involve some identifiable change. Innovation can involve a political process that activates organizations to launch a significant new project for changing rules, regulations, procedures, and structures related to the communication and exchange of information within the organization and with its external environment. While these projects may not require the invention of new technologies, they do require organizational change.

A key challenge for organizations is how to encourage and manage innovation. Innovation is perhaps the most pressing challenge facing organizations today. Influential management consultant Peter Drucker stated, "Innovation is the specific function of entrepreneurship . . . It is the means by which the entrepreneur either creates new wealth producing resources or endows existing resources with enhanced potential for creating wealth."[1] Essentially, innovation is the effort to create purposeful, focused change in the economic and social environment. Founders of innovative new ventures such as Herb Kelleher (Southwest Airlines), Pierre Omidyar (eBay), Jeff Bezos (Amazon.com), Niklas Zennstrom (Skype), Michael Dell (Dell Computer), and Mark Zuckerberg (Facebook) are highly innovative entrepreneurs in comparison to entrepreneurs who establish less innovative ventures such as a McDonald's franchise, a Mercedes-Benz dealership, a newsstand, or a consulting business.

The innovation process is more than creating a good idea. While the origin of an idea is important, and the role of creative thinking is fundamental to its development, innovation is a dynamic process involving both structural and social conditions. The sequence of steps in the innovation process typically starts with the awareness of a need and ends with the implementation of an innovation to satisfy the need. Rosabeth Moss Kanter, a Harvard Business School professor, outlines four major innovation tasks, which correspond roughly to the logic of the innovation process as it unfolds over time and to empirical data about the history of specific innovations.[2] These tasks are:

1. Idea generation and activation of the drivers of the innovation
2. Coalition building and acquisition of the power necessary to move the idea into reality
3. Idea realization and innovation production, turning the idea into a model in order to use the product, plan, or prototype
4. Transfer or diffusion—the commercialization of the product, the adoption of the idea

Corporate Innovation and Creativity

Corporate entrepreneurship can occur only in an organization that is conducive to innovation and creativity. Some traits that facilitate innovation and creativity in an organization include:

- Resources available for innovation and creativity
- Open communication at all levels throughout the organization and among people with conflicting opinions
- Decentralized structures that provide open access to innovation role models and coaches
- Cohesive work groups with open, constructive, conflict resolution approaches that integrate and develop individual creativity
- Low staff turnover
- Personnel policies that reward and motivate innovative and creative behavior without fear of retribution for failure or too much success
- Development of effective mechanisms to deal with environmental uncertainty and the ability to adapt to change

The most successful organizations incorporate knowledge obtained from their past innovative experiences into their strategies and future innovations. This then leads to the development of key capabilities that can improve the organization's performance and improve profitability, development, and growth.

Barriers to Innovation and Creativity

A number of barriers to innovation and creativity that are prevalent in bureaucratic organizations include:

- **Delivery pressures and administrative burdens.** Limited time to dedicate to thinking about how to do things differently causes individuals to miss innovations in delivery service that might be more time- and cost-effective.
- **Guidelines, rules, and policies.** While these are important for day-to-day work life, over time they become roadblocks for out-of-the-box thinking.
- **Short-term budgets and planning horizons.** Inability to think outside of day-to-day pressures on how things could be improved is exacerbated by short-term budgets and planning horizons. Innovative strategies are reduced to tactical responses to immediate needs.
- **Poor rewards and incentives to innovate.** The tradition of higher penalties for failed innovations versus rewards for successful ones remains within large bureaucratic organizations.
- **Culture of risk aversion.** Patterns and routines with primary concerns of accountability, standards, and continuity induce a culture of risk aversion, which impedes and blocks innovation and creativity.
- **Poor skills in active risk or change management.** While opportunity and motivation may be present, there is a relative paucity of skills in change and risk management.
- **Technologies available but constraining cultural or organizational arrangements.** Innovation and creativity are often impeded because there is a resistance to implement innovation

into the organizational culture sometimes resulting from political power issues or the difficulty in learning something new.

Overcoming Barriers to Innovation and Creativity

There are various ways of overcoming these barriers to innovation and creativity:

- **Overcoming the bureaucratic inertia, guidelines, rules, and policies.** Embrace uncertainty and recognize that if failure occurs, it is leading the way toward future progress and advancement. Art Fry, an entrepreneur at 3M, invented the highly profitable Post-it Notes using glue that was not appropriate for its initial use. He did not disregard the glue but found an alternative use for it.
- **Persuasion and motivation.** Highlight the benefits of innovation and creativity by encouraging individuals to think beyond their own job responsibilities and explore the way other disciplines approach problem solving. This will broaden their focus and allow them to see the bigger picture.
- **Facilitation.** Ensure that resources are available for investigation and implementation of innovation.
- **General concepts.**
  o Finding additional resources to support individuals
  o Overcoming any structural or cultural barriers to innovation and creativity
  o Preserving and exerting continuous effort
  o Gaining political support and building alliances

Probably most essential is the support of top-level management and managers throughout the organization. This can be achieved by:

- Establishing clear organizational goals that encourage staff to grow in innovative ways

- Consultation and communication with staff
- Establishing innovation awards and providing informal recognition for innovators
- Relaxing constraints upon innovators
- Protecting innovators by ensuring that their projects have a fair chance for demonstration
- Providing resources for innovators

Innovation and creativity must be effectively managed and should conform to the organizational strategy. Innovation and creativity do not just happen; they need to be integrated into the culture of the organization and be a fundamental part of organizational behavior.

Corporate Entrepreneurial Behavior

Corporate entrepreneurial behavior is a set of actions through which organizations take advantage of entrepreneurial opportunities unrecognized by competitors. Corporate entrepreneurship is considered both an individual and an organizational level phenomenon. Behaviors such as entrepreneurship, renewal, innovation, risk taking, and proactivity differentiate entrepreneurship from non-entrepreneurship in large organizations. Companies like 3M and Microsoft consistently maintain high levels of entrepreneurship. Research on corporate entrepreneurial performance has found that organizations that are more entrepreneurially orientated have a higher level of performance, making corporate entrepreneurship important for organizational success and development.

Five aspects of corporate entrepreneurial attitudes and behaviors are corporate venturing, renewal, innovation, risk taking, and proactiveness. Corporate venturing refers to pursuing and entering businesses related to the organization's current products or services. Renewal emphasizes strategy reformulation, reorganization, and organizational change. Innovativeness reflects supporting new ideas, experimentation, and creative processes, thereby moving away from established practices and technologies. Risk taking is a willingness to commit the needed amounts of resources to projects where outcomes are unknown and the cost of failure could potentially be high. Proactiveness is anticipating and acting on future needs, wants, and expectations in the external environment. Corporate entrepreneurship is a strategic construct that includes certain organizational outcomes and management related preferences, goals, objectives, beliefs, and behaviors.

Corporate entrepreneurship incorporates both attitudinal and behavioral components. It refers to the willingness of an organization to embrace new opportunities and take responsibility for effecting creative change. This individual or group can be considered the entrepreneurial agent. Behaviorally, the components include the set of activities required to identify an opportunity, develop the concept, assess the required resources, acquire the necessary resources, and manage and harvest the venture. These activities are considered an entrepreneurial event.

Studies on entrepreneurial behavior have focused on psychological and behavioral characteristics. The psychological school of thought states that private and corporate entrepreneurs share a common type of personality that explains their behavior. This common type of personality differentiates them from the general population, and this difference can be explained in terms of their personality profile. Entrepreneurs such as Richard Branson (Virgin), Michael Dell (Dell Computer), Bill Gates (Microsoft), Steve Jobs (Apple), Martha Stewart (Living Omnimedia), Meg Whitman (eBay), and Mark Zuckerberg (Facebook) are frequently recognized as heroes with celebrity status and as role models.

One major contributor to this theory was American psychological theorist David C. McClelland.[3] According to this psychological view, a range of personality traits can be identified to indicate high need achievement individuals who are likely to exhibit these entrepreneurial characteristics. Personality characteristics include a need for achievement, need for responsibility, need for power, motivation, risk taking propensity, locus of control, and innovation.

Defining this need for achievement as "a desire to do well, not so much for the sake of social recognition or prestige, but for the sake of an inner feeling of personal accomplishment," McClelland wrote, "A society with a generally high level of need for achievement will produce more energetic entrepreneurs who, in turn, produce more rapid economic development."[4] According to McClelland, entrepreneurship is an intervening variable between need-achievement (nAch) and economic growth. By increasing the level of nAch in a society, there will be a subsequent stimulation of entrepreneurship and economic development. Not only did he find that entrepreneurs were high on nAch, but they also:

- Desire to take personal responsibility for their decisions
- Prefer decisions involving a moderate degree of risk
- Are interested in concrete knowledge of the results of decisions
- Dislike repetitive, routine work

Similarly, corporate entrepreneurial attitudes and behaviors include:

- The desire and motivation to achieve and compete within the organization
- Taking ownership and being accountable for key projects
- Having the necessary autonomy and empowerment to make independent and self-directed decisions
- Being flexible and open to new information, people, and practices
- Being able to tolerate ambiguity and uncertainty within the organizational boundaries and the external environment
- Innovative and creative thinking, problem solving, and decision making

- The ability to see and capture opportunities within the constraints of the organization
- Awareness of the risks attached to choices, actions, and potential consequences
- The capacity to manage and ultimately reduce risks in line with organizational goals and objectives
- Persistence, optimism, and determination in the face of challenge or lack of immediate reward
- Considering, discussing, and formulating a vision as part of the organizational strategy
- The capacity to make an impact

Corporate entrepreneurs are driven by the challenge and opportunity to achieve. They tend to be independent and self-reliant. When accomplishing a task, they prefer to take ownership and have a degree of autonomy and flexibility. The very nature of the corporate entrepreneurship process requires that the corporate entrepreneur have a tolerance for ambiguity and uncertainty. The most successful corporate entrepreneurs appreciate that if the process achieves success, it will diverge from the initially anticipated path. This tolerance for uncertainty combined with flexibility and adaptability is a fundamental part of the process itself.

The corporate entrepreneur demonstrates innovation and creativity combined with taking ownership for the idea and assuming responsibility for its implementation. Creativity is not just about idea generation but is also a fundamental part of the implementation process, which requires further creativity in problem solving and decision making to overcome any obstacles. Bruce Griffing was the corporate entrepreneur behind General Electric's digital X-ray project that became a major division of the company.

Corporate entrepreneurs are also calculated risk takers. Calculated risk taking is pursuing a course of action that has a reasonable chance of failing. An individual attempts to manage the potential risk factors through effective contingency planning, problem solving, and decision making. Corporate entrepreneurs demonstrate persistence and determination in formulating a vision aligned with the vision of the organization. Examples of such corporate visions include 3M's Post-it Notes and Scotch Tape, General Electric's lightbulbs and appliances, and Motorola's cellular phones. Some corporate entrepreneurs go beyond their duty as entrepreneurs by breaking corporate rules to achieve success. Charles House (Hewlett-Packard) continued working on a high-quality video monitor, which led to high sales and profit. Philip Estridge (IBM) led a group to develop and market personal computers through the internal sales force and retail market, breaking major operating rules in the process.

Organizations that enable employees to take ownership and think in a more open and flexible manner encourage corporate entrepreneurial behavior. This strategy led to successful corporate entrepreneurial products such as Post-it Notes and LaserDiscs. Between 1997 and 1999, Lucent Technologies created 19 new ventures in Internet software, networking, and wireless and digital broadcast. In 2006, Lucent merged with Paris-based Alcatel, forming a new entity named Alcatel-Lucent. In early 2007, the new company announced it had acquired Nortel's UMTS radio access business to forward its network development of 3G to 4G technologies. Siemens Nixdorf, led by Gerhard Schulmeyer from 1994 to 1997, produced the turnaround and transformation for the new entrepreneurial culture, bringing in 250 entrepreneurs to head new business units. From 1967 until 1986, DuPont set up 85 new directional businesses resulting in sales of $28 billion and profits of $318 million. Nokia set up new ventures in 1998 to develop ideas with potential for revenues of £500 million within four to five years. Early success with Nokia's Internet communications to commercialize WAP-enabled Nokia to be the world's leading mobile phone supplier. Toshiba created the birth and growth of laptop and notebook computers as a result of the vision, persistence, and championing efforts of Japanese corporate entrepreneurs.[5]

Elements of Entrepreneurial Behavior within Organizations

Three main elements of entrepreneurial behavior in an organization, indicated in Figure 2.1, are (1) opportunity identification, (2) opportunity facilitation, and (3) opportunity desire and motivation. Opportunity identification is the awareness of conditions or prerequisites for the organization and individual managers to change and develop something new. Opportunity identification is the catalyst for the entrepreneurial process and involves having unconstrained relationships and networks, being well informed, having access to acquired information, and having the necessary resources to make decisions and achieve desirable outcomes. In an entrepreneurial-driven organization, individuals throughout the organization not only believe they should be innovative but also are encouraged and permitted to behave in this manner. Common activities include association with key people, networking both formally and informally inside and outside the organization, having access to information on the assigned task, and freely identifying corporate entrepreneurship opportunities.

Second, opportunity facilitation is the way the organization and the individual managers seek to adopt change. The two approaches to initiate change are questioning the assumptions and directions of the organization and having managers as coaches rather than as authority figures. When employees in an organization believe and are encouraged to freely and supportively challenge any other employees in the organization, they can undertake tasks necessary to facilitate opportunities within the organization. Opportunity facilitation does not necessarily achieve desirable outcomes on its own, as it also requires an appropriate system of rewards and motivation.

Finally, opportunity desire and motivation involve the overall willingness to pursue the opportunity. Rewards enhance the motivation of individuals to engage in entrepreneurial behavior. Rewarding employees for success goes beyond the tangible financial returns and includes recognition, feedback, and meaningful work.

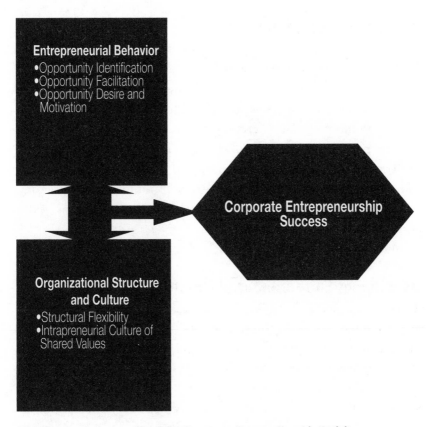

FIGURE 2.1   Behaviors Promoting Corporate Entrepreneurship Activity

Efforts to enhance the performance of organizations partly depend on the ability to successfully reward and motivate employees. An effective reward system that spurs entrepreneurial activity must take into account goals, feedback, emphasis on individual responsibility, and results-based incentives.

Being able to identify and facilitate opportunities, having the desire and motivation to pursue them, and being rewarded establishes an entrepreneurial climate in organizations and is evident in such companies as 3M, DuPont, General Electric, Hewlett-Packard, IBM, Lucent, Microsoft, Nokia, and Toshiba.

An Entrepreneurial Culture

An entrepreneurial culture that promotes the identification and facilitation of opportunities and fosters the desire to pursue these provides an environment for corporate entrepreneurship. This culture fosters managers who achieve desired outcomes by encouraging innovation and creativity. They challenge employees to explore new improved ways of doing things; measure a variety of performance indicators; accept risks and mistakes; support a flexible and fluid organizational structure that minimizes bureaucracy and maximizes adhocracy; and evaluate innovation in terms of the contribution to the strategy.

Developing Entrepreneurial Organizational Behavior

Table 2.1 illustrates behaviors, structure, and culture that promote entrepreneurial actions (opportunity identification, opportunity facilitation, and opportunity desire and motivation). To generate an entrepreneurial structure, there needs to be a move from the traditional bureaucratic structure to a more decentralized organic structure. This allows a greater degree of flexibility and adaptability, and delegation of authority and autonomy.

Organizations that build structures and develop a culture supportive of corporate entrepreneurial behavior have the following characteristics:

- Clearly communicate the vision to all levels
- Reduce bureaucracy by adapting flatter structures that relinquish control and decision making to experts at different levels
- Facilitate a culture of teamwork and a participative management style
- Create systems that support and encourage innovation in pursuit of a distinct mission in line with the organization's vision

TABLE 2.1 Developing Entrepreneurial Behavior in the Organization

Opportunity Identification	Organizational Competencies
• Active • Time Frame • Key Focus	• Active search for dynamism • Long-term orientation • Structural and cultural changes for intra-preneurial success **Individual Competencies** • Active drive and motivation • Future orientation • Transformation from past behavior
Opportunity Facilitation • Structure • Human Resources • Leadership	**Organizational Competencies** • Concise, defined structural change • Effective human resources policies for change, recruitment, motivation, training, and development • Environmental scanning • Individual competencies • Adaptation to embrace change • Drive and motivation to excel • Moderate level of risk taking with the focus on innovative opportunities to improve
Opportunity Desire and Motivation • Motivation and Desire to Change • Drive to Achieve • Intrinsic and Extrinsic Motivation	**Organizational Competencies** • Drive to change • Long-term strategy to change • Focused and goal orientated **Individual Competencies** • Individual desire to change • Overcome past concerns • Focused and motivated to achieve

- Maintain high standards and values in utilization of resources and undertaken activities
- Emphasize reputation, trust, and mutual interdependence
- Drive and highly motivate employees toward innovation and creativity while taking calculated risks
- Instigate performance measures with focus on support, facilitation, training, and development
- Challenge individuals to build skills and be creative
- Focus on the process, not just the end result

Organizational capabilities for corporate entrepreneurship development include:

- Long-term structural change
- Strategic human resources change policies
- Change in recruitment, selection, training, development, and redeployment
- Change in organizational culture
- Desire and support to change
- Environmental scanning
- Challenging job opportunities

Individual competencies for entrepreneurship development include:

- Drive, energy, and motivation to change
- Drive to achieve
- Future and change orientation
- Challenging the past
- Focus on opportunity to excel
- Utilization of core competencies by being innovative and creative
- Moderate risk taking and proactivity

For organizations to enhance performance, they need to develop a culture and a structure that facilitates and supports these behaviors. This type of culture is evident in leading corporate entrepreneurial companies such as 3M, General Electric, Lucent, Microsoft, Nokia, and Toshiba.

Summary

Innovation and creativity are the foundations of corporate entrepreneurial behavior. The corporate entrepreneur develops innovative and creative solutions to an array of problems or challenges facing the organization. Corporate entrepreneurial behavior takes on many forms. While there are some common behavioral attributes—such as calculated risk taking, intrinsic motivation, internal focus of control, achievement, and recognition—there is no one profile.

The challenge is to build congruent organizations both for today's efforts and tomorrow's innovation. A company needs to be organized to build sufficient internal diversity in strategies, structures, culture, people, and processes to facilitate various kinds of innovation at different levels of the organization.

Corporate entrepreneurship does not just happen; it requires the appropriate interaction among management, individuals, and teams where the organization fosters the appropriate strategies, structures, culture, and systems with the external environment. For organizations to develop and grow in dynamic environments, they need individuals who demonstrate entrepreneurial behaviors and who need to adopt the appropriate strategies, structures, and cultures that support and facilitate these behaviors.

3

Understanding and Managing the Entrepreneurial Process

How does a large, established corporation manage the entrepreneurial spirit of its employees? What are the differences between a manager's decision-making process and those made by the corporate entrepreneur? How can a business adjust its culture to capitalize on corporate entrepreneurship?

Scenario: Google Ventures

Google began when Sergey Brin, a student at Stanford, was assigned to show Larry Page, who was considering attending the school, around campus. The first time they met, the two disagreed about everything—but a year later, they joined forces to form a search engine, and in 1997, they named their project Google, Inc., a variation of the mathematical term for the numeral 1 followed by 100 zeros, "googol."

The company experienced what may be one of the most astounding company growth rates in history. In December 1998, just one year after Brin and Page started working together, *PC Magazine* listed Google as one of the top 100 Web sites of 1998. The magazine determined that Google was exceptionally successful in "returning extremely relevant results." By February 1999, Google's eight employees outgrew their original garage office and moved to an office in Palo Alto and then to Silicon Valley in August of the same year. In 2000, Google employees released versions of Google in 13 languages and later that year launched another project called Google AdWords, a pay-per-click service enabling companies big and small to be located online by potential buyers of their products. In November 2000, Google released Google Analytics, a program that helped companies measure the effectiveness of their AdWords campaigns as well as their Web sites. The AdWords program helped Google double profits between 2006 and 2008, from $6.3 billion to $13.1 billion.

In 2001, Google became accessible in 26 languages, and 3 billion documents were indexed and available to users. By early 2002, Google's language version count rose to 72 (including Klingon), and in January 2003, the American Dialect Society had decided that "Google" was the most used word in 2002. By early 2004, Google had indexed 6 billion items and moved its headquarters to a new and larger office where employees were given a campuslike environment. Google Local (later renamed Google Places), a local search service, was then launched, allowing users to quickly locate local services. Google Maps was started in early 2005, and by April of that year, Google was featuring satellite views and providing directions to its users from one location to another. In fact, not only was this feature available on the computer, but also on mobile phones. Suddenly users were accessing driving directions through SMS!

Google created a policy early on allowing all employees to spend 20 percent of their working day on personal projects. It was also a policy to not punish failure but accept mistakes as a natural process for innovation. For example, Paul Buchheit developed Gmail, the e-mail service, in 2001 during his "20 percent time." To entice users to Gmail, Google employees decided to make the e-mail service an invitation-only application: in order to get a Gmail account, a potential user had to be invited to create an account by an existing account holder. The clever idea initially made users feel a part of an exclusive group, and by September 2008, Gmail had 26 million account holders. The number of Gmail accounts surpassed the number of Hotmail accounts at the end of 2009. Continuing its improvements, Google Chat was introduced in 2006, allowing Gmail users to converse with one another while logged into their e-mail.

By July 2009, Google programs and inventions by employees included Google Voice, Google Earth (also available on iPhone and iPod mobile devices), Google Translate (between 41 languages), Google Book Search, OpenSocial, Google Romance, Google Docs, Google Finance, Picasa, Google Reader, Google Scholar, Google Chrome, and Froogle. By June 2006, "Google" had become a formally recognized verb by the Oxford English Dictionary.

Throughout its growth, Google maintained a laid back and friendly atmosphere—dogs were allowed at the office, company employees engaged in cook-off contests, scholarships were offered, and April Fool's Day hoaxes became a tradition. The company also knew the importance of investing in people and projects, and in being involved with its users. One program, started in 2005, focused on educating students in computer science by launching programs such as Summer of Code, which challenged participants to write codes for technology-based projects such as dealing with development and licensing issues. Another activity consisted of asking its users to interpret how Gmail travels around the world; Google received over 1,100 fascinating video responses from users across 65 countries. Additionally, in October 2002, Google introduced the first ever Code Jam—a competition for programmers to work complex coding problems in Java, C++, C#, or VB.NE. The goal of the competition was to find the best programming engineers to rewrite the world's information infrastructure. Code Jam continued on a frequent basis. By January 2006, the competition was in China, with over 13,000 participants, and by July 2010, it was in Europe, with over 10,000 attendees. This competition continues to produce effective solutions for Google's past programming problems and provide those answers in an educational, online format.

Google, Inc., went public in August 2004 with an opening price of $85 per share. By May 2008, the stock price was $580 per share, though the economic downturn in 2009 caused it to drop to $400. The incredible rise was largely attributed to Google's entrepreneurial environment, where new products and inventions were created by its empowered and entrepreneurial employees. In 2009, Google began considering restructuring options in order to promote more flow of new and innovative ideas.

The goal of Google Ventures, established in March 2009, was to follow the strategies and techniques of venture capital firms while integrating Google's technology expertise and encouraging further innovation. Over the first year, Google Ventures expected to invest roughly $100 million not only in existing Google corporate entrepreneurs but also in outside technology businesses. The most important consideration was ROI expectations instead of strategic decisions; particular industries of interest included consumer Internet, software, hardware, cleantech, biotech, and health care. The goal was to invest in businesses that were finding a solution to a problem in creative and innovative ways.

With a simple four-page Web site written in friendly and conversational wording, Google Ventures invested in seed and early stage start-ups. The first two portfolio investments were Pixazza, Inc., and Silver Spring Networks. Pixazza, originally founded in 2008, turns static images into engaging content. Silver Spring Networks builds real-time networks that allow a public utility such as power using "smart meters" to make changes in its business that will help improve efficiency, reliability, and customer service.

Ultimately, Google hopes and expects to continue its innovation well into the future and to capitalize on the next big opportunity.

www.google.com/ventures/faq.html
www.techcrunch.com/2009/04/04/the-google-ventures-cheat-sheet/
http://pixazza.com/
www.silverspringnetworks.com/

www.businessweek.com/technology/content/sep2007/
  tc20070831_697591.htm
www.informationweek.com/news/internet/google/showArticle.
  jhtml?articleID=213300662
http://methainternet.wordpress.com/2009/04/04/google-forms-
  venture-group-to-find-next-big-thing/
www.google.com/corporate/history.html

The Entrepreneurial Process

As is indicated in the case of Google, organizations are interested in creating an environment that will empower all employees to act entrepreneurially and to pursue the entrepreneurial process inside the organization. The process of starting a new venture is embodied in the entrepreneurial process, which involves more than just problem solving of a typical management position. This process has four distinct phases: (1) identification and evaluation of the opportunity, (2) development of the business plan, (3) determination of the required resources, and (4) management of the resulting enterprise (see Figure 3.1). Although these phases proceed progressively, no one stage is dealt with in isolation or is totally completed before the work is begun on other phases.

Identify and Evaluate the Opportunity

Opportunity identification and evaluation is a very difficult task. Most good business opportunities do not suddenly appear, but rather result from a corporate entrepreneur's alertness to possibilities and unmet customer needs or, in some cases, the establishment of mechanisms that identify potential opportunities such as Google's use of Google Ventures.

Although most corporate entrepreneurs do not have formal mechanisms for identifying business opportunities, some sources

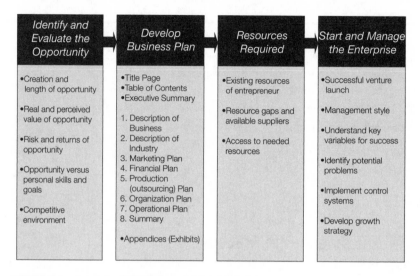

Identify and Evaluate the Opportunity	Develop Business Plan	Resources Required	Start and Manage the Enterprise
•Creation and length of opportunity •Real and perceived value of opportunity •Risk and returns of opportunity •Opportunity versus personal skills and goals •Competitive environment	•Title Page •Table of Contents •Executive Summary 1. Description of Business 2. Description of Industry 3. Marketing Plan 4. Financial Plan 5. Production (outsourcing) Plan 6. Organization Plan 7. Operational Plan 8. Summary •Appendices (Exhibits)	•Existing resources of entrepreneur •Resource gaps and available suppliers •Access to needed resources	•Successful venture launch •Management style •Understand key variables for success •Identify potential problems •Implement control systems •Develop growth strategy

FIGURE 3.1   Aspects of the Entrepreneurial Process

are often fruitful: consumers and business associates, members of the distribution system, and technical experts. Often, consumers are the best source of ideas for a new venture. How many times have you heard someone comment, "If only there was a product that would . . ."? This comment can result in the creation of a new business. One corporate entrepreneur's evaluation of why so many business executives were complaining about the lack of good technical writing and word-processing services resulted in the creation of a business unit to fill this need.

Due to their close contact with the end user, channel members in the distribution system also see product needs. Many corporate entrepreneurs have identified business opportunities through a discussion with a retailer, wholesaler, or manufacturer's representative of the company.

Finally, technically oriented individuals often conceptualize business opportunities when working on other projects. One corporate entrepreneur's business resulted from seeing the application of a plastic resin compound in developing and manufacturing a new type of pallet while developing the resin application in another totally unrelated area—casket moldings—in the company.

Whether the opportunity is identified by using input from consumers, business associates, channel members, organized competitions (as in the case of Google's Code Jam), or technical experts, each opportunity must be carefully screened and evaluated. This evaluation of the opportunity is perhaps the most critical element of the entrepreneurial process, as it allows the corporate entrepreneur to assess whether the specific product or service offers the returns needed compared to the resources required. As indicated in Figure 3.1, this evaluation process involves looking at the length of the opportunity, its real and perceived value, its risks and returns, its fit with the personal skills and goals of the corporate entrepreneur, and its uniqueness or differential advantage in its competitive environment.

The market size and the length of the *window of opportunity* are the basis for determining the risks and rewards. The risks reflect the market, competition, technology, and amount of involved capital. One company that delivered bark mulch to residential and commercial users for decoration around the base of trees and shrubs added loam and shells to its product line. These products (called follow-on products) were sold to the same customer base using the same distribution (delivery) system. Follow-on products are important for a company expanding or diversifying in a particular channel.

Finally, the opportunity must fit the personal skills and goals of the corporate entrepreneur. It is particularly important that the corporate entrepreneur be able to put forth the necessary time and effort required to make the venture succeed. A corporate entrepreneur needs to believe in the opportunity and make the necessary sacrifices to develop the opportunity.

Opportunity analysis, or what is frequently called an *opportunity assessment plan*, is one method for evaluating an opportunity and will be discussed in Chapter 5.

Develop a Business Plan

A good *business plan* must be developed in order to exploit the defined opportunity. This is a very time-consuming phase of the entrepreneurial process. A corporate entrepreneur often has not prepared a business plan before and does not have the resources available to do a good job. Since the preparation of the business plan is the focus of Chapter 9, it is important to note here the basic issues involved as well as the three major sections of the plan (see Figure 3.1). A good business plan is essential to developing the opportunity and determining and obtaining the resources required.

Determine the Resources Required

The resources needed for addressing the opportunity must also be determined. Any critical resources need to be differentiated from those that are just helpful. Care must be taken not to underestimate the amount and variety of resources needed. The downside risks associated with insufficient or inappropriate resources should also be assessed—in other words, a worst-case scenario.

Start and Manage the Enterprise

After acquiring resources, the corporate entrepreneur must use them to implement the business plan. A successful launch is often very difficult to achieve. A control system must be established so that any problem areas can be quickly identified and resolved.

Managerial versus Corporate Entrepreneurship Decision Making

The difference between the corporate entrepreneurship and the managerial can be viewed from five key business dimensions—strategic orientation, commitment to opportunity, commitment of resources, control of resources, and management structure.

Strategic Orientation

The corporate entrepreneurial strategic orientation depends on the perception of the opportunity. This orientation is most important when (other) opportunities have diminishing returns accompanied by rapid changes in technology, consumer economies, social values, or political rules. When the strategic orientation involves the use of planning systems as well as measuring performance to control current resources, the administrative (managerial) domain is operant.

Commitment to Opportunity

In terms of the commitment to opportunity, the second key business dimension, the two domains vary greatly with respect to the length of this commitment. The *entrepreneurial domain* is pressured by the need for action, short decision windows, a willingness to assume risk, and few decision constituencies. This creates a short time span in terms of opportunity commitment. The administrative (managerial) domain is not only slow to act on an opportunity, but once action is taken, the commitment is usually for a long time span, too long in some instances. There are often no mechanisms established to stop and reevaluate an initial resource commitment.

Commitment of Resources

A corporate entrepreneur is accustomed to having resources committed at periodic intervals that are often based on certain tasks or objectives being reached. This process forces the corporate entrepreneur to maximize any resources used to produce a high level of efficiency. This multistage commitment allows the resource providers (such as venture capitalists or private investors) to have as small an exposure as possible at each stage of business development and to constantly monitor the established track record. Even though the funding may also be implemented in stages in the administrative domain, the commitment of the resources is for the total amount needed. Administratively oriented individuals respond to the source of the rewards offered and receive personal rewards by effectively administering the resources under their control.

Control of Resources

Control of the resources follows a similar pattern. Since the administrator (manager) is rewarded by effective resource administration, there is often a drive to own or accumulate as many resources as possible. The pressures of power, status, and financial rewards cause the administrator (manager) to avoid rental or other periodic use of the resource. The opposite is true for the corporate entrepreneur who—under the pressures of limited resources, the risk of obsolescence, a need for flexibility, and the risks involved—strives to rent, or otherwise achieve periodic use of, the resources on an as-needed basis.

Management Structure

The final business dimension, management structure, also differs significantly between the two domains. In the administrative domain, the organizational structure is formalized and hierarchical in nature, reflecting the need for clearly defined lines of authority and responsibility. The corporate entrepreneur, true to his or her desire for independence and, in general, owning a smaller firm with fewer employees, employs a flat organizational structure with informal networks throughout.

Causes for Interest in Corporate Entrepreneurship

These differences in the corporate entrepreneurial and managerial domains have contributed to an increased interest in corporate entrepreneurship. This interest has increased due to a variety of events occurring on social, cultural, and business levels. On a social level, there is an increasing interest in "doing your own thing" and doing it in your own way. Individuals who believe strongly in their own talents frequently desire to create something accompanied by a need to take on new risks and challenges. They want responsibility and have a strong need for individual expression and freedom in their work environment. When this freedom is not there, frustration can cause that individual to become less productive or even leave the organization to achieve self-actualization elsewhere. This new search for meaning, and the impatience involved, has recently caused more discontent in structured organizations than ever before. Corporate entrepreneurship—developing a spirit of entrepreneurship within the existing organization—is one method of stimulating and then capitalizing on individuals in an organization who think that something can be done differently and better, as was the case of Google's success with Google Venture.

Most people think of Xerox as a large bureaucratic Fortune 100 company. Yet Xerox has done something unique in trying to ensure that its creative employees do not leave like Steve Jobs did to form Apple Computer, Inc. In 1989, Xerox set up Xerox Technology Ventures (XTV) for generating profits by investing in the promising technologies of the company, many of which would have otherwise been overlooked. Xerox wanted to avoid mistakes of the past by having "a system to prevent technology from leaking out of the company," according to Robert V. Adams, president of XTV.

The fund has supported numerous start-ups like Quad Mark, the brainchild of Dennis Stemmle, a Xerox employee of 25 years. Stemmle's idea was to make a battery-operated, plain paper copier that would fit in a briefcase along with a laptop computer. While for 10 years Xerox's operating committee did not approve the idea, XTV and Taiwan's Advanced Scientific Corporation funded the idea. As is the case with all the companies funded by XTV, the founder and key employees own 20 percent of the company. This provides an incentive for employees like Dennis Stemmle to take the risk of leaving Xerox to form a technology-based venture.

XTV provides both financial and nonfinancial benefits to its parent, Xerox. The funded companies provide profits to the parent company as well as the founders and employees. Xerox managers now pay closer attention to employees' ideas as well as internal technologies. Is XTV a success? If replication is any indication, then yes. The XTV concept contains an element of risk in that Xerox employees forming new ventures are not guaranteed a management position if the new venture fails. This makes XTV different from the new ventures created in most companies. This aspect of risk and no guaranteed employment is the basis for AT&T Ventures, a fund modeled on XTV.

What Xerox recognized is what hundreds of executives are also becoming aware of in their organizations: it is important to have the entrepreneurial spirit in an organization in order to innovate and grow. In a large organization, problems often occur that thwart creativity and innovation, particularly in activities not directly related to the organization's main mission. The growth and diversification that can result from this flexibility and creativity are particularly critical for the future of the company.

Corporate entrepreneurship is most strongly reflected in entrepreneurial activities as well as in top management orientations in organizations. These corporate entrepreneurial endeavors consist of the following four activities: new business venturing, innovativeness, self-renewal, and proactiveness.

New *business venturing* (sometimes called corporate entrepreneurship) refers to the creation of a new business within an existing organization. These entrepreneurial activities consist of creating new value by redefining the company's current products or services, by developing new markets, or by forming more formally autonomous or semi-autonomous units or firms. Formations of new corporate ventures are the most salient manifestations of corporate entrepreneurship. The second key element of entrepreneurial endeavors, *organizational innovativeness,* refers to product and service innovation with an emphasis on development and innovation in technology. It involves new product development, product improvements, and new production methods and procedures.

Self-renewal is the transformation of an organization through the renewal of the key ideas on which they are built. It has strategic and organizational change connotations and includes a redefinition of the business concept, reorganization, and the introduction of systemwide changes to increase innovation.

Proactiveness involves taking initiatives and risks while building competitive aggressiveness and boldness that are particularly reflected in the orientations and activities of top management. A proactive organization tends to take risks by conducting experiments, taking initiative, and being bold and aggressive in pursuing opportunities. Organizations with this proactive spirit attempt to lead rather than follow competitors in such key business areas as the introduction of new products or services, operating technologies, and administrative techniques.

Managerial versus Corporate Entrepreneurial Culture

Business and sociological conditions have given rise to a new era in business: the era of the entrepreneur. These smaller, aggressive, entrepreneurially driven firms are developing more new products and becoming major factors in select markets. Recognizing the results that occur when employees in other large corporations catch this "entrepreneurial fever," many companies are now attempting to create the same spirit, culture, challenges, and rewards of entrepreneurship in their organizations. What are the differences between corporate and entrepreneurial cultures? What are the differences among managers, entrepreneurs, and corporate entrepreneurs?

The typical *corporate culture* has a climate and a reward system that favors conservative decision making. Emphasis is on gathering large amounts of data as the basis for a rational decision and then using the data to justify the decision should the intended results not occur. Risky decisions are often postponed until enough facts can be gathered or a consultant can be hired to "illuminate the unknown." Caution is valued more highly than new opportunities as a wrong turn has the potential to negatively affect the entire corporation and the individual's career. Frequently, there are so many sign-offs and approvals required for a large-scale project that no individual feels personally responsible. Some corporate cultures emphasize decision-making initiatives funneling from a top down, hierarchical structure. Few have the power and responsibility to create entrepreneurial changes.

The traditional corporate culture differs significantly from a *corporate entrepreneurship culture.* Guiding principles in a traditional corporate culture include: adhere to the instructions given from top management, do not make any mistakes, do not fail, do not take the initiative but wait for instructions, stay on your own turf, and protect your backside by avoiding direct responsibility. This restrictive environment is, of course, not conducive to creativity, flexibility, independence, ownership, or risk taking—the guiding principles of corporate entrepreneurship. Rather, it is an environment directed at promoting the efficiency of current resources.

There are also differences in the shared values and norms of the two cultures. The traditional corporation is hierarchical in nature, with established procedures, reporting systems, lines of authority and responsibility, instructions, and control mechanisms. These support the present corporate culture and do not encourage new product, service, or venture creation. The culture of a corporate entrepreneurial firm is in stark contrast to this model. Instead of a hierarchical structure, a corporate entrepreneurial climate has a flat, fluid organizational structure encouraging networking, teamwork, sponsors, and mentors. Close working relationships help establish an atmosphere of trust that facilitates the accomplishment of visions and objectives. Tasks are viewed as fun, personalized events, not chores, with participants gladly putting in the number of hours necessary to get the job done. Instead of building barriers to protect turfs, individuals make suggestions within and across functional areas and divisions, resulting in a cross-fertilization of ideas. This approach can also produce an internally competitive environment where barriers still exist as certain projects or functions compete to create the next best idea, as in the case of Microsoft's culture.

These two cultures produce and hire different types of individuals and have different management styles. A comparison of traditional managers, entrepreneurs, and corporate entrepreneurs reveals several differences (see Table 3.1). While *traditional managers* are motivated primarily by promotion and typical corporate rewards, entrepreneurs and corporate entrepreneurs thrive on independence and the ability to create.

There is a different time orientation in the three groups, with managers emphasizing the short run, entrepreneurs the long run, and corporate entrepreneurs somewhere in between. Similarly, the primary mode of activity of corporate entrepreneurs falls between the delegation activity of managers and the direct involvement of entrepreneurs. Whereas corporate entrepreneurs and entrepreneurs are moderate risk takers, managers are much more cautious about taking any risks. Protecting one's corporate career and turf is a way of life for many traditional managers, and risky activities are avoided at almost any cost.

Whereas traditional managers tend to be most concerned about those at a higher level in the organization, entrepreneurs serve themselves and their customers, and corporate entrepreneurs add sponsors to these to entrepreneurial categories. This reflects the respective background of the three types of individuals. Instead of building strong relationships with those around them the way entrepreneurs and corporate entrepreneurs do, managers tend to follow the relationship explicitly outlined in the organizational chart.

TABLE 3.1 Comparison of Traditional Managers, Entrepreneurs, and Corporate Entrepreneurs

	Traditional Managers	Entrepreneurs	Corporate Entrepreneurs
Primary Motives	Promotion and other traditional corporate rewards, such as office, staff, and power	Independence, opportunity to create, and money	Independence and ability to advance in the corporate rewards
Time Orientation	Short-term, meeting quotas and budgets, weekly, monthly, quarterly, and annual planning horizons	Survival and achieving 5- to 10-year growth of business	Between entrepreneurial and traditional managers, depending on urgency to meet self-imposed and corporate timetable
Activity	Delegates and supervises more than direct involvement	Direct involvement	Direct involvement more than delegation
Risk	Careful	Moderate risk taker	Moderate risk taker
Status	Concerned about status symbols	Not concerned about status symbols	Not concerned about traditional corporate status symbols; desires independence
Failure and Mistakes	Tries to avoid mistakes and surprises	Deals with mistakes and failures	Attempts to hide risky projects from view until ready
Decisions	Usually agrees with those in upper management positions	Follows dream with decisions	Able to get others to agree to help achieve dream
Who Serves	Others	Self and customers	Self, customers, and sponsors
Family History	Family members worked for large organization	Entrepreneurial small-business, professional, or farm background	Entrepreneurial, small-business, professional, or farm background
Relationship with Others	Hierarchy as basic relationship	Transactions and deal making as basic relationship	Transactions within hierarchy

Source: A modified version of a table in G. Pinchot, *Intrapreneurship*, New York: Harper & Row, 1985, pp. 54–56.

Aspects of Corporate Entrepreneurship

While there can be many aspects of corporate entrepreneurship that can vary significantly from organization to organization, the four most significant ones that affect the level occurring are indicated in the formula below:

$$L = I + O + C^2$$

Where: L = Level of Corporate Entrepreneurship
    I = Innovation
    O = Ownership
    C = Creativity
    C = Change

Each of these four aspects—innovation, ownership, creativity, and change—will be discussed in turn.

Innovation

While innovation is highly valued and a central aspect of most organizations as indicated in the speeches of their top administrators and the aggressive expenditures on it, few organizations are satisfied with the return on their spending, as was discussed in Chapter 2. According to a survey on corporate innovation by the Boston Consulting Group, which drew responses from about 3,000 global executives, innovation is at or near the top of the company's agenda with 43 percent of the respondents considering it one of their three most important strategic priorities and 23 percent considering it their top priority.

Yet in spite of its priority, satisfaction with the return on innovation spending decreased from 52 percent in 2006 to 46 percent in 2007 to 43 percent in 2008. This dissatisfaction with the return on the spending has also caused a decrease in the amount of spending on innovation from 72 percent (2006) to 67 percent (2007) to 63 percent (2008).

Dissatisfaction with the return on spending on innovation occurs at all levels of many organizations regardless of the industry. Many factors affect this poor return, such as a noncorporate entrepreneurial culture; an aversion to risk; the inability to select the right ideas to commercialize; a lack of internal coordination; a long development time from idea to market launch (as discussed in Chapter 5); an inability to institute "best practices" to capitalize on the idea; and the desire to always hit a home run. This last concern reflects a wrong assumption. Venture capitalists' track records show that out of ten investments, generally there are: one very big success; two successes; four walking wounded or living dead (not good, not bad), in which exit would be desired if the money invested would be recouped; and three failures.

One way to gain a perspective on this aspect is to understand the nature of the types of innovations generated as discussed in Chapter 2. As is indicated in Figure 3.2, the majority of innovative events are ordinary innovations—innovations that represent a small change in the way things are generally done; how the product looks, tastes, or performs; or even in the packaging itself. The next most frequent in occurrence are the technological innovations. These are innovations that have some more advanced technological aspect than what is presently occurring in the market. Frequently these are protected by a patent or copyright. Big successes come from breakthrough innovations, the smallest number of innovative events where a radical transformation occurs from what is then taking place in the market. The personal computer, cell phone, social networks, and the Internet are indeed breakthrough innovations. Organizational managers need to manage their expectations and realize that although a breakthrough innovation and a resulting home run can occur, most innovative events in their organizations will be technological or ordinary ones. However, these can produce significant benefits and results as well.

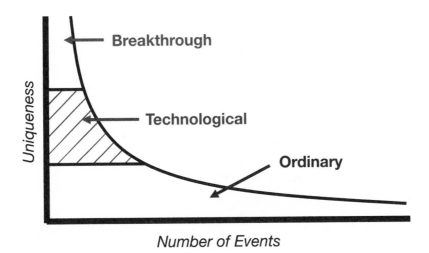

FIGURE 3.2   Innovation Chart

Ownership

Ownership is also essential to corporate entrepreneurship in an organization and reflects the overall organizational environment or culture. In this sense, ownership means owning and feeling responsible for one's job, having the desire to perform the job in the most efficient and effective manner, and in essence loving to go to work.

The overall characteristics of a good corporate entrepreneurial environment, which encourages ownership to occur, are summarized below. The first of these is making sure the organization operates on the frontiers of technology. Since research and development are key sources for successful new product ideas, the firm must operate on the cutting edge of the industry's technology, encouraging and supporting new ideas instead of discouraging them, as frequently occurs in firms that require a rapid return on investment and a high sales volume.

Corporate Entrepreneurial Environments
- Organization operates on frontiers of technology
- New ideas encouraged

- Trial and error encouraged
- Failures allowed
- No opportunity parameters
- Resources available and accessible
- Multidiscipline teamwork approach
- Long time horizon
- Volunteer program
- Appropriate reward system
- Sponsors and champions available
- Support of top management

Second, experimentation—trial and error—is encouraged. Successful new products or services usually do not appear fully developed; instead, they evolve requiring time and money. It took time and some product failures before the first marketable computer appeared. A company wanting to establish a corporate entrepreneurial spirit has to establish an environment that allows mistakes and failures in developing new innovative products. The failures of the corporate entrepreneurs should be viewed more as indirect investments for creating the successful innovative products. This is in direct opposition to the established career and promotion system of the traditional organization. Yet without the opportunity to fail in an organization, few if any corporate entrepreneurial ventures would be developed. Almost every entrepreneur has experienced at least one failure in establishing a successful venture.

Third, an organization should make sure that there are no initial opportunity parameters inhibiting creativity in new product development. Frequently in an organization, various "turfs" are protected, frustrating attempts by potential corporate entrepreneurs to establish new ventures. In one Fortune 500 company, an attempt to establish a corporate entrepreneurial environment ran into problems and eventually failed when the potential corporate entrepreneurs were informed that a proposed new product and venture was not possible because it was in the domain of another division.

Fourth, the resources of the firm need to be available and easily accessible so that the firm supports its corporate entrepreneurs. As one corporate entrepreneur stated, "If my company really wants me to take the time, effort, and career risks to establish a new venture, then it needs to put money and people resources on the line." Often, insufficient funds are allocated not to create something new, but instead to solve problems that have an immediate effect on the bottom line. Some companies—like Xerox, 3M, and AT&T—have recognized this problem and established separate venture-capital areas for funding new internal as well as external ventures. This is discussed in Chapter 11. Even when resources are available, all too often the reporting requirements become obstacles to obtaining them.

Fifth, the corporation needs to encourage a multidisciplined team approach. This open approach, with participation by needed individuals regardless of area, is the antithesis of the typical corporate organizational structure. An evaluation of successful cases of corporate entrepreneurship indicated that one key to success was the existence of "skunkworks" involving relevant people. Developing the needed teamwork for a new venture is further complicated by the fact that a team member's promotion and overall career within the corporation are based on his or her performance in the current position, not on his or her contribution to the new venture being created.

Besides encouraging teamwork, the corporate environment must establish a long time horizon for evaluating the success of the overall program as well as the success of each individual venture. This patient attitude toward money in the corporate setting is no different from the investment-return time horizon used by venture capitalists and others when they invest in an entrepreneurial effort.

Sixth, the spirit of corporate entrepreneurship cannot be forced upon individuals; it must be on a volunteer basis and cultivated. There is a difference between corporate thinking and corporate entrepreneurial thinking, with certain individuals performing much better on one side of the continuum or the other. Most managers in a corporation are not capable of being successful corporate entrepreneurs, and those who are need the opportunity and the accompanying reward of completing the project.

The seventh characteristic is a reward system. The corporate entrepreneur needs to be appropriately rewarded for all the energy, effort, and risk taking expended in the creation of the new venture. Rewards should be based on the attainment of established performance goals and are discussed in Chapter 10.

Eighth, a corporate environment favorable to corporate entrepreneurship has sponsors and champions throughout the organization who not only support the creative activity but also have the planning flexibility to establish new objectives and directions.

Finally, and perhaps most important, the corporate entrepreneurial activity must be wholeheartedly supported and embraced by members of top management, both by their physical presence and by their making sure that the personnel and the financial resources are available. Without top management support, a successful environment cannot be created.

Creativity

The third aspect of successful corporate entrepreneurship is creativity. Creativity—the ability to bring into being from one's imagination something unique and original—is very important and yet often lacking in many organizations, as was discussed in Chapter 2. Eight of the most frequently used creative problem-solving techniques are discussed on the following pages.

Some Creative Problem-Solving Techniques
- Brainstorming
- Reverse brainstorming
- Checklist method
- Free association
- Collective notebook method
- Attribute listing
- Big-dream approach
- Parameter analysis

Brainstorming
The first technique, *brainstorming*, is probably the most well known and widely used for both creative problem solving and idea generation. In creative problem solving, brainstorming can generate ideas about a problem within a limited time frame through the spontaneous contributions of participants. A good brainstorming session starts with a problem statement that is neither too broad (which would diversify ideas too greatly so that nothing specific would emerge) nor too narrow (which would tend to confine responses). Once the problem statement is prepared, 6 to 12 individuals are selected to participate. Finding individuals who are diverse from one another can also add extra value and insight to a brainstorming session. To avoid inhibiting responses, no group member should be a recognized expert in the field of the problem. All ideas, no matter how illogical, must be recorded, with participants prohibited from criticizing or evaluating during the brainstorming session. With this in mind, excluding certain upper level management in the initial brainstorming session may be an effective way to reduce pressure and concern about possible repercussions.

Reverse Brainstorming
Reverse brainstorming is similar to brainstorming, except that criticism is allowed. In fact, the technique is based on finding fault by asking the question, "In how many ways can this idea fail?"

Since the focus is on the negative aspects of a product, service, or idea, care must be taken to maintain the group's morale. Reverse brainstorming can be effectively used before other creative techniques to stimulate innovative thinking. The process usually involves the identification of everything wrong with an idea, followed by a discussion of ways to overcome these problems. Reverse brainstorming usually produces some worthwhile results, as it is easier for an individual to be critical about an idea than to come up with a new idea.

Checklist Method

In the *checklist method,* a new idea is developed through a list of related issues or suggestions. The corporate entrepreneur can use the list of questions or statements to guide the direction of developing entirely new ideas or concentrating on specific "idea" areas. The checklist may take any form and be of any length. One general checklist is as follows:

- Put to other uses? New ways to use as-is? Other uses if modified?
- Adapt? What else is like this? What other ideas does this suggest? Does the past offer parallel opportunities? What could I copy? Whom could I emulate?
- Modify? New twist? Change meaning, color, motion, odor, form, shape? Other changes?
- Magnify? What to add? More time? Greater frequency? Stronger? Larger? Thicker? Extra value? Plus ingredient? Duplicate? Multiply? Exaggerate?
- Minify? What substitute? Smaller? Condensed? Miniature? Lower? Shorter? Lighter? Omit? Streamline? Split up? Understated?
- Substitute? Who else instead? What else instead? Other ingredient? Other material? Other process? Other power? Other place? Other approach? Other tone of voice?

- Rearrange? Interchange components? Other pattern? Other layout? Other sequence? Transpose cause and effect? Change track? Change schedule?
- Reverse? Transpose positive and negative? How about opposites? Turn it backward? Turn it upside down? Reverse roles? Change shoes? Turn tables? Turn other cheek?
- Combine? How about a blend, an alloy, an assortment, an ensemble? Combine units? Combine purposes? Combine appeals? Combine ideas?

Free Association

One of the simplest yet most effective methods that corporate entrepreneurs can use to generate new ideas is *free association.* This technique is helpful in developing an entirely new slant on a problem. First, a word or phrase related to the problem is written down, then another and another, with each new word attempting to add something new to the ongoing thought processes, thereby creating a chain of ideas ending with a new product idea emerging. It may be beneficial to do the first round of free association as individuals so that ideas from the group do not constantly sidetrack from completing the ideas of each individual. Then bring the participants together for a group free association.

Collective Notebook Method

In the *collective notebook method,* a small notebook that easily fits in a pocket—containing a statement of the problem, blank pages, and any pertinent background data—is distributed. Participants consider the problem and its possible solutions, recording ideas at least once, but preferably three times, a day. At the end of a week, a list of the best ideas is developed, along with any suggestions. This technique can also be used with a group of individuals who record their ideas, giving their notebooks to a central coordinator who summarizes all the material and lists the ideas in order of frequency of mention. In addition, ranking the ideas by importance might be more helpful than ranking by frequency as most people initially think of generic solutions at first and then begin to develop more creative, valuable ideas later. The summary becomes the topic of a final creative focus group discussion by the group participants.

Attribute Listing

Attribute listing is an idea-finding technique that requires the corporate entrepreneur to list the attributes of an item or problem and then look at each from a variety of viewpoints. Through this process, originally unrelated objects can be brought together to form a new combination and possible new uses that better satisfy a need.

Big-Dream Approach

The *big-dream approach* to coming up with a new idea requires that the corporate entrepreneur dream about the problem and its solution—in other words, think big. Every possibility should be recorded and investigated without regard to all the negatives involved or the resources required. Ideas should be conceptualized without any constraints until an idea is developed into a workable form.

Parameter Analysis

A final method for developing a new idea—*parameter analysis*—involves two aspects: parameter identification and creative synthesis. Step one (parameter identification) involves analyzing variables in the situation to determine their relative importance. These variables become the focus of the investigation, with other variables being set aside. After the primary issues have been identified, the relationships between parameters that describe the underlying issues are examined. Through an evaluation of the parameters and relationships, one or more solutions are developed; this solution development is called creative synthesis.

Change

In order for corporate entrepreneurship to thrive in an organization, the final "C" of the formula—change—must continuously be allowed and encouraged. Organizational change should ideally be the result of an accumulation of smaller steps (changes) taken over time. Adam Smith in his *Theory of Moral Sentiments* referred to this as "gradual greatness." People tend to be more accepting of change if they can see and experience the steps slowly. New technologies, strategies, structures, and/or rapid business expansion originate from smaller experimental steps and reflect the transference of knowledge and continual practice in the organization.

The idea that change in an organization should occur incrementally and collectively rather than suddenly suggests that an entrepreneurial organization should be continually experimenting and modifying around the edges of the core business. Change, discovery, and renewal are fundamental aspects of this type of organization. As this becomes more apparent, managers are encouraged to develop creative, individualistic approaches and unexpected solutions to problems. This leads to charismatic individual leadership and inventive, creative decision making. Yet it might be necessary, in order to begin this process, to let go some of the existing managers who neither possess the skills nor desire to develop these softer skills.

One approach to instituting and institutionalizing organizational change is the nine-step approach indicated in the following list. This step-by-step process developed by Kotter is a systematic approach to transform the organization.[1]

Nine Steps to Transforming Your Organization
1. Establish a Sense of Urgency
   - Examining market and competitive realities

- Identifying and discussing crises, potential crises, or opportunities
- Develop appropriate guidelines for time frame
- Implementation must be achievable within the existing scope of organizational resources

2. Forming a Powerful Guiding Coalition
- Assembling a group with enough power to lead the change effort
- Encouraging and allowing the group to work together as a team
- Organize a team of established leaders who can implement and obtain buy-in of others and also work toward organizational goals without blocking tasks with personal agendas

3. Creating a Vision of End Result
- Creating a vision to help direct the change effort
- Developing a strategic plan (mission, goals/objectives, strategies/tactics) for achieving that vision

4. Communicating the Vision
- Using every vehicle possible to communicate the new vision and strategies
- Teaching new behaviors by example of the guiding coalition
- Measuring progress toward the end goal must be visible and continually communicated to all

5. Selecting a Champion
- Selecting a champion who can spearhead the transformation
- Champion needs to be able to communicate the vision in a powerful way

6. Empowering Others to Act on the Vision
   - Getting rid of obstacles to change
   - Changing systems that undermine the vision and discourage risk taking
   - Rewarding creative thinking and implementation at any level
   - Acknowledge that employees are the ones responsible for achieving success

7. Planning for and Creating Short-Term Wins
   - Planning for visible performance improvements
   - Recognizing and rewarding employees involved in the improvements with more than token rewards
   - Stair step achievements: Winning small battles to "win the war"
   - Build in accomplishments which lead to the end goal and reward those that add value to that achievement

8. Consolidating Improvements and Producing Still More Changes
   - Using increased credibility to change systems, structures, and policies
   - Hiring, promoting, and developing employees who can implement the vision
   - Giving employees the opportunity to initiate change

9. Institutionalizing New Approaches
   - Articulating the connections between new behaviors and success
   - Developing the means to ensure leadership development and succession
   - Standardizing the process for all future change initiatives

The first steps are to establish a sense of urgency and form a strong guiding coalition. Since an organization is focused on short-term results without establishing the need for change due to the external environment and competitive landscape, the appropriate time frame will not be established. And if a group is not established that has enough power and credibility, nothing will be implemented.

The group needs to establish a vision and strategic plan (step 3) and communicate this throughout the organization by every means possible (step 4). Following the identification and selection of a champion (step 5), limit the obstacles, establish the appropriate new system, and reward all creative thinking (step 6). The next step (step 7) is to ensure to the extent possible that the first initiatives are successful with visible performance improvements. This will make failures easier to handle when they occur, which they will. It is easier to be successful at smaller changes than larger ones. Eventually, the new changes need to be consolidated, producing still more changes (step 8) with change approach and change attitude institutionalized in the organization (step 9). This procedure allows for the successful implementation of the difficult aspects of change involved in the intrapreneurial formula.

Summary
This chapter focused on understanding and managing the corporate venturing process. Attention was paid to the four aspects of the corporate entrepreneurial process—identifying and evaluating the opportunity, developing a business plan, determining the resources required, and starting and managing the venture. This corporate entrepreneurial process needs to be modified for specific corporate cultures in order to facilitate corporate entrepreneurship. The differences between managerial and corporate entrepreneurial decision making were discussed in terms of five business decisions—strategic orientation, commitment to opportunity, commitment to resources, control of resources, and management structure. Following a discussion about the reasons for the increasing interest in

corporate entrepreneurship, the differences between a corporate and a corporate entrepreneurial culture were presented.

The four major aspects of corporate entrepreneurship in an organization were then articulated—innovation, ownership, creativity, and change. This included a discussion of some of the most frequently used methods in a company to generate creativity—brainstorming, reverse brainstorming, checklist method, free association, collective notebook method, attribute listing, big-dream approach, and parameter analysis.

4

Identifying, Evaluating, and Selecting the Opportunity

How can creating an opportunity analysis help an organization generate and assess new ideas? What are the roles of product planning and product development in the corporate entrepreneurship process?

Scenario: 3M Post-it Notes

According to the Gallup Organization, in 1998 an average U.S. professional was receiving roughly 11 Post-it Note messages every day. Stunning statistics for a product that was invented by mistake in the mid-1970s! But even more impressive is the resulting unique corporate entrepreneurial culture created and promoted by 3M.

Art Fry, a 3M researcher, is credited with the coinvention of Post-it Notes. Born in 1931 in Minnesota, his early years of education began in a one-room rural schoolhouse, where he initially expressed interest in engineering. In the early 1950s, he started to study chemical engineering at the University of Minnesota and in 1953 accepted a position with 3M as a new product development researcher.

The invention of masking tape in 1925 significantly helped grow and establish 3M as a well-known company; similar product inventions like Fry's Post-it Notes have provided the company with sustainable success through the last century. To ensure this constant influx of new ideas and innovation, 3M has been instilling a unique corporate culture since its early beginnings, focusing on seven core pillars, the "Seven Habits of Highly Innovative Corporations."

The first pillar concerns the commitment to innovation through the dedication of monetary resources. In 2008, 3M spent $1.4 billion, about 5.5 percent of its revenue, on research and development, more than is typically spent on R&D by industrial companies. The company's Genesis Grant offers 12 to 20 grants between $50,000 and $100,000 to scientists who want to work on projects outside of the company. The researchers selected can put the money toward hiring additional staff or purchasing equipment.

The second pillar involves actively maintaining the corporate culture. 3M believes every employee should feel part of the organization; to ensure this, the company hires exceptional people, orally teaches the company history, grants the employees independence to do their jobs in their own way, and tolerates mistakes.

In pillar three, 3M spreads its technological know-how across all its divisions. The company has expertise in 42 different technologies and extends that expertise through cross-divisional communication.

Pillar four encourages both formal and informal networking among the researchers. Such networking and sharing of information is promoted through conferences and Webcasts hosted by individual labs, ongoing seminars, and an annual symposium where all 3M researchers are in attendance. The objective is to make sure researchers know whom to contact with a specific question or when they are in need of advice.

Pillar five involves the setting of expectations for each individual employee and properly rewarding outstanding work. Employees are all treated as unique people, and awards are often given out individually, including a vacation for two to the 20 highest performers.

The sixth pillar focuses on constant quantification to evaluate R&D efforts in creating products that generate adequate revenue. 3M makes sure research money is being spent effectively by comparing the past four years' worth of research with profits generated from the new developments.

The final pillar—seven—focuses on the customer. 3M employees spend a significant amount of time interacting with customers to determine inadequacies of existing products and unmet needs of customers. They then return to the lab to develop corresponding products to match the observed and change needs into reality.

Perhaps the most significant aspect of 3M's innovative success, at least in terms of Fry's Post-it Note invention, is the "bootlegger" rule. The company allows researchers to devote 15 percent of their work time to "pursue unique ideas they believe might have merit for the company." Fry dedicated this bootlegging time toward exploring the possibilities, opportunities, development, and ways of promoting the award-winning Post-it Note.

In 1968, Dr. Spencer Silver, a 3M chemist, developed a formula for an adhesive that stuck slightly and could be repositioned due to the limited amount of surface area contact between the adhesive and the substrate caused by the microspheres. However, he was unable to find good use for the adhesive and the product was deemed a failure. Art Fry was living in Minnesota where on weekends he was involved in singing in the church choir. He became frustrated when the bits of paper he used as bookmarks to mark the hymn page kept falling out of the hymnal. He felt that if he could find a piece of paper that would stick to the pages but not damage them upon removal (as would adhesive tape), he would solve his problem. He began to reflect on one of Dr. Silver's seminars, which he had attended through 3M's open communication policy, where he learned of the "failed" adhesive. The following day Fry requested a sample of Dr. Silver's adhesive and began spending his bootlegging time working on creating precisely what he was in need of: a piece of paper with some adhesive on the tip so it would stick in the book without damaging it.

It did not take Fry long to recognize his invention had more use than just as a bookmark—it could be used to organize and communicate too. He introduced the product to management who initially did not see the benefits of the invention. So in order to promote interest in his idea, he began communicating with his boss by leaving him messages on the sticky notes, and he proceeded to produce enough of them to distribute to 3M employees at the headquarters office. People quickly became addicted and began consistently asking him for more.

In 1977, persuaded by the positive feedback from employees, 3M named the sticky notes "Post-it Notes" and in 1978 tested them in Boise, Idaho. The test market proved to be an overwhelming success, as 90 percent of the people who tried Post-it Notes said they would buy them. Further test results gave 3M the confidence to launch Post-it Notes nationally in 1981 and expand to Canada and Europe in 1990.

Art Fry and Dr. Spencer Silver did not go unnoticed. In accordance with 3M's corporate values, the entire Post-it Note team was awarded 3M's Golden Step Award in both 1980 and 1981, the highest honor offered by 3M. In 1986, Art Fry was named a corporate research officer and became a member of the 3M Carlton Society and Circle of Technical Excellence.

Today, Post-its are in over 100 countries, in 8 standard sizes, 25 shapes, and 60 colors, and have been recyclable from the beginning. The product now has many varieties, such as Post-it Flags, Post-it Note Pads, Post-it Labeling & Cover-up Tape, and Post-it Pop-up Notes and Dispensers.

www.inventhelp.com/articles-for-inventors-art-fry.asp
www.businessweek.com/innovate/content/may2006/
   id20060510_682823.htm
www.3m.com

Introduction

Art Fry's recognition of an unmet need and then solving it occurs daily in organizations throughout the world. But without a process to recognize and harness this corporate entrepreneurial spirit, organizations often miss these innovative opportunities. These opportunities frequently use internal and external sources to obtain the much-needed ideas that can fuel growth, increase sales or efficiency, and, where applicable, enhance profitability. This chapter focuses on this important aspect by first addressing sources and methods of generating new ideas and determining trends. Following this is a discussion on evaluating these ideas and building an opportunity analysis and an opportunity analysis plan. In addition, there is a section about product planning and the development process. The chapter concludes with a discussion of some company innovative idea strategies.

Sources of New Ideas

Some of the more frequently used sources of ideas include consumers, existing products and services, supply chain system, the federal government, and research and development.

Consumers

Close attention needs to be paid to consumers and their buying habits. This monitoring can take the form of informally monitoring potential ideas by observing customers or more formally by arranging for consumers to have an opportunity to express their opinions.

Existing Products and Services

Competitive products and services on the market should also be evaluated. Frequently, this analysis uncovers ways to improve the present offerings that may result in a new product or service that has more market appeal and better sales and profit potential than the existing offering. This can result in the replacement of an older company product with a newer model.

Supply Chain System

Members of the supply chain are also excellent sources for new ideas due to their familiarity with the needs of the market at different stages of production. Not only do supply chain members frequently have suggestions for completely new products, but also they can help in marketing the company's newly developed products.

Federal Government

The federal government can be a source of new product ideas in two ways. First, the files of the U.S. Patent and Trademark Office (USPTO) contain numerous new product possibilities. Although the patents themselves may not be feasible, they can frequently suggest other more marketable product ideas. Several government agencies and publications are helpful in monitoring patent applications. The *Official Gazette*, published weekly by the USPTO, summarizes each patent granted and lists all patents available for license or sale. The USPTO also provides online full-text access for patents issued since 1976 (www.uspto.gov).

Second, new product ideas can be developed in response to changing government regulations. For example, the Occupational Safety and Health Act (OSHA) mandated that first-aid kits be available in business establishments employing more than three people. The kits had to contain specific items that varied according to the company and the industry.

Research and Development

The largest source of new ideas is the company's own "research and development" efforts, which may be a formal endeavor or even a more informal one. One research scientist in a Fortune 500 company, Hillenbrand Industries, developed a new plastic resin that became the basis of a new product, a plastic molded modular cup pallet.

Methods for Generating Ideas

Even with such a wide variety of sources of ideas available, coming up with an idea to be the basis for a new venture can still be a problem. Several methods help generate and test new ideas, including focus groups, brainstorming, and problem inventory analysis.

Focus Groups

In a *focus group*, a moderator leads a group of people through an open, in-depth discussion rather than simply asking questions to solicit participant response. For a new product area, the moderator focuses the group discussion in either a directive or a nondirective manner. The group of 8 to 14 participants is stimulated by comments from other group members in creatively conceptualizing and developing a new product idea to fill a market need. One company interested in the women's slipper market received its new product concept for a "warm and comfortable slipper that fits like an old shoe" from a focus group of 12 women from various socioeconomic backgrounds in the New York area. The concept was then developed into a new women's slipper that was a market success. Even the theme of the advertising message came from comments of focus group members.

In addition to generating new ideas, the focus group is an excellent method for initially screening ideas and concepts. With the use of one of several procedures available, the results can be analyzed more quantitatively, making the focus group a useful method for generating new product ideas.[1]

Brainstorming

Although most of the ideas generated from the group are not further developed, in the *brainstorming* method, sometimes a good idea emerges. A good idea has a better chance of occurring when the brainstorming effort focuses on a specific product or market area. The rules of brainstorming were discussed in Chapter 3.

A large commercial bank successfully used brainstorming to develop a journal that would provide quality information to its industrial clients. The brainstorming among financial executives focused on the characteristics of the market, the information content, the frequency of issue, and the promotional value of the proposed new journal for the bank. Once a general format and issue frequency were determined, focus groups of vice presidents of finance for Fortune 1000 companies were held in three cities— Boston, Chicago, and Dallas—to discuss the new journal format and its relevancy and value to them. The results of these focus groups provided the basis for a new financial journal that was well received by the market.

Problem Inventory Analysis

Problem inventory analysis uses individuals in a manner that is analogous to focus groups to generate new product ideas. However, instead of generating new ideas themselves, consumers are provided with a list of problems in a general product category. They are then asked to identify and discuss products in this category that have the particular problem. This method is often effective since it is easier to relate known products to suggested problems and arrive at a new product idea than to generate an entirely new product idea by itself. One of the most difficult problems in using this technique is in developing an exhaustive list of problems.

Results from product inventory analysis need to be carefully evaluated, as they may not actually reflect a new business opportunity. For example, General Foods's introduction of a compact cereal box in response to the problem that the available boxes did not fit well on the shelf was not successful, as the problem of package size really had little effect on actual purchasing behavior.

Trends

A trend often provides a good opportunity for starting a new venture area within the organization. Here are seven trends of the next decade.

Trends of the Next Decade

- Green
- Clean energy
- Organic orientation
- Economic
- Social
- Health
- Web

Green Trend

The green sector is brimming with opportunities around the world. Water is one aspect of this green trend that provides opportunities, particularly in the area of irrigation, such as reclamation programs for golf courses, parks, and smart irrigation systems. It is also an opportunity to find ways to increase water use efficiency. Other business areas worth looking at include eco-friendly printing, recycling, and green janitorial services. Green trends are especially effective when firms connect green actions with reduced costs or long-term savings for consumers.

Clean Energy

One of the most pressing environmental concerns of consumers is clean energy. Many feel that the power of the twenty-first century will come from the sun, wind, and geothermal sources. Smaller businesses and homeowners are a significant untapped market in this area. For example, in the construction industry, there are recent trends geared toward improvements in insulation and windows that reduce heating and cooling expenses for homeowners.

Organic Orientation Trend

The organic trend is increasing significantly, particularly in the food sector, which has been accelerated by the reduction in the price gap between organic and nonorganic foods. The sales growth in all organic foods, including meat, dairy, fruits, vegetables, breads, and snack foods, averages about 25 percent per year. Total organic nonfood sales are also growing, particularly in apparel.

Economy Trend

The impact of the credit crunch, bank failures, the housing slide, and foreclosures has forced consumers to be much more careful in their spending. This increase in frugal spending provides significant opportunities in such areas as garden products, business coaching, discount retailing, credit and debt management, virtual meetings, outsourcing, and do-it-yourself culture. According to *Business Times*, IKEA, a do-it-yourself, low-priced furniture outlet, had experienced record sales in 2008–2009 (an increase of 1.4 percent) during the economic downturn (www.btimes.com).

Social Trend

The social trend is evident throughout the world, with more networking events and opportunities occurring each week. These include Facebook, Myspace, LinkedIn, and Twitter as well as social networking for businesses. In addition to maintaining current relationships, there is also a trend of starting relationships online. Another avenue of socializing online is through the gaming industry, where strangers meet and join forces through self-created characters in order to defeat the game. The social trend also provides opportunities in related areas of financial planning and travel as individuals want to have the ability to be financially solvent and viable in their longer life spans and enjoy the benefits of seeing new places with their children and grandchildren. Longevity Alliance, for example, is a one-stop advisory service offering counseling in long-term care and financial planning.

Health Trend

Maintaining your health and concerns about health-care provision is one of the biggest trends today that will continue in the next decade as the world population ages and as life expectancy increases. This provides many opportunities, including cosmetic procedures, mind expansion such as the "brain gym" of Vibrant Brains, personal health portals, point-of-care testing facilities, nutritional experts, fitness centers, fitness toys such as the latest Fit-Flops and Wii Fit peripherals, fit food, convenient care clinics, and wellness coaches.

Web Trend

The Web trend is creating many new forms of communication and purchasing potential, which is opening up massive new opportunities. The opportunities, with low-cost barriers to entry, include Web 2.0 consulting, blogging, online video, mobile apps, and Wi-Fi apps as well as the new iPhone with its many applications. There is also the B2B customer who can benefit from online activity, as organizations constantly need updated, relevant information about their changing customers.

Evaluating the Idea

The key to successful domestic and international venture creation is to develop an idea that solves a problem satisfying a need for a large market or adds extensive value to the product thereby increasing profit margins in a niche strategy. The result of the creativity and idea developed in Chapter 3 needs to be thought of in terms of satisfying a specific market need or, as one corporate entrepreneur stated, "Making the customer more profitable."

What is deemed "profitable" varies by the product or service idea and particularly whether the idea is in the business-to-business market or the business-to-consumer market. The uniqueness of the idea, its competitive advantage, and the market size and characteristics can be determined through the development of an opportunity analysis (assessment).

Opportunity analysis is often best accomplished by developing an opportunity analysis plan. An opportunity analysis plan is *not* a business plan. Compared to a business plan, it should:

- Be shorter
- Focus on the opportunity, not the venture
- Have no financials, marketing plan, or organizational plan
- Be the basis to make the decision on whether to act on an opportunity or wait until another, better opportunity comes along

An opportunity analysis plan has four sections—two major sections and two minor sections. The first major section develops the product or service idea, analyzes the competitive products and companies, and identifies idea differentiation in terms of its unique selling propositions. This section includes:

- The market need for the product or service
- A description of the product or service
- The specific aspects of the product or service (as detailed as possible)
- The competitive products already available filling this need and features
- The companies in this product market space
- The unique selling propositions of the new product or service in light of the competition

Some data sources for determining competition and market size discussed below can also be used in Chapter 9, "Developing the Business Plan."

The second section of the opportunity analysis plan focuses on the market—its size, trends, characteristics, and growth rate. It includes:

- The market need being filled
- The social condition underlining this market need
- Any market research data available to describe this market need
- The size and characteristics of the domestic and/or international market
- The growth rate of the market

The third section focuses on the corporate entrepreneur and the management team in terms of their skills and experience. It should include answers to the following questions:

- Why does this opportunity excite you? What will keep you going when the business becomes difficult?
- How does the product or service idea fit into your background and experience?
- What business skills do you have to provide as equity capital?
- What business skills are needed?
- Where will you find these needed skills?

The final section of the opportunity analysis plan develops a timeline indicating the steps needed to successfully launch the venture and translate the idea into a viable business entity. This section should focus on:

- Identifying each step
- Determining the sequence of activities and putting these critical steps into some expected sequential order
- Determining the time and money required at each step

- Determining the total amount of time and money needed
- Identifying the source of this needed money if not currently available

Product Planning and Development Process

Once ideas emerge and are analyzed through the opportunity analysis plan, they will need further development and refinement. This refining process—the product planning and development process—is divided into five major stages: idea stage, concept stage, product development stage, test marketing stage, and commercialization. These stages result in the start of the *product life cycle* (see Figure 4.1).

Establishing Evaluation Criteria

At each stage of the product planning and development process, there need to be established criteria for evaluation of the product and process. Criteria should be established to evaluate the new

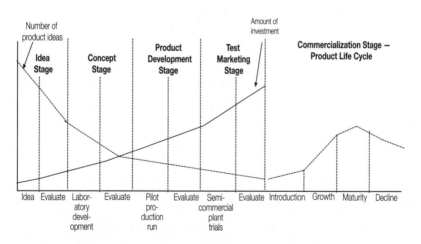

FIGURE 4.1   The Product Planning and Development Process

idea in terms of market opportunity, competition, marketing system, and financial and production factors.

A market opportunity exists in the form of a new or current need for the product idea. The determination of market demand is by far the most important criterion of a proposed new product idea. Assessment of the market opportunity and size should consider: the characteristics and attitudes of consumers or industries that may buy the product, the size of this potential market in dollars and units, the nature of the market with respect to its stage in the life cycle (growing or declining), and the share of the market the product could reasonably capture.

Current competing producers, prices, and marketing efforts should also be evaluated. The new idea should be able to compete successfully with products or services already on the market by having features that will meet or overcome current and anticipated competition. The new idea should have some unique differential advantage based on an evaluation of all competitive products or services filling the same consumer needs in the same market.

The new idea should have synergy with existing capabilities and marketing strategies of the company. The company should be able to use its marketing experience and other expertise in this new product effort. For example, General Electric would have a far less difficult time adding a new lighting device to its line than Procter & Gamble would. Several factors should be considered in evaluating the degree of fit: the degree to which the ability and time of the present sales force can be transferred to the new product; the ability to sell the new product through the company's established channels of distribution; and the ability to "piggyback" the advertising and promotion required to introduce the new product.

The proposed product or service idea should be able to be supported by and contribute to the company's financial well-being in a reasonable amount of time. The manufacturing cost per unit, the marketing expense, and the amount of capital need to be determined along with the break-even point and the long-term profit outlook for the product. Management should also evaluate the compatibility of the new product's production requirements with existing plant, machinery, and personnel. If the new product idea cannot be integrated into existing manufacturing processes, it will involve more initial investment costs such as plant and equipment, which have to be taken into account as part of the product's long-term profit potential. This overall evaluation should result in a go or no go decision at the end of each stage.

Idea Stage

Promising new product or service ideas should be identified and impractical ones eliminated in the *idea stage,* allowing maximum use of the company's resources. One evaluation method successfully used in this stage is the systematic market evaluation checklist, where each new idea is expressed in terms of its chief values, merits, and benefits. Consumers are presented with clusters of new product or service values to determine which, if any, new product or service alternatives should be pursued and which should be discarded. Care should be taken so that consumers are not biased by the presentation of the product values to avoid skewing results.

It is also important to determine the need for the new idea as well as its value to the company. If there is no need for the idea or it does not have any value or benefit to the company, the new product or service idea should not be developed. To accurately determine the need for a new idea, it is helpful to define the potential needs of the market in terms of timing, satisfaction, alternatives, benefits and risks, future expectations, price-versus-product performance features, market structure and size, and economic conditions. A form for helping in this need determination process is indicated in Table 4.1. The factors in this table should be evaluated not only in terms of the characteristics of the potential new product or service but also in terms of the new product or service's competition.

In the determination of the value of the new product or service to the company, financial scheduling—such as cash outflow, cash inflow, contribution to profit, and return on investment—needs to be evaluated in terms of other product or service ideas as well as investment alternatives. With the use of Table 4.2, the amount of each of the considerations essential to the new idea should be determined as accurately as possible, which of course will be revised as the idea moves forward.

Concept Stage

After a new product or service idea has passed evaluation in the idea stage, it should be further developed and refined through interaction with consumers. In the *concept stage,* the refined idea is tested to determine consumer acceptance. It is appropriate to gather initial reactions to the concept from potential customers or members of the distribution channel. One method of measuring consumer acceptance is the conversational interview in which selected respondents are exposed to statements that reflect the physical characteristics and attributes of the product or service idea. These statements can also compare these primary features to the competition. Features, price, and promotion are evaluated for both the concept being studied and for any major competing products. Favorable as well as unfavorable product features can be discovered by analyzing consumers' responses, with the favorable features then being incorporated into the new product or service.

Product Development Stage

In the *product development stage*, consumer reaction is determined in relation to the physical product or service. One tool frequently used in this stage is the consumer panel, where a group of potential consumers is given product samples. Participants keep a record of their use of the product and comment on its virtues and deficiencies. This technique is more applicable for product ideas but also works for some service ideas.

TABLE 4.1   Determining the Need for a New Product or Service Idea

Idea Factor	Aspects	Competitive Capabilities	New Product Capability
Type of Need			
Continuing need			
Declining need			
Emerging need			
Future need			
Timing of Need			
Duration of need			
Frequency of need			
Demand cycle			
Position in life cycle			
Competing Ways to Satisfy Need			
Doing without			
Using present way			
Modifying present way			
Perceived Benefits/Risks			
Utility to customer			
Appeal characteristics			
Customer tastes and preferences			
Buying motives			
Consumption habits			
Price versus Performance Features			
Price-quantity relationship			
Demand elasticity			
Stability of price			
Stability of market			
Market Size and Potential			
Market growth			
Market trends			
Market development requirements			
Threats to market			

TABLE 4.1 Continued

Idea Factor	Aspects	Competitive Capabilities	New Product Capability
Availability of Customer Funds			
General economic conditions			
Economic trends			
Customer income			
Financing opportunities			

Source: Robert D. Hisrich and Michael P. Peters, *Marketing Decisions for New and Mature Products*, 2nd edition, Upper Saddle River, NJ: Pearson Education, Inc., 1991, 186. Reprinted by permission.

The panel of potential customers can also be given a sample of the product and one or more competitive products simultaneously. In this case, one of several methods is used to discover customer preference, such as multiple brand comparisons, risk analysis, level of repeat purchases, or intensity of preference analysis.

Test Marketing Stage

Although the results of the product development stage provide the basis of the final marketing plan, a market test can be done to increase the certainty of successful commercialization. This last step in the evaluation process, the *test marketing stage*, provides actual sales results, which indicate the acceptance level of consumers. Positive test results indicate the degree of probability of a successful product launch and company formation.

Selecting the Foreign Market

When considering an international market, one of the critical issues is correct market selection. Although there are several market selection models available, one effective method employs a five-step approach: (1) develop appropriate indicators, (2) collect data and convert into comparable indicators, (3) establish an appropriate

TABLE 4.2   Determining the Value of a New Product or Service Idea

Value Consideration	Cost (in $)
Cash Outflow	
R&D costs	
Marketing costs	
Capital equipment costs	
Other costs	
Cash Inflow	
Sales of new product	
Effect on additional sales of existing products	
Salvageable value	
Net Cash Flow	
Maximum exposure	
Time to maximum exposure	
Duration of exposure	
Total investment	
Maximum net cash in a single year	
Profit	
Profit from new product	
Profit affecting additional sales of existing products	
Fraction of total company profit	
Relative Return	
Return on shareholders' equity (ROE)	
Return on investment (ROI)	
Cost of capital	
Present value (PV)	
Discounted cash flow (DCF)	
Return on assets employed (ROA)	
Return on sales	
Compared to Other Investments	
Compared to other product opportunities	
Compared to other investment opportunities	

Source: Robert D. Hisrich and Michael P. Peters, *Marketing Decisions for New and Mature Products*, 2nd edition, Upper Saddle River, NJ: Pearson Education, Inc., 1991, 196. Reprinted by permission.

weight for each indicator, (4) analyze the data, and (5) select the appropriate market from the market rankings.

In step one, appropriate indicators need to be developed based on past sales, competitive research, related experiences, and management discussions. Specific indicators for the company need to be developed in three general areas: overall market indicators, market growth indicators, and product indicators. Market size indicators generally center on population; per capita income; market for the specific product, for business-to-consumer products, and for types of companies and its sales; and profits of particular business-to-business products. In terms of market growth, the overall country growth (gross domestic product, or GDP) should be determined as well as the growth rate for the particular market of the venture.

Step two involves collecting data for each of these indicators and converting the data in order to make appropriate comparisons. At this stage the organization needs to collect both primary data (original information collected for the particular requirement) and secondary data (existing published data). Typically, secondary data is collected first to establish what information still needs to be collected through primary research. When collecting international secondary data, there are several possible problems that vary based on the stage of economic development of the country.

These problems include: (1) comparability (the data collected for one country will not be the same as data gathered for another); (2) availability (some countries have much more country data than others, usually reflecting the stage of economic development); (3) accuracy and reliability (sometimes the data has not been collected using vigorous standards and can even be biased due to the interests of the government of the country; the latter is particularly a problem in nonmarket-oriented economies); and (4) cost (the United States has the Freedom of Information Act, which makes all government collected data that does not pertain to security or defense free and available to all; at least some of the collected data is available but only for a price in most other countries).

One company, HB Associates, was interested in opening the first western health club in Moscow. The firm planned to charge two rates: a higher hard currency rate to foreigners and a lower ruble rate to Russians and other citizens of countries in the former Soviet Union. In determining the best location, it was important to locate areas of the city most populated by foreigners. After significant searching and a high degree of frustration, the required data was purchased from the former KGB (Soviet Union security branch).

When researching foreign markets, organizations typically want economic and demographic data such as population, GDP, per capita income, inflation, literacy rate, unemployment, and education levels. There are many sources for this foreign information at government agencies, Web sites, embassies, and intergovernmental unions. For example, the continent of Africa is often considered a risky investment as its business environment is still largely unknown and unfamiliar to the western world. Yet intergovernmental unions and organizations such as the African Union (AU), East African Community (EAC), Southern African Development Community (SADC), and Economic Community of West African States (ECOWAS) are gradually amassing relevant information to increase the ease of doing business and attract foreign investors to Africa. Much of this information is easily accessible through Web sites and news articles.

One important overall source of data is the National Trade Data Bank (NTDB), which is managed by the U.S. Department of Commerce. There are a large number of international reports released regularly such as Country Reports, Country Analysis Briefs (CABS), Country Commercial Guides (CCG), Food Market Reports, International Reports and Reviews, Department of State Background Notes, and Import/Export Reports.

Another relevant source of data is through trade associations with U.S. and foreign embassies. Although trade associations are a good source of domestic and international data, sometimes more specific information can be obtained by contacting the U.S. Department of Commerce industry desk officer or the economic attaché in the appropriate U.S. or foreign embassy.

The collected data then needs to be converted for each selected indicator to a point score so that each indicator of each country can be numerically ranked against the other countries—essentially standardizing data to compare apples to apples. Various methods are used to achieve this, each of which involves some judgment by the global entrepreneur. Another method is to compare country data for each indicator against global standards.

The third step establishes appropriate weights for the indicators. For one company manufacturing hospital beds, the number and types of hospitals, the age of the hospitals and its beds, and the government expenditure on health care and its socialized system were the best country indicators in selecting a foreign market. This procedure results in each indicator receiving a weight that reflects the relative importance of the indicator.

Step four involves analyzing the results. When looking at the data, the organization should carefully scrutinize and question the results because it is easy to make and overlook mistakes. Also, a "what if" analysis should be conducted by changing some of the weights and measuring the variation of the results.

The fifth and final step is selection of the foreign market. It is important for the organization to select an appropriate entry strategy for the targeted market as well as options for follow-up markets in order to develop a market plan. China, Germany, India, and Ireland are countries that ICU Global, a videoconferencing provider, is targeting, according to founder and chief executive Stephen McKenzie. The company currently employs six people in the UK with profits of approximately £3 million this year. Yet despite its size, according to McKenzie, the countries in question have been selected because they offer the greatest opportunities for ICU Global. "It's good to have a base in Germany because you can easily access the rest of Europe," he says.

Internal Company Indicators

Several internal company indicators can be used to develop foreign market indicators, including competitive information, information from fellow global corporate entrepreneurs, previous leads and sales, and trade show information. Strong indicators of foreign markets with good potential are often the markets entered by a company's competitors.

Another effective internal method to establish foreign market indicators is to discuss the various markets with noncompeting global companies. The time and experience of the noncompeting company in these countries can supply exceptional inside knowledge and perhaps even establish a mentoring relationship. In order to build this relationship further and benefit both parties, do not hesitate to offer your own areas of expertise for current or future ventures of your mentor.

A third source for developing marketing indicators is your own company's past sales and leads. Leads and actual sales, while doing business domestically, from out-of-country markets are by far the best indicators of foreign market potential. Actual sales to a foreign country are another matter because this signifies that your product is competitive for at least one customer in that foreign market.

The final source for developing foreign market indicators is leads from domestic and foreign trade shows. Trade shows occur in most all industries and in locations throughout the world. Some of the ones in the computer industry include Computer Assisted Radiology and Surgery Trade Show, Vietnam Computer Electronics World Expo, and WSEAS International Conference on Computers. Trade shows in the gifts, games, and hobbies sector include Babytime, Sibtoy, South of England Postcard Fairs, D&K Craft Fairs, Malaysia International Gift and Premium Fair, Kuwait International Trade Fair, and Bucklers Craft Fair. Trade shows and fairs in more than 50 industries from agriculture, horticulture, and farming to industrial and manufacturing to travel and tourism and hotel and resorts can be found at the Trade Show News Network

Web site (www.TSNN.com). These trade shows usually supply important information for firms and buyers in a particular product area and, as such, provide a great opportunity to gather market information for determining market potential in various countries as well as competitive information.

Company Innovative Idea Strategies

The following are some innovation strategies employed by several companies.[2]

Southwest Airlines

Recognizing that innovative ideas often arise internally, Southwest Airlines selected a group of employees and arranged for these people to meet and brainstorm for 10 hours every week. The intent of the project was to pinpoint the most significant changes that could be made in terms of the impact they would have on Southwest's aircraft operations. These brainstorming sessions went on for six months, and because the members had been selected from various departments including maintenance, dispatch operations, ground, and in-flight, the functional diversity enabled them to create a list of 109 ideas that were brought to senior management. From the ideas presented, three involved large and significant operational changes, including an idea that helped streamline the "swap" process (switching out one aircraft for another when mechanical problems arose).

Nokia

Many high-tech companies rely on patents to promote innovation strategies. In order to increase the number of patents held by employees, Nokia motivated its engineers by creating "Club 10"—an exclusive group that employees joined once they had earned 10 patents. The prestige of the club is enhanced by a yearly formal awards ceremony that publicly honors those who are inaugurated into the club.

3M

To further promote an entrepreneurial atmosphere, 3M distributes its Genesis Grant to a select number of researchers who have the desire to work on outside projects. Roughly 60 scientists and engineers apply for the grant every year, and the applications are reviewed by 20 senior scientists. Anywhere between 12 and 20 receive a monetary award that ranges from $50,000 to $100,000. Funds are typically applied to hiring extra staff members or purchasing supplies.

Starbucks

Typically, upper-level executives do not have direct, daily contact with the end customers who keep their business afloat. Starbucks, understanding this trend, relies on the baristas to communicate customer insights and trends to the upper executives. Starbucks even requires certain senior executives to spend a few days as a barista in order to understand the processes in action, the point of view of the baristas, and the needs of the customers. In addition, Starbucks also sponsors field trips for departments such as product development to visit other facilities. The idea is for the employees to gain insight into customers and trends and return inspired to their home office. One team, for example, took a trip to Paris, Düsseldorf, and London, to better understand the local cultures and ways of life. They returned with a unique understanding and entirely different perception that cannot be attained through a lecture or by reading a book. These actions also attest to the amount Starbucks is willing to invest in its employees and how much Starbucks values their input.

Infosys Technologies Ltd.

Keeping in touch with the younger generations can lead to some brilliant ideas while remaining close to a wide market segment. In order to take full advantage of its human capital, Infosys Technologies chairman N. R. Narayana Murthy created the Voice of

Youth program that directly involves upper management in innovation. Infosys picks nine of its best young employees (all are under 30 years of age) and has them take part in all eight of the yearly senior management council meetings. The young employees are given the opportunity to share their voices, as they are encouraged to present and confer about their ideas with the top company leaders.

BMW
When communication is simplified by eliminating miles, time zones, and telephones, innovation is enhanced. Following this strategy, BMW moves between 200 to 300 employees from around the organization into its Research and Innovation Center for a period of three to five years. This shifting occurs when BMW takes on a new project, which helps decrease the number of conflicts surrounding change, prevents possible model defects, and accelerates effective communication.

Toyota Motor Corporation
The Japanese auto manufacturer Toyota expends significant effort on innovating and improving its manufacturing process. Toyota took it a step further after releasing the new and innovative Prius, earning the company respect as an innovator of products, not just processes. In addition, Toyota began teaming up with its suppliers not only to cut costs but also to improve the whole design process. Toyota named this approach its "Value Innovation" strategy.

Summary
This chapter focused on an essential element of corporate venturing—identifying, evaluating, and selecting opportunities. Various sources of ideas were discussed, including consumers, existing products and services, supply chain systems, governments, and research and development. Chapter 5 also presents several methods

for generating ideas—focus groups, brainstorming, and problem inventory analysis.

Some major trends were identified that will provide opportunities in the next decade. These included green trends, organic orientation trends, economic trends, social trends, health trends, and Web trends.

A method for evaluating the opportunity—the opportunity analysis plan—was presented in detail, including sources for the needed information. Following a discussion of the four stages of the product planning and development process (idea stage, concept stage, product development stage, and test marketing stage), the chapter concludes with describing foreign market selection and various innovation idea strategies of several prominent companies.

Part Two

Organizing Corporate Entrepreneurship

5

Locating the Venture in the Organization

How do companies identify and develop the entrepreneurial spirit within their employees? How do you develop a corporate entrepreneurship program? What reporting system should be established?

Scenario: American Express

American Express originally opened for business in 1850 as a successful express delivery service for freight and valuables, not as a charge card company or a financial institution. At the time, the U.S. Postal Service was slow, expensive, and would not deliver anything larger than a package the size of a letter envelope. American Express seized the opportunity and became an early and important player in the westward expansion of America.

Though originally not a financial institution, most of American Express's customers were banks. American Express found itself delivering small packages that held stock certificates, currency, notes, and other financial instruments. The company scaled down its delivery services and began selling its own financial products. By 1891, American Express was selling the first internationally accepted traveler's checks. This globally focused product created the need to establish worldwide locations; in 1895, American Express opened its first European office in Paris and by 1910 had ten European branches.

American Express survived World War I and the Great Depression and by 1950 was experiencing solid growth, employing 5,500 employees spread across 173 countries. At the risk of cannibalizing its own product—the traveler's check—American Express established its charge card.

At the turn of the century, American Express had two main motivations for corporate entrepreneurship. First, executives recognized the importance of adapting to changing times and were concerned about how the newly popularized and easily accessible Internet would affect their business. Second, American Express recognized that it was missing out on attracting and developing talented employees. Corporate entrepreneurship would expand the recruitment network and provide an increase in talent.

Management of American Express understood the risk of diverging too much from its core business and ensured that all of its corporate entrepreneurship would leverage its core business and strategies. Members of management were determined to learn from other companies' mistakes and recognized early on that the way to success was staying close to what they knew best. As their corporate entrepreneurship took effect, American Express became an example of a firm that was successful in its entrepreneurial activities.

American Express began the corporate entrepreneurship process by clearly defining its core business and competitive boundaries. For example, American Express kept all its venturing investments within the boundaries of the charge card business. Essentially, American Express established three operating requirements for its corporate entrepreneurship. First, the venture must provide superior value to American Express's customers. Second, the venture must provide this value by achieving best-in-class economics. Third, the venture must enhance the American Express brand. Though simple sounding, following all three rules prior to launching ventures proved challenging. Yet implementing these principles clearly defined the venture criteria that allowed this company to successfully implement the corporate entrepreneurship process.

One example of American Express's corporate entrepreneurship is MarketMile. In March 2001, American Express invested $17 million in MarketMile, a start-up venture focused on helping mid-sized companies (between $100 million and $2 billion in annual revenue) cut costs by streamlining processes for purchasing goods and services. The investment in MarketMile allowed American Express to get started in this midsized market through its core business, the charge card. Essentially, MarketMile provides the streamlining to cut a company's indirect buying and service procurement from $95 to a mere $5—but only if these customers pay with an American Express card.

American Express began its early years of corporate entrepreneurship informally but successfully. In fact, Ken Chenault, CEO of American Express, recalls that he was not even aware of the initial venturing investments until American Express created a formal entrepreneurship group. The purpose in formalizing an entrepreneurship group was to guide investments, generate management participation, and grow both American Express's core business as well as its brand.

Through more than 100 years of corporate entrepreneurial endeavors, American Express has developed five methods that significantly enhance the success of its new ventures. Most important, the company understands the value of prudently selecting its investments. American Express understands that the same due diligence is needed when selecting partners as when hiring employees. The company implemented three methods to avoid pitfalls: stringent management of cash by the partner, never moving too quickly from one step to the next, and never engaging in an incomplete product or service offering.

Currently, American Express's two main operating divisions consist of the Global Consumer Group and the Business-to-Business Group. Though both groups offer services for their customers, the company's main source of revenue continues to be the charge card with its annual fee. The customers are rewarded through the accumulation of points, which can be redeemed for rewards. As of 2009, American Express had over 92 million charge cards in circulation with revenues in 2008 at $31.9 billion.

www.independent.co.uk/news/business/sme/roger-trapp-corporate-venturing-does-it-really-pay-off-526032.html
www.bain.com/bainweb/publications/publications_detail.asp?id=5623&menu_url=publications.asp
www.AmericanExpress.com

Introduction

As indicated in the scenario, corporate entrepreneurship can be a risky and expensive investment of company resources, yet if identified and applied correctly, corporate entrepreneurship has the potential to greatly increase a firm's value and growth opportunities. American Express's corporate entrepreneurship success implies that it understood several important aspects of corporate venturing—first, the need for adaptation to the changing times both internal and external to the organization; second, the importance of not straying too far from the company's core business; and third, the prudent selection of locating new ventures.

American Express is an excellent example of a firm succeeding through instilling an entrepreneurial culture and reaping the financial benefits. Listening to customers, expanding globally, accepting creative criticism, identifying the need for change, staying close to the firm's core competencies, and carefully selecting new ventures are critical components of establishing corporate entrepreneurship.

This chapter deals with these aspects of the corporate entrepreneurship process in terms of the location of the new entrepreneurial activity. The chapter first describes the barriers to corporate entrepreneurship in an organization followed by a discussion on the various structures. Following a discussion of the procedures for implementation, the chapter concludes with the indicators of an entrepreneurial climate in an organization.

Organizational Barriers to Corporate Entrepreneurship

There are several barriers to overcome in order to successfully implement and practice corporate entrepreneurship in an organizational culture. The first is part of the inherent nature of large organizations. Whereas entrepreneurial firms are very flat with start-ups consisting of one to three people, large organizations generally have extensive procedures and reporting systems in order to facilitate growth. These procedures and reporting systems are not problematic until they become so strictly enforced that they inhibit change and creativity. The rigidity of the procedures and reporting systems becomes a barrier to empowering individuals in the organization to think creatively about their own position and the operations of the organization itself.

The second barrier concerns the need for the organization to accomplish its short-term objectives. The implementation and establishment of a corporate entrepreneurial culture requires time and internal resources in order to capture returns in addition to successfully running the organization. One of the authors of this book will not take on a corporate entrepreneurship consulting project unless the senior management commits five years and a specified amount of money each year to facilitate the process. This focus on the long term does not fulfill short-term expectations and results needed by most organizations. Just think of how difficult it would be for a publicly traded company that reports sales and profits each quarter to heavily invest in a long-term idea in corporate entrepreneurship.

The lack of corporate entrepreneurial talent is the third barrier. As organizations expand and grow, there is more emphasis on managerial processes than on entrepreneurial methods. The larger the organization and the longer it functions without a corporate entrepreneurial element, the fewer corporate entrepreneurs remain and the harder it is to start and instill this mindset.

In order to locate the corporate entrepreneurial talent, it is important to identify certain individual characteristics that constitute a successful corporate entrepreneur. As summarized below, these include understanding the environment, being visionary and flexible, creating management options, encouraging teamwork, supporting open discussions, building a coalition of supporters, and being persistent.

Corporate Entrepreneurial Leadership Characteristics

- Understands the environment
- Is visionary and flexible
- Creates management options
- Encourages teamwork
- Encourages open discussion
- Builds a coalition of supporters
- Persists

A corporate entrepreneur needs to understand current and possible future aspects of the environment. Part of this ability is reflected in the individual's level of creativity, which generally decreases with age and education in most individuals. To establish a successful corporate entrepreneurial venture, the individual must be creative and have a broad understanding of the internal and external aspects of the corporation.

The person who is going to establish a successful new corporate entrepreneurial venture must also be a visionary leader—a person who dreams great dreams. Although there are many definitions of leadership, the one that best describes what is needed for corporate entrepreneurship is: A leader is like a gardener. When you want a tomato, you take a seed, put it in fertile soil, and carefully water under tender care. You do not manufacture tomatoes; you grow them. Another good definition is, "Leadership is the ability to dream great things and communicate these in such a way that people say 'yes' to being a part of the dream." Martin Luther King Jr. in his "I Have a Dream" speech further demonstrated that dreams brought to life by visionary leaders could inspire thousands to follow in spite of overwhelming obstacles. To establish a successful new venture, the corporate entrepreneurial leader must have a dream strong and clear enough to overcome obstacles and to continue inspiring followers.

The third necessary characteristic is that the corporate entrepreneur must be flexible and create management options. A corporate entrepreneur does not "mind the store" but rather is open to and even encourages change. By challenging the beliefs and assumptions of the organization, a corporate entrepreneur has the opportunity to create something new in the organizational structure. This desire is exceptionally effective when coupled with an optimistic attitude for facing the uncertainty that comes with change. So instead of focusing only on the problems, the corporate entrepreneur views change as a challenge for new opportunities and growth.

The corporate entrepreneur needs a fourth characteristic: the ability to encourage teamwork in a multidisciplined approach. This oftentimes violates the organizational practices taught in most business schools that operate in established organizational structures. In forming a new venture, putting together a variety of skills requires crossing established departmental structures and reporting systems. To minimize disruption, the corporate entrepreneur needs to be a good diplomat. One company, Xeta Technology Inc., launched a successful new entrepreneurial venture due in large part to the corporate entrepreneur being able to have the technologist see the wisdom of making the changes to the technology prescribed by the sales manager due to market feedback.

Open discussion needs to be encouraged in order to develop an effective team for creating something new. Many corporate managers have forgotten the frank, open discussions and disagreements that are part of the educational process. Instead, they spend time building protective barriers and insulating themselves in their corporate empires. A successful new corporate entrepreneurial venture can be formed only when the team involved feels the freedom to disagree and to critique an idea in order to reach the best solution. The degree of openness among the team members depends on the degree of openness of the corporate entrepreneur leader.

Openness also leads to the establishment of a strong, invested coalition of supporters and encouragers. The corporate entrepreneur needs to encourage and affirm each team member, particularly during difficult times. This encouragement is very important, as the usual motivators of career paths and job security are not operational in establishing a new entrepreneurial venture. A successful corporate entrepreneur makes everyone a hero and, in turn, relies upon this support system in times of doubt.

Last but not least is persistence. Throughout the establishment of any new corporate entrepreneurial venture, frustration and obstacles will occur. Only through the persistence of the corporate entrepreneur and the supporting team will a new venture be created with a successful commercialization result.

The final major barrier to establishing corporate entrepreneurship in an organization is not having an appropriate compensation system for the corporate entrepreneur. This is perhaps the most difficult barrier to overcome for two reasons. First, the expectations of the corporate entrepreneur often need to be managed. Although the individual is doing something new and creative in the organization, he or she must understand that the operative words are "in the organization." The organization has concerns about resources, expertise, market knowledge, established customer base, and an established distribution system, which an entrepreneur does not have when starting a new venture outside an organization. The corporate entrepreneur should not expect the high compensation level that many successful entrepreneurs receive as corporate entrepreneurs do not take the same risks (particularly financial) and have access to these additional organizational assets.

The second problem is how to actually reward the corporate entrepreneur and keep compensation levels and systems in parity. In managing expectations and keeping parity, many creative approaches can be used to reward corporate entrepreneurial behavior and leadership, which are discussed in Chapter 10. These range from a reserved parking spot to awards such as Innovator of the Day to pools of money for distribution to point systems to 15 percent of out-of-pocket savings or 3 percent of first year sales. Remember, it is not as important to have a large financial incentive for the corporate entrepreneurs in an organization as it is to make sure every corporate entrepreneur is recognized and receives some incentive. Since autonomy is generally valued, having certain rewards that increase the individual's independence within the company is a good motivation.

Various Structures for Corporate Entrepreneurship

Corporate entrepreneurship can be a part of an organization through a wide variety of structures. Sometimes it involves the formation of an autonomous venture capital unit. This internal venture capital unit, which is further discussed in Chapter 11, "Funding the Venture," can fund both internal and external proposals that meet normal venture capital criteria. The four major structures used for corporate entrepreneurship include a section within the human resources department, new products subsidiary, new products division, or the process occurring throughout the organization.

Some organizations use a more careful approach to corporate entrepreneurship by establishing a section devoted to the area inside the human resources department. This section usually has minimal impact on the output of the organization as it focuses on training or sending managers to corporate entrepreneurship conferences. These trained managers can later be used to facilitate corporate entrepreneurship as now one of the organization's previously discussed barriers has been eliminated—lack of corporate entrepreneurial talent.

As corporate entrepreneurship often results in a different culture and way of doing things, some organizations separate the activity through a new products subsidiary. While separated from the rest of the organization, the unit evaluates proposals from individuals throughout the organization. The accepted proposals are then brought into the new subsidiary, and the individual develops the idea further with support and resources provided by the firm.

An even more formalized corporate entrepreneurship structure is the multidisciplinary new products division. This division is usually formally established at the vice presidential level and encourages creativity and submission of new product or service ideas. Individuals with accepted proposals are given time and resources to further develop their project. By being established at such a high level in the organization, it signifies to all employees that corporate entrepreneurship is an important initiative.

The final structure for corporate entrepreneurship makes the concept and process occur throughout the entire organization. Creativity and innovation are encouraged and rewarded with new products, services, and processes constantly occurring and flowing across the organization. Change and flexibility are central to this organic structure, allowing corporate entrepreneurship to flourish and spread.

Developing a Corporate Entrepreneurial Program

Each corporate entrepreneurial program is customized to fit the culture and the objectives of the specific organization. The procedure for developing the specific program reflects this and varies from organization to organization as does the final program itself. Even though this is the case, a procedure that has worked well in establishing a corporate entrepreneurship program in different organizations varying according to size, profit versus nonprofit status, and industry is discussed in the final chapter, Chapter 12.

This procedure has been accomplished at Genentech, a company that has a long history of developing revolutionary drugs. Genentech has established a culture that emphasizes and rewards curiosity and creativity and encourages risk taking. Employees are encouraged to initiate projects that are high risk with management knowing that most will not be successful. However, those that are successful, such as the cancer-fighting drug Avastin, are true breakthroughs.

Genentech is the only pharmaceutical company to have a postdoctoral program where an employee with a Ph.D. can receive a fellowship for four years. During this time, the selected employee can focus on fundamental research of his or her interest that could later result in a new product. This program keeps the innovative entrepreneurial spirit flowing inside the research group, which, in turn, encourages corporate entrepreneurial work throughout the company while also attracting top-caliber new talent. Key findings of the research are published in scientific journals, establishing credibility and an innovative status for Genentech in the pharmaceutical research community.

Evaluation Criteria

Similar to the procedure for developing a corporate entrepreneurship program and the actual program itself, the evaluation criteria vary widely across organizations. The initial reaction by members of the organization is typically that the program will not be around long since new changes often do not last in the company culture. That is why companies need a longer time and resource commitment. Some of the standard evaluation criteria are indicated below, and the aspect of control is the focus of Chapter 7. Specific guidelines must be established for each criterion using quantitative measures where possible and a one-through-five or one-through-seven evaluation criteria with more qualitative measurements.

Criteria for Evaluating Corporate Entrepreneurial Proposals
- Degree of organizational fit
- Low initial investment
- Experienced venture champion
- Experience with product or service industry
- Low competitive threat
- Proprietary technology
- High gross margin
- High rate of return

One very important criterion for proposal evaluation in many corporate entrepreneurship cultures is the degree to which the proposal fits with the organization's vision and core business, as in the case of American Express. While many organizations understand this criterion, using it to grow in scale, others use corporate entrepreneurship to expand the scope of the organization into new areas. Care needs to be taken so that there are no perceived, significant barriers stunting creative ideas, especially concerning the response from upper management. In one division of a Fortune 500 company, the corporate entrepreneurship process, which was enthusiastically endorsed by many participants, was severely set back when the head of the division's response to a corporate entrepreneurship proposal was, "That is not possible as it is in the realm of another division." The enthusiasm of the participating members in this volunteer program was severely damaged and never fully recovered.

While the degree of fit needs to be established, it also reflects two other criteria—an experienced venture champion and the organization's experience with the product or service proposed. A corporate entrepreneurship proposal has a higher probability of success if both these aspects are in the proposed corporate venture. This is particularly true for the first ventures as it is most important to have early success stories to build enthusiasm and maintain top management support. A midmarket company in Cleveland, Ohio, was able to do this with all of its initial ventures funded through a very careful selection process.

Other more specific proposal criteria frequently used include low initial investment, low competitive threat, proprietary technology, high gross margin, and high rate of return. Given the success rate of new enterprises whether inside or outside the corporation, it is generally better to spread the risk by allocating the amount of money set aside over more proposals of lower investment than one or two proposals requiring higher investment. A proprietary technology proposal, particularly if it has protected intellectual property, is much better in terms of a sustainable, successful launch if the funds are spread out than a proposal requiring significant capital at the start. A high gross margin at least conceived initially is also important as many corporate ventures end up costing about 30 percent more than anticipated and taking 30 percent longer than anticipated to generate revenues. While this and a high rate of return are useful criteria, care needs to be taken to avoid "marginitis"—having an unmovable fixed rate of return. This creates a hurdle rate that can stifle the funding of some corporate entrepreneurship proposals that may provide returns in other ways.

Indicators of Climate

Before launching a corporate entrepreneurship program, a benchmark needs to be established to evaluate the present corporate entrepreneurial climate of the company. Periodic measurements, at least every six months, should then be taken to see if the climate has changed and is moving toward a more corporate entrepreneurial one. By establishing a monitoring system, the company can measure the effects of its corporate entrepreneurship program and find areas for improvement. While benchmark indicators are organizational specific and can vary significantly from organization to organization, the more frequently used indicators are presented below.

Indicators of a Corporate Entrepreneurship Climate
- Self-selection
- No handoffs
- New ideas encouraged
- Failures allowed
- No home-run philosophy
- Tolerance of risk, failure, and mistakes
- Patient money
- Crossfunctional teams
- No opportunity parameters
- Longer time horizon
- Support of top management
- Resources available and accessible
- Percentage of yearly sales from products or services introduced in last five years
- Percentage of yearly sales from customers obtained in last three years

Some of these have already been discussed in this or previous chapters, such as not having a home-run philosophy, long time horizon, patient money, and support of top management. Several other indicators are also important and should be monitored.

One of these is the percentage of sales each year stemming from new products or services introduced in the market in the last five years. While the metric development should take into account the nature of the industry and market, if one objective of the corporate entrepreneurship program is creating the next generation of products or services, then this percentage should be increasing. Some companies rely significantly on continual new products or services. Invacare, for example, a leader in home health-care products, particularly wheelchairs, has the goal of having 40 percent of its revenue stream from new products introduced within the last 24-month period. In order to achieve this, the company is continually increasing its investment in research, development, and innovation. According to A. Malachi Mixon III, chairman and CEO of Invacare, "You have to continually focus on delivering new quality products to your customers." Regardless of the metrics established, this percentage should be measured on a six-month basis to ensure that the organization is delivering new quality products or services and is creative and innovative.

Another critical indicator of a corporate entrepreneurial climate that should be regularly tracked is the percentage of sales each year coming from new customers obtained in the last three years. Although creative, innovative organizations want to retain a loyal customer base and have low customer turnover, these firms also want to continue adding new customers. This will allow the company to grow by increasing purchases for present customers as well as generating new sales from new customers. The climate of corporate entrepreneurial organizations fosters new innovative products or services along with new customers.

Summary

The focus of this chapter was the corporate entrepreneurship process. First, the organizational barriers to corporate entrepreneurship were discussed. This was followed by a presentation of the four major structures commonly used: a section with the human resources department, a new products subsidiary, a new products division, and a diffusion of the concept and process throughout the entire organization.

Following a discussion of the evaluation criteria needed to ascertain the spirit of corporate entrepreneurship, the chapter concludes with the indicators of a corporate entrepreneurship climate.

6

Organizing the Venture

How can an organization develop a culture that fosters corporate entrepreneurial activity? What are the most appropriate structure(s) for new corporate ventures? What are the dangers of the new venture evolving into a bureaucratic structure? How can corporate entrepreneurial activities be effectively organized and managed?

Scenario: Siemens

Siemens was founded in Berlin in 1847 by Ernst Werner von Siemens as the Telegraphenbauanstalt von Siemens & Halske. Werner von Siemens was a German electrical engineer who was a visionary inventor and entrepreneur and made a significant contribution to technological advancement in the nineteenth century. Within a few decades, the enterprise developed from a small engineering workshop into one of the world's largest companies in electrical engineering and electronics.

For over 160 years, Siemens has been associated with international focus and worldwide presence. Siemens is a global powerhouse with activities in more than 190 countries all over the world providing customers with fast, local, tailor-made solutions. It has approximately 405,000 employees working in over 190 countries. Few industrial corporations can reflect on such a long history of success in the way Siemens made the transition from a small back building workshop in Berlin to a global firm.

From 1847 to 1865, Siemens began its initial expansion following the design of the pointer telegraph in 1847. Within a few years, the craftsman's workshop founded in Berlin developed into an internationally active corporation. From 1865 to 1890, Werner von Siemens pushed the global expansion of the company and increased agencies in European countries. Through the discovery of the dynamoelectric principle in 1866, potential applications for electricity were limitless.

Between 1890 and 1918, there was growth through consolidation and partnerships. Werner von Siemens retired from operational management in 1890 and died in 1892. His successors followed the course he had set, identifying market opportunities arising from technical developments and constantly advancing and developing the company. In 1897, Siemens & Halske transformed into a joint-stock corporation and targeted acquisitions and collaborative agreements to cover all aspects of electrical engineering. Lighting, medical engineering, wireless communication, and, in the 1920s, household appliances were followed after World War II by components, data processing systems, automotive systems, and semiconductors. Siemens was the only company in its industry to operate in telecommunications and power engineering. Because of World War I, Siemens lost almost 40 percent of its business assets, including the majority of its patent rights abroad. In the mid-1920s, the House of Siemens became again one of the top five electrical concerns in the world.

The beginning of the National Socialist regime in 1933 and the outbreak of war in 1939 meant that German companies were increasingly integrated into military preparations and the war economy. At the end of World War II, most of Siemens's buildings and manufacturing facilities in Berlin were destroyed. Between 1945 and 1966, Siemens reconstructed itself and emerged as a global player. Due to political uncertainty in April 1949, Siemens & Halske moved to Munich, and Siemens-Schuckertwerke, a German electrical engineering company headquartered in Berlin, moved to Erlangen and Nuremberg and was incorporated into Siemens AG in 1966. The company focused on reinforcing traditional core expertise and investing in business areas of strong growth such as semiconductor and data technology, and successfully returned to the global markets.

In 1966, in order to pool the various activities and competencies of the company, Siemens & Halske AG, Siemens-Schuckertwerke AG, and Siemens-Reiniger-Werke AG merged as of October 1 to form Siemens AG. Commencing in the 1970s, Siemens pushed forward the expansion of its position in the electrical markets of the United States, Western Europe, and Asia. The combination of outstanding technological achievements, organic growth, and an active investment policy brought Siemens strong market positions in strategically significant areas like power, data, and communications technology.

The years 1989 to 2008 marked the era of deregulation and globalization. Late 1980s management introduced a structural reform that created a basis for operating successfully in the globalized marketplace. In the 1990s, Siemens changed from a company dealing mainly with public customers in regulated markets to a global competitor. To increase efficiency and effectiveness, the company reformed its approach with programs based on the strategic pillars of productivity, innovation, and growth. During this time, the company pursued active portfolio management. In 1990, the creation of the largest European company in the computer industry occurred, Siemens Nixdorf Informationssysteme AG (SNI). In the United States, Siemens acquired Westinghouse's fossil power plant activities in 1998 with the goal of boosting earnings in the power generation sector. Since the late 1990s, Siemens has been focusing more on optimization of its business portfolio through divestments, acquisitions, the formation of new companies, and the founding of joint ventures. The spin-off of the semiconductor sector and the listing of Epcos and Infineon Technologies on the stock exchange in 1999 included the acquisition of a majority stake in Atecs Mannesmann AG and the merging of Siemens's nuclear activities with the French company of Framatome.

Siemens has demonstrated innovations in technologies and major projects since its founding in 1847. Innovation milestones at Siemens are focused in the following areas: (1) information and communications (the Pointer Telegraph, Russian Telegraphy Network, Indo-European telegraph line, transatlantic cable, Telex Network, Raisting Earth Station, and fingerprint sensor); (2) power generation, transmission, and distribution (Dynamo, Benson Boiler, Shannon Power Plant, expansion circuit breaker, Cabora Bassa Power Plant, fuel cell, and gas turbines); (3) transportation (electric streetcar, Budapest subway, first traffic signal installation, Dortmund suspended railway, InterCity Express (ICE), diesel catalytic converter, and the Transrapid); (4) health care (X-ray sphere, electron accelerator, echocardiography, cardiac pacemaker, ultrasound diagnosis, nuclear magnetic resonance tomography, and PET scanner); (5) industry automation and building technology (rolling mill motor, mercury vapor rectifier, totally integrated automation, postal automation, augmented reality, and the Intelligent Fire Detector); (6) lighting technology (differential arc lamp, tantalum lamp, circolux fluorescent lamp, and the light-emitting diode); and (7) household appliances and radio (dust suction pump, cookers and washing machines, television set, dishwasher, aquastop system, and the shirt ironing machine).

From the beginning, Siemens had landmark inventions, an immense readiness to innovate, and a strong international commitment, all of which have driven the company's success. Siemens's 160-year history illustrates how visions can become reality. Since it was founded under Werner von Siemens, a visionary inventor and entrepreneur who made an enormous contribution to technological progress in the nineteenth century, the company has grown into a global network of innovation uniting approximately 405,000 employees at 1,640 locations around the globe including 176 research and development facilities. Siemens is a global powerhouse with activities in over 190 regions. Entrepreneurial organizations like Siemens can leverage their people at all levels to be innovative through its flexibility, responsiveness, innovativeness, and openness.

www.siemens.com

Introduction

There are few decisions that are more important to corporate entrepreneurship organizations than deciding how best to organize new corporate venture projects. The nature of implementation results in the degree of venture autonomy. To ensure effective development and commercialization of new venture activities, the relatedness between the two must be clearly defined and autonomy must be carefully assigned. Certain organizational issues, such as the level of autonomy assigned for the new venture project, will be influenced by the degree of relatedness or unrelatedness in the organization.

Corporate entrepreneurship will be a key success factor for organizations in the future, particularly when linked to organizational culture, structure, relatedness, and degree of autonomy. The culture, structure, relatedness, and degree of autonomy allow opportunities for corporate entrepreneurship to occur. CEOs of a company need to be organized in such a way that they have sufficient internal diversity in strategies, structures, people, and processes to facilitate different kinds of corporate entrepreneurship.

This chapter addresses four major aspects of organizing corporate entrepreneurship—culture, organizational structure, relatedness and degree of autonomy, and organizational effectiveness.

It discusses the various organizational cultures, structures, and degree of autonomy found in new corporate entrepreneurship activities.

Culture

Organizational culture refers to the ideas, values, and beliefs shared by an organization regarding its opportunities, problems, practices, and goals. Culture is a fundamental part of an organization's commitment to excellence as well as being a determinant of employee behavior and commitment. A shared organizational vision is an important aspect of culture as it can overcome potential boundaries between the existing organization and venture by creating a common language and mutual understanding. A shared language is vital for effective communication and knowledge exchange. A shared vision can help recognize the value and knowledge within the organization. At 3M, there is an unwritten guideline that researchers can spend 15 percent of their time working on an idea without approval from management.

Effective management of corporate entrepreneurship involves managing a culture that applauds successes, learns from failures, and provides screening mechanisms to facilitate innovation and creativity. A distinctive reputation and culture occur in organizations such as 3M, Dell, Hewlett-Packard, IBM, Lucent, Microsoft, Nokia, and Sharp Corporation. Organizational culture is an influential factor and is the first step in fostering a venturing activity within an organization. It determines "the way things are done around here." Positive cultures are in line with an organization's vision, mission, and strategies and help promote desired behavior.

The challenge for corporate entrepreneurial organizations is to determine the cultural features that are conducive to entrepreneurship in their organizations. Various aspects of corporate entrepreneurship culture such as risk, emotional commitment, empowerment, involvement, experimentation, visible management, clarity, recognition, and esprit de corps have been identified by many researchers. The following are important features of a corporate entrepreneurship organizational culture:

- **Innovations.** New innovative and creative ideas with future possibilities are encouraged and supported at all levels of the organization.
- **Supportive environment.** Drive, motivate, and facilitate employees to independently innovate, create, and invent.
- **Teamwork.** Encourage and facilitate a multidisciplinary team approach that works toward greater synergy. The existence of "skunkworks" has generated corporate entrepreneurship success through using groups of people with the appropriate skills to instill a high level of group identity and loyalty.
- **Availability and accessibility of required resources.** Human and financial resources must be available and readily accessible to quickly capture the "window of opportunity." The organization needs to eliminate any obstacles or restrictions that could inhibit the venturing process.
- **Tolerance of mistakes.** Trial and error is encouraged, and mistakes are tolerated and recognized as inevitable in the corporate entrepreneurship process. For example, Nokia has a culture that permits and supports mistakes. BMW has a "successful failures" program that awards employees whose innovative ideas fail during implementation by giving a "flop of the month" award.
- **A proper reward system.** Employees are recognized as valuable members of the venturing process and rewarded for their drive, energy, effort, and perseverance in creating a new venture. Rewards should be based on the attainment of established performance goals and objectives.
- **Long-term orientation.** The corporate environment must establish long-term orientation as it takes time and patience to assess and evaluate the benefits of a venture.

- **Corporate venture champions.** It is favorable for the venture to have individuals who support innovative and creative activity.
- **Support of top management.** Corporate entrepreneurship needs to be totally supported and embraced by top management. Without top management support, corporate venturing cannot exist.

Corporate entrepreneurship organizations need to develop a culture that encourages innovation, creativity, and experimental efforts. They must also eliminate obstacles that inhibit opportunities, promote teamwork, ensure availability of resources, and enlist top management support. Organizations including Adobe, Intel, Lucent, Sun Microsystems, and Xerox have introduced corporate entrepreneurship capital programs to promote greater innovation and creativity. In addition to being innovative and creative, the CEO needs to have flexibility and a vision that encourages teamwork within the corporate structure and across established structures. Lucent created its New Venture Group (NVG) in 1997 in order to commercialize technologies out of its Bell Laboratories that did not fit with any of Lucent's established businesses. Lucent learned that the challenge for the NVG was to develop a more entrepreneurial spirit in the culture of the organization.[1]

Core Ideology and Envisioned Future

A core ideology is a shared understanding of an organization's "reason for being." It addresses the question of why the organization was created in the first place. A core ideology deals with the "character" of the organization. What are the most important tenets, guiding principles, values, and expectations from everyone in the organization? It is based on the concept that organizational culture develops over time in response to external and internal stimuli. A good ideology, well executed, will shape the attitudes, habits, and behaviors of individuals in the organization. Corporate entrepreneurship organizations are guided by a vision, which consists of core ideology (core values and core purpose) and envisioned future. The core values and purpose are unchanging while the envisioned future is what the organization is aspiring to become and achieve. The envisioned future varies in complexity and scope depending on the difficulty of the goals the organization commits to achieve over time. During his time as CEO of General Electric, Jack Welch had a goal that every division of GE should to be number one or number two in its respective industry; if this was not achievable, he felt GE should exit that specific business. Few business leaders have had such a clearly defined and tightly knit business philosophy as Jack Welch.

Core values are the essential and enduring principles of an organization that do not require external justification. *3M Corporation*'s core values include "thou shalt not kill" a new product idea, absolute integrity, respect for individual initiative and personal growth, tolerance for mistakes, and product quality and reliability. *Merck*'s core values include corporate social responsibility, unequivocal excellence in all aspects of the organization, science-based innovation, honesty and integrity, and profit from work that benefits humanity. *Sony Corporation*'s core values include being a pioneer, doing the impossible, and encouraging individual ability and creativity. *Walt Disney Company* preserves and controls the Disney magic as part of its core values.

The core purpose is the organization's reason for being. This is not to be confused with a goal, objective, or strategy. It is the idealistic motivation for undertaking the organization's work. *3M*'s core purpose is to solve unsolved problems innovatively. *Hewlett-Packard*'s core purpose is to make technical contributions for the advancement and welfare of humanity. *McKinsey & Company*'s core purpose is to help leading corporations and government become more successful. *Merck*'s core purpose is to preserve and improve human life. *Nike*'s core purpose is to experience the emotion of competition, winning, and crushing competitors.

Sony Corporation's core purpose is to experience the joy of advancing and applying technology for the benefit of the public. *Telecare Corporation*'s core purpose is to help people with mental impairments recognize their full potential. *Walt Disney Company*'s core purpose is to make people happy. The organizations that enjoy continued success have core values and a core purpose that remain constant while their strategies and practices continuously adapt to a fast-paced, rapidly changing environment. Examples of these organizations include 3M, Hewlett-Packard, Johnson & Johnson, Merck, Motorola, Procter & Gamble, and Sony Corporation.

If the organizational goal is to create a corporate entrepreneurship environment, then culture underlies all other components of that work environment. Structure, relatedness, and degree of autonomy along with other aspects of the work environment need to be congruent with the key aspects of the organizational corporate entrepreneurship culture.

Designing the Corporate Venture

Generally, the design of the new corporate venture is simple. The CEO may in fact perform all the functions of the new venture alone or with one or two others. Regardless of whether one or more individuals are involved in the new venture start-up, as the workload increases, the organizational structure will need to expand to include additional team members with defined roles in the new venture. Effective interviewing and hiring procedures will need to be implemented to ensure that new employees will effectively grow and mature with the new venture as will be discussed in Chapter 10. All the design decisions involving personnel and their roles and responsibilities reflect the formal structure of the organization. In addition, an informal structure or organizational culture that evolves over time needs to be addressed by the CEO. In terms of the organizational culture, the CEO can have some control over how it evolves and help ensure that it is separate from the parent company.

The design of the organization will be the CEO's decision, which indicates what is expected of members of the organization. These can usually be grouped into the following five areas:

- **Organizational structure.** This defines individuals' jobs, chain of command, and channel of communication. These relationships are reflected in an organizational chart.
- **Planning, measurement, and evaluation schemes.** All organizational activities should reflect the goals and objectives of the new venture. It must be clearly communicated how these goals will be achieved, how they will be measured, and how they will be evaluated.
- **Compensation and rewards.** Members of an organization will require compensation and rewards in the form of equity, bonuses, promotions, recognition, and so on.
- **Recruitment and selection.** A set of guidelines is needed for recruiting, selecting, and retaining appropriate individuals either internally from the parent company or externally for each position (see Chapter 10).
- **Training and development.** Training and development, on or off the job, need to be specified. This training may be in the form of formal education or learning skills.

The organization's design can be very simple—that is, one in which the CEO and his or her team perform all the tasks (usually indicative of a start-up) or more complex, in which other employees are hired to perform specific tasks. As the organization becomes larger and more complex, the expectations become more relevant to facilitate the growth and development of the new venture.

As the organization evolves, the CEO or venture manager decision role becomes very critical for an effective new venture. The CEO's primary concern is to adapt to changes in the environment and seek new innovative and creative ideas. When a new idea is found, the CEO will need to initiate its development. In addition, the CEO will also need to respond to pressures such as an unsatisfied customer, a supplier reneging on a contract, or a key employee threatening to quit. Much of the time at the start-up phase will be spent dealing with pitfalls.

Another role for the CEO and venture manager is effective allocation of resources. This involves the delegation of budgets and responsibilities. The allocation of resources can be a very complex and difficult process since one decision affects other decisions. The final decision role is that of negotiator. Negotiations of contracts, salaries, and prices of raw materials are an integral part of the job.

Organizational Structures for Corporate Entrepreneurship

While structures and systems are necessary for the management and control of a corporation, they need to have some flexibility for a corporate venture. The adoption of the right corporate entrepreneurship organizational structure depends on the size of the organization, type of market, organizational and venturing objectives, and the availability of human resources. Bureaucracy is a formal organizational structure characterized by tight control systems, rigidity, structured channels of communication, specialization, hierarchy, and positions held based on expertise. These bureaucratic characteristics can inhibit organizational corporate entrepreneurship. The more hierarchical the organizational structure, the greater the difficulty for an organization to identify opportunities, achieve top management support, reallocate resources, and take calculated risks. Bureaucracy fails to provide the flexibility, adaptability, speed, or incentives for innovation and creativity that are critical for corporate entrepreneurship.

When Jack Welch took over GE, he "delayered" GE's management tiers from nineteen to eleven organizational layers and a decade later reduced these eleven to six. GE used the term "boundarylessness," which focused on eliminating bureaucracy. Organic structures are more adaptable, flexible, and loosely controlled where power is decentralized and communication is open, resulting in faster decision making and delegation of autonomy.

Since corporate entrepreneurship requires innovative and creative thinking, it becomes even more important when environments become more dynamic. Since corporate entrepreneurship is communication intensive and since much of that communication is informal and unplanned, the corporate reporting system must facilitate effective lateral and vertical communication throughout. This means that corporate entrepreneurial organizations need to ensure that an organic structure is in place.

Corporate entrepreneurship is most likely to occur in an organic structure, which facilitates a high level of venturing. A corporate entrepreneurship organic structure has the following characteristics:

- Venture managers have the flexibility and resources to promote corporate entrepreneurship.
- The organizational structure has as few layers as possible.
- Authority is delegated on individual skills and expertise.
- Focus is on results rather than the process of achieving them.
- Decision making is decentralized.
- There is apparent open communication and an informal control system.
- Teamwork is an integral part of the corporate entrepreneurship process.

In large corporate entrepreneurial organizations, the responsibility for development and planning can be located at the corporate level, division level, or both. Locating this responsibility at the corporate level may be the only option when divisions do not have the required competencies for new product or service development. This is particularly beneficial when the corporate level of innovation and creativity exceeds beyond the current business and can serve as a cost saving measure for the initial stages of the venture.

Venturing at the divisional level is appropriate when the divisions are large and autonomous. Divisional managers are often more sensitive to the needs, wants, and expectations of customers. A combination of both corporate and divisional level entrepreneurship is appropriate when there is high risk associated with the new product or service needing the responsibility located at the corporate level. This allows divisional managers to have the required level of control, while corporate managers focus on the long-term issues of the new product or service. However, this can result in additional conflicts as it can be difficult to create consensus.

The degree of autonomy is influenced by the overall structure of the organization, management style, type of industry, and risk of developing new products or services. Kao Corporation, an imported fancy goods wholesaler, has a management style that is based on three fundamental principles: maintain a customer-oriented spirit, all individuals have equal value, and combine abilities and goals to maximize effectiveness. These principles drive Kao's three main managerial practices: total system management, group management, and R&D career focus. Whatever reporting system is in place, the chain of command and the channels of communication must support the key goals and objectives of the corporate entrepreneurship so that innovation and creativity are facilitated throughout the organization.

Structures to support the new product or service development process require the organization to take ownership of the project. Several challenging questions need to be addressed: Who has the required skills and expertise to be involved and at what level? How does the organization structure itself to achieve open communication, trust, cooperation, and teamwork across departments, divisions, and management in terms of entrepreneurship activities? Primary responsibility for corporate entrepreneurship can be handled in various ways.

The alternative structures for the new product or service development aspect of corporate entrepreneurship generally comprise the following:

- Corporate venture department
- Corporate venture committee
- Autonomous venture units
- Professional consultants
- Corporate venture manager
- Divisional venture units
- Corporate venture teams

The corporate venture team structure is most suited to large corporations focused on new product or service development rather than product or service extensions. Smaller organizations that do not have the budget for full-time personnel required for this or new product or service planning and development are likely to use the committee approach. Organizations with multiple product or service lines might want to adopt the corporate venture manager approach as it provides the organization with a focused new product or service development effort involving unique products. This is especially beneficial when development involves product or service extension, improvements, new markets, or repositioning decisions.

Arm & Hammer is an organization that exhibits both "new products" and "new markets." The company has been able to achieve desirable financial returns through the creative introduction of its core product—baking soda—into new product market arenas. Arm & Hammer capitalized on emerging product market opportunities that were not recognized and valued by its competitors; these included the introduction and development of baking soda toothpaste and deodorizing products. New corporate ventures need to enhance and develop venturing activities within the existing organization that can be integrated into and be facilitated by the existing organization.

An essential requirement to the success of any organizational structure is top management support. Members of top management must recognize that their attitudes and behavior toward corporate entrepreneurship will be part of the organizational culture and will be reflected in the decisions made. Any negative attitudes demonstrated in relation to venturing will weaken its development and stifle innovation and creativity. Whatever structure is in place, there needs to be a strong, visible level of top management support.

Relatedness and Degree of Corporate Venture Autonomy

Corporate entrepreneurship organizations require systems that emphasize open communication, employee empowerment, and rewarding employees for their performance. Open communication is a way of information sharing and empowerment that is recognized as corporate entrepreneurship. Communication is important for success.

A barrier-free philosophy is also important as barrier-free organizations typically feature fewer layers of management, smaller-scale business units, promote the creation of teams and interdisciplinary work groups, open communications vertically and laterally, and have accountability for results.[2] For corporate entrepreneurship to occur, managers at all levels within the organization must listen, challenge, endorse, facilitate, sponsor, and invest in the ideas of employees.

Organizational autonomy is a key ingredient of corporate entrepreneurship. Autonomy creates appropriate boundaries from the existing organization, which increases the efficiency and effectiveness of the venturing process. In order for autonomy to support and facilitate corporate entrepreneurial projects, corporate entrepreneurs need to operate within the organizational culture and structure that promote independent action and seeking out opportunities. Autonomy provides corporate entrepreneurial projects with a sense of freedom and ownership. This results in higher levels of innovation and creativity and facilitates greater adaptation in implementing a specific project.

The degree of relatedness of the new venture to the existing organization will influence the level of autonomy. Relatedness indicates the degree the new venture can utilize the existing organization's knowledge and resources and the degree it needs to explore new knowledge and obtain additional resources. Explorative new business development activities require searches, discovery, experimentation, risk taking, innovation, and the generation of new knowledge. On the other hand, exploitative activities result from reducing the variety and enhancing the efficient application of existing sources of knowledge.[3]

Research on corporate entrepreneurship has indicated that exploration and exploitation activities require substantially different strategies, cultures, structures, processes, and capabilities and may have different impacts on organizational adaptation and performance.[4] Explorative organizations generate greater diversity in performance by experiencing substantial success as well as failure, while exploitative organizations are likely to generate more stable performance.[5] Corporate entrepreneurship autonomy needs to be contingent on the degree to which projects can use and leverage available knowledge within the existing organization versus the exploration of new knowledge.[6]

There can be variations in the degree of relatedness in terms of product, service, process, market, technology, and required resources. This construct may vary from being closely related to completely unrelated to the organization's current activities, leading to variation and the challenge of required learning for effectively managing the new corporate venture. The more related these constructs are to the existing organization, the greater the opportunity to identify the required resources and competencies needed within the organization. The more unrelated the new venture is to the existing organization, the greater the challenges facing the organization. Assessing how projects are related to the existing organization is important, as it identifies potential synergies as well as obstacles. Technological synergies could be achieved, for example, by sharing production facilities and benefiting from the existing distribution and sales systems that drive marketing synergies.

The greater the level of alignment or fit between the new corporate venture and the existing organization, the greater the degree of legitimacy and continuous access to existing resources. New corporate ventures that have high relatedness to the existing organization have access to key resources. Those key resources can give the new venture competitive advantage, increase the speed to market, and provide technological advancement. The corporate entrepreneur managing the new venture needs to recognize the internal politics of venturing in terms of resource allocation and comply with the existing corporate culture, structure, relatedness, and degree of autonomy.

Related corporate entrepreneurship projects are within the existing organization's knowledge and resources. During the development stage, related projects benefit from tighter integration with the existing organization. Chrysler Corporation brings managers and employees from across the organization to achieve functional integration. Chrysler has been recognized as a company that has sustained its position in the global automobile industry due to its product development cycle, time and product quality, and process reengineering principles. Lower levels of autonomy facilitate knowledge sharing and resource utilization, preventing unnecessary duplication between the venture project and the existing organization. During commercialization, corporate entrepreneurship projects targeting related markets should have less autonomy to maximize the potential for leveraging existing market knowledge and capabilities.

Unrelated corporate entrepreneurship projects are outside the existing organization's knowledge and resources. During the development stage, research has indicated that there is a need to provide more autonomy. The greater the diversity of the new corporate entrepreneurship project to the existing organization, the higher the degree of autonomy required to reduce potential interference and unnecessary delays in the project development. Then the entrepreneurship project can adopt its own work methods that are most suitable, resulting in more efficient project development and better utilization of resources. To facilitate the exploration of market knowledge and capabilities, a greater level of autonomy needs to be given to unrelated corporate entrepreneurship projects in the commercialization stage.

Developing the Corporate Entrepreneurship Team and a Successful Culture

There are some key issues to address before assembling and developing the corporate entrepreneurship team. The team must be able to accomplish three functions:

- Execute the new venture business plan.
- Identify fundamental changes in the new venture as they emerge.
- Make adjustments to the venture plan based on changes in the environment and market that will maintain and develop profitability and growth.

Although these functions may appear straightforward, the individuals who have been recruited and the culture that is promoted are critical in their being able to be achieved. Not only are individual core competencies important, but also the personality and characteristics of each individual. The organization culture will be a blend of values, attitudes, behaviors, dress, and communication styles that make one organization different from another. There are some important considerations and strategies in recruiting and assembling an effective corporate entrepreneurship team and in creating an effective and positive organizational culture. These include:

- The culture must fit the business strategy as specified in the new corporate entrepreneurship business plan.
- The corporate entrepreneur heading the new venture must create a workplace where employees are motivated and rewarded for good work.
- The corporate entrepreneur heading the new venture needs to be flexible and adaptable to new opportunities and methods for accomplishing better results.
- Time and commitment need to be given to the recruitment and selection process so that the right people are selected to be part of the new venture team. The recruitment and selection processes need to establish the procedures for screening, interviewing, and assessing all candidates. Job descriptions and person specifications that will match the desired culture should be documented as part of this process.
- The corporate entrepreneur heading the new venture needs to understand the importance of leadership. Leadership should help to establish core values and provide the appropriate tools so that employees can effectively complete their jobs.

Finding the most effective team and creating a positive organizational culture is indeed a major challenge. Figure 6.1 indicates the importance of ensuring effective interactions among the parent company, the new venture, and the innovative environment. The opportunities for new venture success can be improved by ensuring that interaction of the new venture with the innovative environment is as strong as its interaction with the parent company. Sadly, few organizations evaluate a new venture based on how effective it is at attracting advisors, consultants, and external talent early in the life cycle.

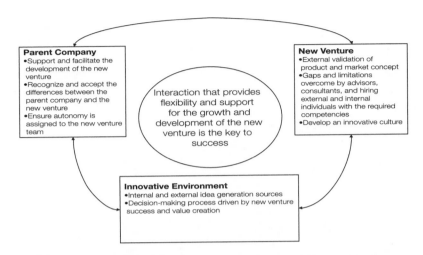

FIGURE 6.1 Interactions between Parent Company, New Venture, and the Innovative Environment

Effectively Organizing Corporate Entrepreneurial Activities

To effectively organize corporate entrepreneurship, organizational culture needs to be established with the appropriate culture and support systems (see Tables 6.1 and 6.2).

A culture supportive of the corporate entrepreneurship makes it easier to effectively manage the resulting activities. The culture needs to establish core ideology, present and future practices, and behavioral norms that fit requirements for the execution of a strategy that motivates employees to be innovative and creative. The decision to move toward a more participative culture that rewards corporate entrepreneurship will fail if it is not supported by top management who need to provide appropriate training, encouragement, and tolerance of mistakes. New employees need to be culturally integrated into the organization if they are to become participative members of the team.

Corporate cultures that value innovation and change will be more willing to provide the required resources (human, physical,

TABLE 6.1   Structures for Corporate Entrepreneurship

Supporting Structure	Favorable Factors	Unfavorable Factors	Reporting Mechanism
Corporate venturing department. A department within a division.	Centralized coordination, control, and decision making, increasing responsiveness to opportunities.	Duplication of effort; inefficient use of resources.	Vice President
Corporate venturing committee. Somewhat informal, serving special functions with diverse representation.	Ideas and expertise of key executives pooled; required for special purpose such as brainstorming, idea generation, and screening ideas.	Lacks clear lines of authority and responsibility; can be time consuming.	Product or Service Manager
Autonomous venture units. Members are chosen from various functional areas. Suitable when product or service is unrelated to existing business or requires special attention.	Allows the organization to take on new products that would not be viable without the existing organization; full-time commitment to the venture team; combining group talent can achieve synergy.	Interdepartmental conflict can occur; conflict if the department head will not cooperate and assign staff to the team.	Division Head
Professional consultants. Specialist external consultants.	The consultants have specialized training; they are not involved in the internal politics; they bring credibility and outside perspective to the process.	Can be costly and time consuming to bring in an outside service; there can be internal resistance to the consultant.	Corporate Venturing Manager
Corporate venturing manager. One manager who is responsible for a new product or service.	Specialists in a particular market and generalists in the marketing mix.	Burdened with responsibility regarding existing products or services that there is little time for new product or service development.	President
Divisional venture units. A large, self-sufficient division.	Centralized control and coordination, which enhances efficiency and effectiveness; commitment and long term orientated; top management support; availability of resources.	Coordination with other organizational divisions.	Division Head

TABLE 6.2 Summary of Organizing Corporate Entrepreneurship

Culture	Supporting Systems
✓ Visionary	✓ Organic organizational structure
✓ Values	✓ Innovative managers and leaders
✓ Beliefs	✓ Open communication
✓ Consistent language	✓ Delegation of autonomy and responsibility
✓ Innovative	associated with the specific venture
✓ Learning	✓ Flexibility and adaptability
✓ Commitment	✓ Team orientation
✓ Empowerment	✓ Resource utilization
✓ Teamwork	✓ Motivation system that recognizes and
✓ Flexibility	rewards innovation and creativity

and financial) to corporate entrepreneurial activities. Problems have occurred when organizations may use resources, such as personnel, because they are available even if they do not adequately match the criteria and competencies needed. The resources must not only fit the needs of corporate entrepreneurship but also be available in a timely manner. The possible use of inappropriate resources or the inadequate sharing of resources between the existing organization corporate entrepreneurship will radically affect any possible success.

Summary

The most successful corporate entrepreneurship organizations are those that incorporate knowledge obtained from past innovation experiences into their strategies and future innovations. Successful corporate entrepreneurship can be achieved through challenging employees to explore new markets and diversification; measuring a variety of performance indicators; accepting risks and mistakes; supporting a flexible and fluid organizational structure that minimizes bureaucracy and maximizes adhocracy; and evaluating innovation schemes in terms of their contribution to a cogent, coherent, and understandable strategy.

The effective organization of corporate entrepreneurial activities into organizational strategy is fundamental to developing innovative and creative approaches designed to develop new ideas and ways of doing things. Corporate entrepreneurial projects should be more tightly integrated with the existing organization to realize potential synergies. Unrelated corporate entrepreneurial projects need to receive more autonomy to increase the chances of venture success.

7

Controlling the Venture

What is the nature of a control system for corporate entrepreneurship? How should corporate entrepreneurial activities be evaluated? Should organizational control change from the traditional control system in place? Why are financial and nonfinancial methods of control important?

Scenario: American Greetings Corporation

American Greetings Corporation, the largest publicly traded greeting card company in the world, was started in 1906 by a Polish immigrant, Jacob Sapirstein, who moved to Cleveland, Ohio. He borrowed $50 to buy a supply of penny postcards, which he sold to drug stores, novelty shops, and confectioners. After the first week, he had sold enough cards to repay the loan and had an extra $50 to fund the following week's business. Soon thereafter, American Greetings Corporation became a family operation. In 1921, family business sales totaled $11,500, equivalent to approximately $100,000 today.

In 1929, American Greetings introduced the first self-serve greeting card display fixtures. This innovation is still the standard worldwide display for greeting cards today. By 1936, the company was printing its own cards. The company achieved significant growth in 1952, leading to its first public offering of stock with the sale of 200,000 shares at $12 per share. In 1956, American Greetings operated nine plants in Cleveland, turning out 1.8 million cards daily, and acquired Carlton Cards. In 1957, American Greetings introduced a new kind of greeting card, Hi Brows, which featured short, comic punch lines and cartoon-style artwork. In 1967, American Greetings introduced Holly Hobbie, whose peaceful patchwork captured the fancy of millions. By 1977, Holly Hobbie was one of the most sought after female licensed characters in the world. American Greetings purchased Feliciataciones Nacionales in 1968. American Greetings established AG Industries, Inc., in 1978 as the largest display fixture company in the nation. In 1979, American Greetings purchased Plus Mark Canada, a manufacturer of Christmas wrap, boxed cards, and accessories.

Strawberry Shortcake, a new character personifying spunky innocence, made her debut in 1980. By 1981, the rag doll–style character generated $500 million in retail sales. In less than one year, over 600 different Strawberry Shortcake products were available. In 1980, American Greetings purchased the rights to Rust Craft Greeting Cards of Toronto and acquired Celebration Arts Group Ltd. (CAG), based in Corby, Northamptonshire. In 1982, they created the Care Bears. In the first five years, Care Bear merchandise accounted for over $2 billion in retail sales. In 1986, the company reached the $1 billion milestone. The acquisitions of John Sands in Australia and New Zealand and S.A. Greetings in South Africa strengthened the company's international presence. American Greetings launched its own Web site in 1996, featuring paper greeting cards, electronic cards, candy, flowers, and gifts. Currently, AG Interactive offers one of the largest creative selections available on the Web through its flagship site, AmericanGreetings.com, as well as its family of other sites, including Egreetings.com and BlueMountain.com. The company introduced DateWorks in 1998 as a separate business unit to market and distribute the company's calendar line. In 2002, the Care Bears reemerged from Care-a-lot, and in 2003, Classic Strawberry Shortcake was reintroduced as "Strawberry Shortcake and Friends." As a result of mobile technology in 2004, AmericanGreetings.com announced the formation of AG Mobile, the company's new wireless division. Because of the expansion into a new medium, the company changed its named from AmericanGreetings.com to AG Interactive. In 2008, American Greetings purchased PhotoWorks and Webshots, two online photo sharing and personal publishing sites. In 2009, American Greetings acquired the Recycled Paper Greetings and Papyrus brands.

American Greetings constantly innovates ways to reduce waste, create environmentally friendly products, and explore options to make its operations more energy efficient. It promotes sustainability through its:

- **Communities**. Supports the United Way of Greater Cleveland with a variety of local organizations through donation drives, volunteering, and select sponsorships.
- **Associates**. Helps associates reduce waste and energy consumption through a paperless communications system and corporate sponsored events.
- **Retailers**. Values sustainability and has several initiatives including the introduction of a new car fleet for the sales force to reduce greenhouse gas emissions.
- **Operations**. Ensures that a sustainability program runs throughout its business chain.
- **Final product**. Ensures a more sustainable final product through initiatives around waste management.

The dedication to innovate that drove Jacob Sapirstein in 1906 is alive and well today, driving the company to assist consumers in enhancing its relationships through self-expression.

www.corporate.americangreetings.com/aboutus/history.html

American Greetings Interactive Sites
AmericanGreetings.com
BlueMountain.com
Egreetings.com
Kiwee.com
PhotoWorks.com
WebShots.com

Introduction

Traditionally, control evokes images of bureaucracy, rigidity, and conformity to the rules, regulations, policies, and procedures of an organization. While control is needed to ensure that the organization achieves its goals and objectives, it should not be in excess but rather a function of managers who oversee the daily operations of the organization.

As the organization develops and grows, control systems become more complex. Additional rules, regulations, policies, and procedures are implemented to establish a work environment that could restrict an employee's ability to be more innovative and creative. While structures and systems are necessary for the management and control of an organization, these policies should not inhibit flexibility, innovation, or creativity.

Control in this way means monitoring and evaluating organizational activities while anticipating events that could potentially occur and determining appropriate courses of action. Control is concerned with keeping employees motivated, dealing with problems confronting the organization, and working to take advantage of opportunities that enhance organizational performance.

The development of a control system has implications for the amount of corporate entrepreneurship occurring in an organization. Effective control systems: (1) monitor and regulate how efficiently an organization and its members are performing the activities necessary to achieve organizational goals; (2) develop the organizational strategy and structure that will allow the organization to use resources to create value for customers; and (3) monitor and evaluate whether the organization's strategy and structure are working as intended and how they could be improved.

In this chapter, the nature of controlling corporate entrepreneurship activities is discussed. First, the elements and roles of management in developing and creating the control and the forms and measures of control are presented. Then the characteristics of an effective control system are discussed followed by approaches to developing a management control philosophy that encourages corporate entrepreneurship. The chapter concludes by looking at financial and nonfinancial methods of control together with identifying key ingredients required for obtaining a high level of innovation and creativity in a corporate entrepreneurial organization.

Nature of Controlling the Venture

Control can be defined as a systematic process through which managers make sure that organizational activities are in line with the goals and objectives established in plans, targets, and standards of performance. Control is often associated with the act of delegation. Effective delegation requires decision rules that are consistent with the organization's philosophy, strategy, and objectives. A control system consists of rules, regulations, policies, procedures, objectives, and guidelines that are integrated into the organization. These can be formally integrated into the organization or can be an informal interaction at a point in time. Regardless, they should not be so complex as to inhibit creativity and innovation.

The type and level of control need to be tailored to the needs of the organization and be linked to other organizational mechanisms. The control mechanisms for corporate entrepreneurship need to allow adequate autonomy and flexibility and provide direct contact with top management to make sure needed information is provided.

To effectively control an organization, managers must plan and set realistic but challenging performance standards, implement a communication system that will provide timely information, and take action to correct any deviations. At the organizational level, management needs to exercise control over the behavior and actions of employees in order to ensure a satisfactory level of performance. An effective control system emerges and develops over time and is responsive to changes occurring.

Elements of a Management Control System

There are generally five elements of a corporate entrepreneurship management control system.

- **Planning what is desired.** Establish clear goals and objectives.
- **Establishing standards of performance.** Establish realistic measurements of the level and quality of the goal(s).
- **Monitoring and evaluating actual performance.** Establish a system of reporting information, which is accurate, relevant, timely, and identifies any deviations.
- **Comparing actual results with desired results.** Interpret and evaluate information in order to give details of progress, disclose deviations, and identify causes.
- **Rectifying deviations and taking corrective action.** Execute the most appropriate course of action, which may involve removing certain processes or employees and/or increase training to improve organizational performance.

Forms of Control

Control of corporate entrepreneurship can serve a number of functions and take a number of forms:

- Control systems can focus on the measurement of inputs (e.g., recruitment and selection), behavior (e.g., performance appraisals), or the outputs (e.g., measuring performance).
- Controls can measure general results or specific actions.
- Controls can evaluate the overall performance of the organization as a whole or with specific parts of it or day-to-day operational activities.

Measures and Strategies of Control in Organizations

The various types of control determine outputs of corporate entrepreneurship (such as sales, productivity, costs, profitability, and growth) and behavior (such as employee behavior, culture, management competencies, rewards, and motivation) and can be grouped into four general categories: personal control, bureaucratic or centralized control, output control, and cultural control. Personal control is direct supervision and leadership with centralized decision making involving reward and punishment reinforcement to produce conformity. Bureaucratic or centralized control is highly formalized with narrowly defined tasks, procedures, and rules applied to undertaking each task, centralized decision making, and reward and punishment systems that reinforce conformity to rules, regulations, and procedures. Output control is having each job or unit designed to be responsible for complete outputs, delegation of decisions on operational matters, and reward and punishment linked to attainment of output targets. Cultural control concerns shared values, norms, and conformance with few formal controls but with a strong emphasis on selection, training, and development of personnel and rewards orientated toward job security and career progression.

Generally, formalized control relies on rules, regulations, policies, and procedures that indicate the required level of output. Cultural controls rely on shared values and beliefs. A formalized control system uses standardized budgets, reporting systems, and policy manuals. Cultural controls require congruence between the individual and the organizational values and norms.

Characteristics of an Effective Control System

While there is a need for some form of control of corporate entrepreneurial activities, the extent and type of control varies. It is important that the controls are different for each task and perhaps each function. Effective controls of corporate entrepreneurship have the following characteristics:

- **Link to strategy.** Controls should reflect where the organization is going in the short and long run.
- **Utilize all the control steps.** The control steps consist of setting realistic standards of performance, gathering information about actual performance, comparing standards to the actual performance, and taking corrective action where deviations exist.
- **Accepted by employees.** The more committed and compliant employees are to the control standards, the more successful the control system will be. This often requires direct involvement by employees in establishing these systems in order to increase ownership and commitment.
- **Balance objective and subjective data.** Managers need to balance quantitative and qualitative performance indicators to ensure that all activities receive attention.
- **Accuracy.** The control system needs to encourage accurate, thorough information to detect deviations.

- **Flexibility.** The control system needs to be flexible enough to make necessary adaptations.
- **Timely.** The control system should provide timely information for management response.

An effective corporate entrepreneurship control system should:

- Contribute to the achievement of efficiency, quality, and responsiveness to customer needs.
- Increase the level of innovation and creativity:
  - Managers create an environment so that employees feel empowered to be creative.
  - Authority is decentralized so employees feel free to experiment and take risks.
- Provide a basis for evaluating the performance of corporate entrepreneurs.
- Assess how efficiently and effectively the organization is functioning.
- Monitor the quality of output so continuous improvements can be made.
- Make the organization more responsive to customers.
- Optimize organizational success by minimizing the cost of failure.

The economic success of an organization's corporate entrepreneurial activities depends on building and developing a corporate framework and top management team that can provide the required resources and control. This requires establishing corporate performance benchmarks.

The objective of the control system of corporate entrepreneurship is to achieve desirable outcomes in line with the organizational strategy. As indicated in Table 7.1, the fundamental control attributes between a bureaucratic organization and corporate entrepreneurship are different. The level of formality and

TABLE 7.1   Controlling a Bureaucracy versus Controlling a Corporate Entrepreneurship

Controlling a Bureaucracy	Controlling a Corporate Entrepreneurship
Narrowly defined rules, regulations, procedures, and policies	Broadly defined rules, regulations, procedures, and policies
Centralization	Decentralization
Autocratic	Empowerment
Inflexible, discretion not permitted	Flexible, discretion permitted
Formal	Informal
Emphasis on conformity	Encourages individuality
Compliance orientated	People orientated
Risk adverse	Risk tolerant

informality, centralization and decentralization, rigidity and flexibility, authority and empowerment, top-down communication and horizontal communication, and compliance and individuality indicate significant differences between the two.

There are also some similarities. An effective control system should be understood by everyone involved and should be linked in the organizational structure to decision centers responsible for performance. It should identify any deviations from the desired standard of performance as quickly as possible and focus on the critical activities fundamental to the success of the organization. To be effective, a corporate entrepreneurship control system needs to be flexible and adaptable to change yet consistent with the objectives established.

Control Philosophy of Corporate Entrepreneurship

The elements of a management control system need to be linked to an organization's philosophy of corporate entrepreneurship. The elements of a corporate entrepreneurship philosophy include:

- Broadly defined with effective control elements
- Ability of management to give up control through delegation and employee trust

- Empowerment and autonomy built into the job
- Understand the relationship between empowerment and control
- Promote and reward entrepreneurial behavior
- Open communication and dissemination of information
- Trust and respect at all levels
- Encourage, motivate, and reward innovation and creativity

Many centralized organizations have such advanced and formalized control systems that innovation and creativity are inhibited. Companies such as DuPont and General Electric had CEOs who understood the process of innovation and applied systems, which helped avoid this problem.

Effective control systems and evaluation processes are important for corporate entrepreneurship. Higher levels of corporate entrepreneurship are generally associated with more informal control systems that focus on results rather than processes. Sometimes those organizational controls are simple in the beginning but can become more sophisticated and complex to the point of encouraging bureaucracy. This type of control system can too tightly monitor behavior and resource utilization and undermine employee empowerment, creativity, and motivation to experiment and take risks. It is not about more or less control, but the type and level of control.

The level of control depends on the degree of corporate entrepreneurship desired by the organization (see Table 7.2). Innovative firms such as Amazon, Dell, General Electric, IBM, Lucent, 3M, and Nokia would not have achieved their level of success if they had not combined the right strategies with effective control systems to facilitate their corporate entrepreneurial activities.

Generally, incremental innovations can be achieved in a more tightly controlled environment, while discontinuous innovations require higher levels of autonomy and empowerment. The degree of control is usually higher with projects that are initiated within a specific functional area or department, such as research and

TABLE 7.2   Level of Control versus Level of Autonomy in Various Types of Innovative Initiatives

Types of Innovative Initiatives	Level of Control	Level of Autonomy
Projects tightly monitored by senior management	High	Low
Centralized projects in specified departments	High	Low to moderate
Department or functional initiatives	Moderate to high	Low to moderate
Independent venture team projects	Moderate	Moderate to high
Independent venture division projects	Low to moderate	Moderate to high
Venture projects	Low	High

development or marketing. Projects in new venture divisions and venturing projects generally have a higher degree of autonomy. Organizational control needs to reflect initiatives within each of the functional areas or divisions, as well as the innovation and creative competencies among individuals at each level. Nokia demonstrates the importance of a flexible and adaptable organizational structure and control system to keep ideas flowing through the company. Every Nokia unit is expected to search for new ideas, and most of those ideas are actually developed within the business group. Likewise, through appropriate systems, Xerox Technology Ventures establishes young firms by capitalizing on ideas that could have easily been dismissed.

Control Systems for Innovation and Creativity

Companies need processes for identifying real opportunities and control systems that allow for addressing and monitoring these opportunities. IBM's struggle with the impact of PC operating systems, AT&T's lack of clarity about its role in the Internet, and Barnes & Noble's challenge to overcome Amazon's increasing sales highlight the problems companies face when identifying the boundaries of their strategies. While these companies engaged in market research studies, they did not actually follow the results until after new ventures entered the market. Unfortunately, sometimes boundaries can keep good ideas out and in effect isolate the organization.

IKEA redefined the company's boundary to incorporate an assembly service of its flat-pack furniture in order to penetrate the Japanese market. While there may be a number of dimensions or underlying characteristics affecting the rigidity of the boundary, some occur more often. Morris et al.[1] present three dimensions that have been linked to strategic and operational aspects of the organization:

- **Administrative formality/informality.** The degree to which the organization relies on clearly defined and/or documented mechanisms (e.g., rules, regulations, procedures, policies) in influencing resource allocation and employee behavior.
- **Managerial flexibility/inflexibility.** The degree to which discretion and/or freedom is given to frontline managers to interpret or ignore rules and procedures in undertaking their assignments.
- **Budgetary tightness/looseness.** The degree to which budgets implement restrictions on how resources are allocated and how performance is evaluated.

The degree of informality in an organization depends in part on the organizational strategy and the level at which individual initiative is encouraged within the context of the overall strategic direction. Similarly, the degree of managerial discretion reflects organizational boundaries and the level of the employee in the organization. Budgetary (resource) control requires discipline, accountability with a degree of flexibility, as well as an awareness and openness to new entrepreneurial opportunities. Corporate entrepreneurial behavior is greater when there is a strong focus on efficiency, freeing up available resources for activities beyond day-to-day activities. The organization can clearly define financial accountability in a broader context that permits certain levels of discretion to promote opportunities for innovation and creativity.

Other important dimensions include: (1) the degree to which controls are centralized, or prescriptive; (2) the priority given to self-control; (3) the relative emphasis on conformance and compliance; and (4) the levels of detail and complexity. Morris et al.[2] suggest that certain characteristics of control can facilitate corporate entrepreneurial behavior. For this innovative behavior to occur, the organization needs to be controlled through transparent processes.

Bureaucracies with their excessive control over individuals can inhibit corporate entrepreneurship; being too informal, flexible, and with little accountability can decrease the opportunities for it as well. A balance between these is needed in an effective control system. There is some relationship between a decentralized structure and corporate entrepreneurship. These include increased autonomy, flexibility, and control over resources. 3M's approach to innovation is widely recognized; the company's culture includes the 15 percent "bootlegging rule," which allows employees to spend up to 15 percent of their week working on a product-related topic of their choice. Google emulated 3M's "bootlegging rule," allowing employees to spend up to 20 percent of their time on projects of interest that are not related to their specific job function. Firms such as Lucent, AT&T, and Hewlett-Packard have created separate entrepreneurial organizations in order to streamline the management of new product concepts.

Organizational Control Focus

Organizational control systems are focused on both human resources and financial resources. All organizations have limited resources, and each area is competing for those resources. In this area, the following are focuses of control:

- **Feed forward control.** Control that focuses on human, material, and financial resources flowing into the organization.
- **Concurrent control.** Control that consists of monitoring ongoing employee activities to ensure their consistency in achieving goals and objectives with established standards of performance.
- **Feedback control.** Control that is directed at the organization's outputs focusing on the quality of the end product or service after the organization's task is completed.

Core Management Control System

Most organizations have core management control systems consisting of the strategic plans, financial forecasts, operating budgets, management by objectives, operation management systems, and management information system (MIS) reports that together provide an integrated system for directing and monitoring organizational activities.

The strategic plan is based on an in-depth analysis of the organization's industry position, internal strengths and weaknesses, and external opportunities and threats. The financial forecast is usually a one- to three-year projection of the organization's sales, revenues, and products. The operating budget is an annual projection of estimated expenses, revenues, assets, and related financial figures for each operating department for the next financial year. Management by objectives typically includes standard forms and rating scales that evaluate employee competencies and performance. Operation management systems are inventory, purchasing, and distribution systems. Management information system reports are composed of data on personnel complements, volume of orders received, percentage of sales returns, and other statistical data relevant to the performance of a department or division.

Methods of Control

There are many methods of control, which can be classified into financial controls and nonfinancial controls as indicated in Table 7.3.

Financial Controls

There are three frequently used financial controls: budgetary control, break-even analysis, and ratio analysis.

Budgetary Control

Budgetary control is the process of having results and comparing these with the corresponding budget. It is one of the most commonly used methods of managerial control as it links all three types of organizational control focus—feed forward, concurrent, and feedback control—depending on the point of application. For budgets to be effective, they must be supported by top management with effective communication and employee participation and be based on realistic, reliable numbers. Corporate entrepreneurial organizations adapt a more flexible approach with budget mechanisms to facilitate innovation and creativity by focusing more on the results rather than the process.

TABLE 7.3   Methods of Control

Financial Controls	Nonfinancial Controls
Budgetary control	Project controls
Break-even analysis	Management audits
Ratio analysis	Inventory controls
	Production control
	Quality control

There are four main types of budgets:

- **Revenue and expense budget.** Sales budget.
- **Time, space, material, and production budget.** Projects machine hours, space allocated, materials required, and production output.
- **Capital expenditure budget.** Expenditure on plant and machinery.
- **Cash budget.** Projects cash receipts and disbursements.

Break-Even Analysis

Break-even analysis uses fixed and variable costs to determine the amount needed to become profitable. Regardless of output, fixed costs remain constant and variable costs change over time. Break-even analysis is useful for decisions regarding eliminating or introducing certain products or projects. This is particularly important for a corporate entrepreneurship to ensure efficiency and effectiveness in utilizing resources. Organizations break even when total costs equal total revenue earned:

$$P(x) = FC + VC(x)$$

Where: P = selling price of the new product
  x = break-even point
  FC = fixed costs
  VC = variable costs

This break-even equation allows various prices to be used to determine various break-even points. These prices should be chosen based on experience and judgment, as well as the prices of competing products.

For example, let us suppose that a firm developed a new non-fogging photochromic ski goggle. The fixed costs are $1,000,000, and the variable costs are $18.00 per unit. What is the break-even point at prices of $18.50, $20.50, and $32.50?

At a price of $18.50 per unit, the break-even point is:

$$18.50(x) = 1,000,000 + 18.00(x)$$

Where: x = 2,000,000 units

At a price of $20.50 per unit, the break-even point is:

$$20.50(x) = 1,000,000 + 18.00(x)$$

Where: x = 400,000

At a price of $22.50 per unit, the break-even point is:

$$22.50(x) = 1,000,000 + 18.00(x)$$

Where: x = 222,223

From this analysis, the firm can estimate demand for the new product idea at the prices being considered and whether or not to proceed and at what price.

Ratio Analysis

An effective approach for checking on the overall health and performance of a corporate entrepreneurship is using financial ratios. *Ratio analysis* examines the relationships between various financial statement items. Key ratios are calculated from selected items on both the income statement and the balance sheet. By examining the financial ratios, management can identify where and how money is being made and determine where best to focus their corporate entrepreneurship efforts.

There are four categories of financial ratios that are frequently used: liquidity, activity, profitability, and leverage. Each of these categories is discussed in Chapter 11, "Funding the Venture."

Nonfinancial Controls

There are five frequently used nonfinancial controls: project controls, management audits, inventory controls, production control, and quality control (see Table 7.3).

Project Controls

Project controls are designed to control the operation of certain projects undertaken by the organization. The two most popular project controls are Gantt charts and Program (or Project) Evaluation Review Technique (PERT) analysis. A Gantt chart (named for Henry Gantt) is a bar chart that illustrates the time relationship between events and their outcome. The chart highlights the activities required to complete a task and allocates a time frame for each. The Gantt chart can be used to identify if a project is ahead, behind, or on schedule. Gantt charts are most useful for activities that are unrelated such as engineering, manufacturing, research, and design. PERT illustrates the most likely time necessary to complete each task required to finish the project and identifies where delays are most likely. The following are the steps needed to develop a PERT chart:

- Identify all events that must be completed and assign a challenging but realistic time frame.
- In chronological order, keep a record of all the tasks that need to be completed and those responsible for the completion.
- Estimate the time needed to complete each task.
- Estimate the total time for each activity in a sequence or path of activities.

Management Audits

Management audits have been developed to evaluate and control conflicts of interest within an organization. Audits can be internal or external. Internal audits investigate the operations of the organization through planning reviews. Internal audits often identify problems such as poor resource utilization, resource duplication, and uneconomical use of plant and machinery.

Through external audits, objective, third-party managers conduct investigations of an organization. External audits assess the strengths and weaknesses of corporate entrepreneurship.

Inventory Control

Inventory control involves the control of stock levels to ensure that the organization has stock when needed while preventing obsolete inventory.

Production Control

In the production area, planning and control systems are intertwined because the outputs of planning are the inputs of the control system. The objective of *production control* is to ensure that goods are produced on time, at the right cost, and conform to quality standards.

Quality Control

Quality and production control are intertwined since *quality control* is a measure of the efficiency of production. A good quality system can offer significant cost savings.

The emphasis on quality has led many organizations to adopt a Total Quality Management (TQM) approach, which is underpinned by the following key principles:

- Quality goods and services will be produced when the meaning of quality is expressed daily and is part of the organizational culture.
- While employees work in the system, managers need to work on the system, to identify ways to continuously find best practices.
- TQM is a strategic choice made by top management and is consistently translated into guidelines for the functioning of the whole organization.

- Monitoring and evaluation of the process is important. This is best achieved by giving the required level of autonomy to workers closest to the process.
- Identify core goals and objectives for the organization and develop a road map on how best to achieve this strategy.

Ingredients to Financial and Nonfinancial Controls in Corporate Entrepreneurship

One key to financial and nonfinancial controls in a corporate entrepreneurship is to motivate and facilitate employees to be innovative and creative. One way to achieve this is to effectively communicate organizational goals and objectives by:

- Open communication where all employees have access to the financial and nonfinancial information
- Training and development provided at all levels to ensure that employees have the required competencies
- Making sure employees know how their work fits into the overall organizational strategy
- Making sure employees are empowered to make decisions in their work based on their core competencies
- Making employees have a stake in the organization's success and share in the risk of failure

Methods of management control are moving more to nonfinancial information analysis since value creation comes from all parts of the business; if an organization wants to create value, it needs to measure the nonfinancial aspects of the business. Most organizations have traditionally focused on the financial related metrics. These financial metrics are outcomes and not "drivers" of performance. Organizations need to evaluate the real drivers behind financial performance such as process efficiency, human resource development, leadership effectiveness, customer retention and growth, and product and service innovation.

DuPont is recognized as an inventor of modern management control. As a result of decentralization and its level of specialization, DuPont saw the need for a performance measurement system. It launched a new accounting measure, Return on Investment (ROI), because it believed it would be more accurate to use than the old measures. DuPont and General Motors are considered pioneers in this area and also created different types of decentralized organizations, budgeting, and planning cycles. IKEA uses both financial and nonfinancial controls. Its financial measures are mostly based on sales and productivity, and nonfinancial measures are based on market, customer, and employee surveys.

Early in 3M's history, CEO William L. McKnight introduced a number of formal and informal controls to enable the company to innovate consistently. Management has continued to expand and embrace these controls, believing innovation is the cornerstone of 3M's future. To make the changes in staff behavior permanent and self-improving, a system of continuous reinforcement needs to be installed, with clear thresholds established. Retailers such as Walmart and Whole Foods Market in the United States or Globus in Germany combine creatively standardized processes with individual initiative to build enthusiasm and raise the level of service.

Nokia and Apple use diverse approaches to manage the increasing development expenses and increase their profitability. Nokia outsources a major part of its chipset business, reducing the financial risk in designing its own chips. Nokia has continued its strategy of focusing on its core competence (developing chipset technologies and improving agility) and outsourcing in other areas. It has approximately 40 percent of the worldwide market, selling over 70 million phones annually. Apple acquired a small boutique microprocessor design house with extensive experience in cell phone technology at a cost of $278 million. The acquisition allowed Apple to innovate, continuously improving the customer experience. Apple's focus on design and software continues, while Apple's decision to retain design control, which was initially costly, has significantly contributed toward Apple's success.

Summary

This chapter looked at control systems and their implications for corporate entrepreneurship. A control system is a combination of rules, regulations, policies, and procedures implemented to achieve desirable employee behavior and organizational performance. Control systems that are either too rigid or too flexible can create a significant barrier to corporate entrepreneurship. Corporate entrepreneurship is facilitated by a more flexible control system with open communication and mutual trust that empowers, encourages, and motivates employees to be innovative and creative and rewards them for those behaviors.

Financial and nonfinancial methods of control need to be implemented throughout the organization. The key is to develop a control system that provides for an adequate level of control without inhibiting corporate entrepreneurial activities.

8

The Internal Politics of Venturing

What are the positive and negative consequences of internal political behavior? What are the political obstacles that can potentially inhibit new corporate entrepreneurship? How can these obstacles be overcome? What political tactics can corporate entrepreneurs use to be more successful?

Scenario: Bord na Móna

Bord na Móna is Ireland's leading environmentally responsible integrated utility service provider in electricity, heating, resource recovery, water, growing media, and related services. Bord na Móna was established in 1934 and began as a final manifestation of an idea—the development of the vast peatlands of Ireland. It is a small company developing a variety of businesses based on the engineering and scientific skills it has built since 1934. The company has strong skills in resource management and development, manufacturing, distribution, science, engineering, and human resource development. It owns 80,000 hectares of peatland, employs approximately 2,000 people, and operates in 20 locations throughout Ireland, the United Kingdom, and the eastern United

States. It had a turnover of 384.4 million in 2009–2010. Bord na Móna focuses on six main business areas:

- **Energy.** Providing secure, dependable, and sustainable energy and power with renewability at its core. Its core business is the supply of peat as a fuel for the generation of electricity.
- **Environmental.** Providing solutions in the areas of wastewater treatment and air pollution abatement systems to the Irish and overseas markets.
- **Fuels.** Supplying solid fuel products within the residential heating market in Ireland.
- **Horticulture.** Manufacturing and supplying growing media products domestically and internationally for the professional and hobby gardener.
- **Resource recovery.** Collecting and environmentally treating of waste.
- **Land and property.** Managing the company's land and property assets.

Bord na Móna expects each of the five business areas to demonstrate sustained profitability through enterprise and creativity, exercise responsibility to customers, show continuous improvement through the development and involvement of its people, operate with care for the environment and society, and carry on its business with integrity and fairness.

The company was originally established in 1934 as the Turf Development Board. Bord na Móna was subsequently established as a statutory body by the Turf Development Act of 1946. The first activities were based on harvesting sod peat, which was used in power stations and as a household fuel. The Turf Development Act of 1950 gave the company further opportunity for development. From the late 1950s, the company decided to move from the highly labor intensive production of sod peat to the highly capital intensive production of milled peat. A U.K. subsidiary selling horticultural peat products was established in 1957. Two other factories were built in Derrinlough and Croghan in 1960. In 1974, Bord na Móna began its Third Development Program, which involved the acquisition and development of a further 35,000 hectares of bog, and the construction of a further briquette factory in County Tipperary.

A program of change, downsizing, and divisionalization commenced in 1988, to reduce costs and make the company more market focused. Productivity was improved by over 100 percent in the core peat production business. New forms of autonomous working by self-directed teams and employees were paid by results. The different businesses became divisions: Peat Energy, Fuels, and Horticulture. In 1990, the Environmental Products Division was established. In 1992, Bord na Móna was a partner in Ireland's first commercial wind farm, and in 1997, the government agreed to remove the historical noncommercial debt carried by Bord na Móna with an injection of £90 million. Between 1996 and 1998, the government invested £108 million equity in Bord na Móna to be used exclusively for the retirement of this debt.

In 1999, Bord na Móna became a public limited company (PLC), and the divisions became limited liability companies. Bord na Móna PLC's shareholder is the Minister for Finance, and its board is appointed by the Minister for Communications, Marine, and Natural Resources. The company accounts show a turnover for the year 2005–2006 of €295.7 million and a strong operating profit of €29.9 million. The company that emerges in 2011 will be significantly different from the one that was initially established in 1934.

Bord na Móna has a vision, "A New Contract with Nature," signifying the beginning of a transition from traditional businesses heavily dependent on peat and fossil fuels to a new, more sustainable business focused on renewable energy, resource recovery, and environmental products and services supported by the traditional businesses of fuels and horticulture. The company considers its commitment to innovation as a competitive advantage and has re-aligned its organizational structure to be more customer-oriented. The energy business unit has been divided into Power Generation and Feedstock Supply. The environmental business unit is now geographically market-focused—North America and Western Europe. In the environmental business units, the increasing requirement for green, sustainable technologies for the treatment of wastewater and air has driven the innovation agenda. Other innovative projects include development of a next generation small-scale wastewater treatment unit and low carbon footprint and novel wastewater treatment systems for small- and medium-sized communities. Other development initiatives include potential technology partnerships with patent holders to develop and commercialize tertiary water treatment technologies.

Bord na Móna continues to invest in research and development to improve its products, processes, packaging, and distribution systems. In 2009–2010, Bord na Móna spent 5.2 million on research and development including business development, exclusive of grants. Besides its facility in Ireland, it also has a dedicated innovation center in North Carolina.

Like many companies nationally and internationally, Bord na Móna has been challenged by the global financial crisis, but it has responded, for example, with reduced prices to customers, combined with tactical changes to reduce excess capacity and cost reduction. Those initiatives, along with its continued innovation and investment in research and development, led the company to perform well in 2009–2010.

www.bnm.ie
www.bnm.annualreport09-10.com
www.bnm.ie/corporate/index.jsp?pID=93&nID=95
www.dcenr.gov.ie/Energy/Peat+Division/Bord+na+M%C3%
   B3na+plc.htm

Introduction

Political behavior is the application of influence in business, and depending upon how that influence is used, it either generates functional or dysfunctional consequences for individuals and organizations. Political behavior may be precipitated by a combination of individual and contextual factors and is not necessarily viewed as self-serving.[1] Management from a political perspective characterizes the workplace as a miniature society with politics pervading all managerial work and individual managers being viewed as "knowledgeable human agents." Influence reinforces the theoretical and practical importance of building alliances and networks of cooperative relationships. Internal politics is inevitable in all organizations large and small and either encourages or inhibits corporate entrepreneurial activity.

Many venture managers who have developed corporate entrepreneurship activities can experience difficulty implementing them due to a lack of understanding the political requirements in their organizations. Given the usual small size and nature of the corporate entrepreneurial activity in comparison to the existing organization, the activity needs to be politically correct to be supported and accepted by the existing organization. Successful corporate entrepreneurs are those who can work out and cope with the unwritten laws and politics within the organization. They can influence and motivate key people, especially the CEO, senior management team, and stakeholders.

The greatest problems that corporate entrepreneurs face at the initial start-up stage are issues with legitimacy, human and nonhuman resource shortages, and resistance to the corporate entrepreneurship activity. Corporate entrepreneurs need to develop political tactics that will influence, persuade, and motivate the right people to embrace the potential opportunity while at the same time gain legitimacy, have available necessary human and nonhuman resources, and overcome any resistance from the parent organization.

This chapter is designed to provide an understanding of the political obstacles and the appropriate political tactics to help overcome these obstacles when developing and engaging in corporate entrepreneurship. First, there is a discussion of the internal politics and obstacles that inhibit corporate entrepreneurial activities. Second, an analysis of the ways of overcoming the obstacles is presented. This is followed by a presentation of the political strategy and tactics that can be used to overcome resistance and build support. Following a discussion of the impact of influence and politics on corporate entrepreneurial activities, the chapter concludes with guidelines on the political tactics needed to increase the necessary influence for corporate entrepreneurship to progress.

Internal Politics

Politics is inevitable in the work environment. Organizations consist of individuals and groups that bring their own interests, desires, wants, expectations, and needs to the workplace, which results in a diversity of interests in which politics occur. Relationships, norms, processes, performance, and outcomes are significantly affected and influenced by organizational politics because they are all integrated into the organizational culture and management system.

Political behavior is a natural and expected characteristic of organizations. The organization has the right to make certain decisions regarding the behavior of individuals in accomplishing organizational goals and objectives. Submitting to the authority of the organization is contingent upon the organization satisfying certain individual goals and objectives. Compensation, terms and conditions of employment, career advancement, and progression are management systems that align organizational and employee interests. Individuals continue to act politically within the organization's political boundary and strive to improve their own benefits and satisfaction. The political capability of an organization is dependent upon its political resources in terms of influence bases. To ensure future political capability, the organization can attempt to expand or consolidate these bases. Table 8.1 summarizes the positive and negative consequences of individual and organizational uses of political behavior.

Internal politics refers to the way influence is distributed throughout the organization. Any level of change has the potential of modifying the balance of power among various formal and informal groups. The uncertainty brought about by change creates ambiguity, which increases the probability of political activity as individuals attempt to create structure by attempting to control their environment. In most companies, political influence is highly concentrated at the top of the organization. The support or opposition of politically influential executives with vested interests in a particular outcome weighs heavily in the actions taken by the parent company in relation to the corporate entrepreneurship activity.

To address this, important questions for corporate entrepreneurs include: Who can underestimate the value of your idea? Who in the organization has the influence to inhibit an idea from being developed? Who has the final word on whether to embrace a new corporate entrepreneurial opportunity? To implement and develop corporate entrepreneurship, an innovative corporate entrepreneur must attempt to motivate and influence the key stakeholders. Failure to identify core stakeholders and effectively bring them on board can severely block the corporate entrepreneurship process and could potentially eliminate it altogether.

One popular method for attracting and aligning key stakeholders from top management for the corporate entrepreneurship is through "stinging." This method is often used by corporate entrepreneurs who need the support of top management to proceed. "Stinging" involves carefully approaching top management individuals with a corporate entrepreneurial activity to determine their level of potential support. In this way, the corporate entrepreneur acts as the bee treating top management as the hive and

TABLE 8.1 Positive and Negative Consequences of Individual and Organizational Uses of Political Behavior

Positive	Negative
Individual	**Individual**
• Inspire confidence, trust, and sincere behavioral attributes	• Frustration, demotivation, dissatisfaction
• Increased assertiveness	• Low morale and loss of confidence
• Reduced anxiety and stress	• Increased anxiety and stress
• Improved position and influence	• Loss of position and influence
• Career advancement and progression	• Damaged reputation
Organizational	**Organizational**
• Support for desirable policies and procedures	• Negative manipulation and game-playing
• Contribute to organizational effectiveness	• Restrain organizational effectiveness
• Implement legitimate decisions	• Unethical decision making and use of resources
• Improve decision-making strategy	• Inhibit communication by increasing barriers
• Develop approaches for effective conflict resolution	• Inhibit goal attainment, which will lead to conflict
• Create an environment that is adaptable to change	• Reduce flexibility and adaptability
• Manage resistance to change	• Block organizational change

"stinging" those members most likely to support the new idea before rolling it out to all top management members. Finding these internal, upper-level champions is crucial for promoting the new idea in its initial stages. Starting in the 1980s, Goldman Sachs approached corporate entrepreneurship using a "stinging" method with high-level champions. This is the way Goldman Sachs successfully introduced and implemented its entrance into junk bonds and investment banking on a global scale.

Many political problems can significantly deter the corporate entrepreneurship process. Obstacles that have political ramifications that can inhibit the corporate entrepreneurship process include:

• Lack of adequate time and support to engage in corporate entrepreneurship

- No compensation and reward system in place to motivate and incentivize innovative individuals
- Failure by corporate entrepreneurs to demonstrate the potential return on investment resulting in the lack of adequate investment from the parent company
- Inappropriate structure in place that focuses on an autocratic style of management
- A high level of skepticism occurring particularly if the idea is diverse and challenging
- Resistance from the parent company for the new corporate entrepreneurial concept or idea, which can result in limited interest or concern, feeling threatened by innovative individuals, lacking resources, direct or indirect competition, and resistance among individuals
- Environment of fear, which constrains innovation and creativity throughout the organization and significantly inhibits any entrepreneurial behavior by fear of failure and punishment

Overcoming the Obstacles

Each of these obstacles and negative implications results from management practices and internal organizational factors. In order to manage and overcome these, the corporate entrepreneur needs to influence, persuade, and motivate the necessary individuals on the potential benefits of the corporate entrepreneurial activity. Any level of change involves modification of the political system. To gain support and influence behavior, the corporate entrepreneur needs to gain legitimacy, have access to the required human and nonhuman resources, and be able to influence individuals at all levels of the organization.

Gaining Legitimacy

The newer the market and idea, the more significant is the issue of legitimacy as there is no history or track record. From the beginning, corporate entrepreneurship needs to create a positive notion of capability, survival, and legitimacy. The basic and most influential tactic for gaining legitimacy is using personal and independent external advisors or consultants to demonstrate the viability and credibility of the new activity. This is validated when the corporate entrepreneur has a reputation for developing new initiatives that have been successful. Internal support from employees with a more objective viewpoint and proven track record can add legitimacy to the project. If the corporate entrepreneur can rapidly acquire legitimacy, then the corporate entrepreneurial activity will quickly gain acceptance throughout the organization.

Human and Nonhuman Resource Requirements

A new corporate entrepreneurial activity needs an adequate supply of both human and nonhuman resources to progress and develop. The corporate entrepreneur needs to determine if individuals with the required skills exist internally within the parent company or if there is a need to recruit key people externally (see Chapter 10). Nonhuman resources include funding, equipment, technology, access to production, and service systems. The corporate entrepreneur usually faces constraints in the amount of resources that are available. To secure adequate resources, the corporate entrepreneur needs to engage in resourceful politicking, relying on persistence and determination to secure the resources needed.

It is important that the corporate entrepreneur not assume that the only way to receive needed resources is to seriously deplete the resources from another department or project. This zero sum mindset is often the cause that turns politics and competition into destructive conflict. Remember that one of the most valuable attributes of a corporate entrepreneur is his or her ability to innovate and create wealth—a positive sum game.

Overcoming Resistance

Corporate entrepreneurial activities are often triggered by the need to respond to new challenges or opportunities occurring in the external environment, such as new products by a major competitor or technological advances. A new creative idea will not benefit the organization until it is in place. One frustration for corporate entrepreneurs is the resistance that occurs for no apparent reason. As indicated in Table 8.2, there are a number of reasons associated with resistance, including self-interest, lack of understanding and trust, risk and uncertainty, and different goals and objectives. To effectively manage the implementation process, corporate entrepreneurs need to be aware of the reasons for resistance and be prepared to use techniques for obtaining cooperation.

Techniques for Obtaining Cooperation

- Gain senior management support for the new venture activity.
- Educate all those about the benefits of the new venture by ensuring that all research has been carried out, providing accurate information.
- Communication with all those affected by the new venture.
- Participation from those individuals who are innovative and creative and can help bring the venture to fruition.
- Create opportunities for people to demonstrate their skills and competence.
- Build support networks inside and outside the organization.

Political Strategy

Political strategies are specific tactics used to increase and effectively use influence. The political tactics needed to obtain resources, achieve agreement and support, and overcome potential barriers and

TABLE 8.2 Sources of Resistance

Individual Resistance	Organizational Resistance
Self-interest (e.g., loss of influence, loss of freedom, or loss of status associated with current position)	Organizational culture
Fear of the unknown	Focus on maintaining stability
Reluctance and resentment	Failure to invest in additional resources required for the new venture
Lack of understanding and trust about new venture	Inadequate financial resources provided to the new venture
Risk and uncertainty associated with new venture activity	Threats to current power and/or influence
Different goals and objectives compared to the new venture	Too much competition for the new venture to adequately survive
Feel the new venture is disturbing the status quo	Disturbs and threatens the current systems in place

resistance differ by organization. There are a number of tactics available to the corporate entrepreneur to deal with problems.

Since the reasons for resistance are legitimate in the eyes of the individual having them, the best procedure for the corporate entrepreneur is not to ignore resistance but to diagnose the reasons for it and to design strategies to gain acceptance before officially announcing the new idea. One political strategy for overcoming the organizational resistance that inhibits the corporate entrepreneurial process has the following steps:

1. **Clarify the short-, medium-, and long-term goals and objectives of the corporate entrepreneurship activity.** By clearly stating the core objectives, the corporate entrepreneur can identify who internally and externally would be affected by the new venture. This will also identify all the individuals, groups, or organizations that would be required to contribute to its success and whether each is willing to give his or her support. It is important to build the maximum consensus for the new idea, preferably prior to any formal decision meeting.

2. **Identify the potential political obstacles that would inhibit corporate entrepreneurship development.** The corporate entrepreneur must review the various interest groups and identify the existing level of support, the internal and external opponents, and the potential actions that could be undertaken by opponents.

3. **Identify individuals and groups that are neutral to the new venture's success.** It is important to use appropriate political strategy to align these individuals and groups rather than risk their becoming opponents of the new venture. The political strategy should be designed and developed in such a way as to: maximize the support, minimize the threats from opponents, convert the neutral group to supporters, and convert the opponents to neutrality, thus reducing the damage they could potentially cause the new venture.

4. **Anticipate possible responses from individuals and groups.** Since human behavior can be unpredictable, it is of significant importance that the corporate entrepreneur be prepared for and able to manage a range of diverse responses and reactions from each individual and group. The corporate entrepreneur needs to be flexible and can adjust the political strategy according to the anticipated response from specific individuals and groups.

5. **Formulate a political strategy.** The analysis and evaluation of critical execution issues help ensure that when the political strategy is applied, it will work. The corporate entrepreneur needs to keep the process as straightforward as possible by focusing on key alliances and opponents. Once agreement is reached with the required individuals and groups, then the strategy needs to be implemented with clear emphasis on the activities that will bring the corporate entrepreneurial activity to the next stage of development.

6. **Monitor and evaluate the progress of the political strategy.** The corporate entrepreneur needs to monitor and evaluate

the political strategy to identify any deviations and take appropriate corrective action.

It is important to keep political matters in perspective. There is room for different views and opinions and using consensus building to come to a decision.

Political Tactics

Corporate entrepreneurs find themselves in a variety of situations where political skills are critical. They normally have limited formal influence, so they need to use their influence to obtain the support needed. To develop and build legitimacy and influence, the corporate entrepreneur can undertake the following:

- **Accurate, precise, and timely communication and information sharing.** Building trust and credibility as well as a support network inside and outside the organization.
- **Generate opportunities for people at all levels to demonstrate their creativity, innovation, skills, knowledge, and abilities.** Allowing the organization to utilize their human resources while creating a positive work environment that allows people to develop and grow within the organization.
- **Teamwork.** The corporate entrepreneur needs to build a team that is able to demonstrate substantial experience and skills.
- **Develop problem-solving strategies that are focused on the organization.** Corporate entrepreneurs need to demonstrate that they have the ability to not only solve problems but also to seek and follow advice from others. This helps gain other types of support.
- **Develop influential alliances and networks.** Corporate entrepreneurs who build appropriate networks inside and outside the organization can draw on these networks to influence, persuade, and motivate any adverse reactions.

Politics

Politics and influence are a part of any organization; there will be people who want to acquire influence, legitimately or illegitimately. Organizations consist of individuals who are there to achieve a common purpose while at the same time are driven by their own need to achieve their own goals. A political approach to management is particularly needed by a corporate entrepreneur in an organization where the clarity of goals is not absolute, where the decision-making process is not clearly defined, and where the authority to make decisions is not evenly or appropriately allocated to the necessary sources. From a corporate entrepreneur's perspective, politics can be used as a process to influence senior management, individuals, and groups within the organization.

Internal politics and the desire for control can significantly inhibit innovation and set the organization on the road to failure. This happens when the organizational structure and culture are valued over corporate entrepreneurship. Internal politics can make it very difficult for the culture of corporate entrepreneurship to flourish.

Microsoft cannot foster innovation if it threatens the corporation's political power and control. Frequently larger software companies are seen in the continuous innovation camp but rarely as creators of discontinuous innovation. In more rigid, less adaptive cultures where senior management is more skeptical about the benefits of corporate entrepreneurship and resistance is the norm, there is a preference to wait until there is more clarity and less risk before engaging in corporate entrepreneurial activities. Resistant cultures place a premium on avoiding mistakes and leaning toward safe options.

A company that does not value managers and employees who are creative inhibits corporate entrepreneurship development. The big risk of this type of culture is that the organization can underestimate competitors and overestimate its own progression. This can create a corporate culture of hubris with a feeling that the organization is "too big to fail." Unhealthy cultures can significantly inhibit organizational performance. Bank of America, Ford, General Motors, Sears, and Xerox are examples of companies that had unhealthy cultures during the late 1970s and early 1980s, which contributed to their poor performance.

When these companies encounter rapidly changing business environments, the failure to move from the traditional ways can result in significant losses. The traditional mechanistic management practices designed and developed to manage large corporations are not conducive to corporate entrepreneurship, as indicated in Table 8.3. In most cases, organizational strategies, systems, structures, rules, regulations, policies, and procedures are designed and developed to achieve organizational goals and objectives rather than engage in corporate entrepreneurial activities. Managers and individuals who are not motivated in their current positions are likely to focus on inputs and controls rather than provide ways to be innovative and engage in new corporate entrepreneurial activities that meet the needs of the organization and customers.

General Motors, IBM, and Sears are examples of companies whose traditional bureaucracies did not adequately respond to the fundamental changes in their markets. Their cultures and behaviors were not suited to achieve market success, and, as a result, these companies struggled during this time. Adaptive cultures, on the other hand, do what is necessary to ensure long-term organizational success. This type of culture supports managers and employees at all levels who propose or initiate new corporate entrepreneurial activities. Technology and software companies are good examples of organizations with adaptive cultures. Companies like Amazon.com, Google, Dell Computer, Intel, Nokia, and 3M rapidly adapt and adjust to the needs of the environment. They are practitioners of corporate entrepreneurship and innovation and have the willingness to take the necessary risks to create new products, new businesses, and new industries. To

TABLE 8.3 Traditional Management Practices That Inhibit Corporate Entrepreneurial Activities

Traditional Management Practices	Negative Implications
Rigidly defined rules, regulations, and procedures	Innovation and creativity inhibited
Mechanistic organizational structure in place	Corporate entrepreneurial activities are limited and diverse
Control system with limited delegation of autonomy and authority	Opportunities to be corporate entrepreneurs are limited and diverse
Avoid any risk and uncertainty to the existing organization	Fear of change and any threat to the existing organization causes potential opportunities to be not recognized or considered
Future decisions based on past performance	Failure to recognize market changes leading to inaccurate decisions
Limited compensation and reward system	Limited motivation and incentives to be innovative
Standard promotion system in place based on years of service and compatibility to organizational ethos	Lack of opportunity for motivated corporate entrepreneurs to add value

create a corporate entrepreneurship culture, these companies staff their organizations with people who are entrepreneurially minded and innovative, have an aptitude for new activities, and embrace emerging opportunities.

In particular, Intel took a corporate entrepreneurship risk with its recent entrance into the Japanese market, where it came up against entrenched government supported competitors. Intel was not a household name in Japan, where branding is a key ingredient for attracting Japanese consumers. Intel internally came up with a new branding strategy of aligning itself with the Walt Disney theme park and cartoon characters in Japan. After conducting market research, Intel discovered that most electronic purchases in Japan were made by women and that Japanese women loved Disney characters. This innovative corporate entrepreneurial venture vaulted Intel to top-of-mind awareness and into the top five electronic firms in Japan within two years.

Political Tactics for Corporate Entrepreneurs to Increase Their Influence

Corporate entrepreneurs use political tactics to increase their influence by increasing the validity and credibility of a new corporate entrepreneurial activity. This can be accomplished by managing and controlling risk and uncertainty, becoming invaluable to the organization, leading and motivating individuals, generating appropriate resources, and building and developing networks and alliances (see Figure 8.1).

- **Manage and control risk and uncertainty.** Corporate entrepreneurs who can manage risk and reduce uncertainty for the organization increase influence and become leaders.
- **Become invaluable to the organization.** Develop valuable core competencies (knowledge, skill, and abilities).
- **Leadership and motivation.** Corporate entrepreneurs can lead and control the organization's activities if they have the right mindset to motivate individuals and gain support.

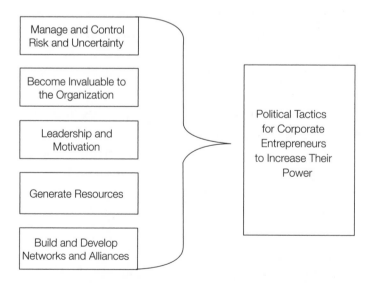

FIGURE 8.1   Political Tactics for Increasing Power in an Organization

- **Generate resources.** Corporate entrepreneurs need to recruit, select, and retain skilled people or attract appropriate financing and investment.
- **Build and develop networks and alliances.** Develop mutually beneficial relationships inside and outside the organization.

Political Tactics for Corporate Entrepreneurs to Exercise Influence

It is important for corporate entrepreneurs to think in terms of short- and long-term goals and objectives for the new venture project. As indicated in Figure 8.2, politically skilled corporate entrepreneurs have an ability to utilize the five political tactics for increasing influence as well as an appreciation for the political tactics to exercise influence.

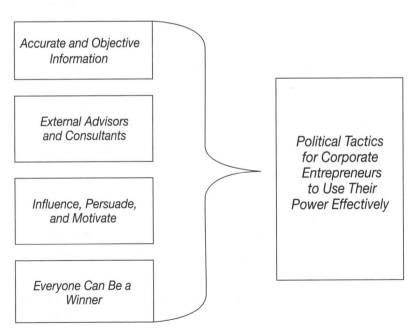

FIGURE 8.2   Political Tactics for Corporate Ventures to Exercise Power

- **Accurate and objective information.** All information needs to be accurate and objective in order to gain trust and integrity within the organization.
- **External advisors and consultants.** Bring in an expert or group of experts who can objectively support the corporate entrepreneurial proposal, as this increases its credibility.
- **Influence, persuade, and motivate.** Use political tactics to influence, persuade, and motivate the behavior of all those involved in the decision-making process.
- **Everyone can be a winner.** Emphasize the benefits of the new corporate entrepreneurial opportunity to everyone whose support is needed as well by highlighting the personal benefits from providing that support.

It is in the political interest of the corporate entrepreneur to identify any source of risk and uncertainty in the parent organization and take the necessary steps to control these sources of uncertainty. The corporate entrepreneur needs to build her own alliances and networks inside and outside the organization to support the progress and development of her new venture idea.

Summary

Corporate entrepreneurs can become so focused and committed to the corporate entrepreneurial activity that they neglect its context. Politics exist in every organization to some extent and need to be managed as effectively as possible. In managing internal politics, the corporate entrepreneur needs to inform and use key supporters, alliances, and networks inside and outside the parent organization. Any individuals and/or groups in opposition need to be managed.

Recognizing the importance of internal politics and the development of political tactics is an important aspect of corporate entrepreneurship. Influence of managers can inhibit even the most opportunistic corporate entrepreneurship—or alternatively it can ensure its progression and success. Corporate entrepreneurial failures are frequently due to the difficulty in gaining legitimacy, inadequate human and nonhuman resource requirements, and inability to overcome resistance. The corporate entrepreneur needs to devote appropriate time and effort to managing and overcoming the obstacles created from the internal politics.

Corporate entrepreneurs need to determine the core issues and problems, identify their key supporters, and recognize and manage problematic individuals. They should cautiously move forward while developing political tactics that will manage and solve the problems through supporters and networks inside and outside the organization.

Part Three

Operationalizing Corporate Entrepreneurship

9

Developing the Business Plan

How does Apple Inc. capture and encourage innovation? How does this affect its bottom line and overall corporate and cultural strategies? What are the steps in creating a business plan that will develop and sustain corporate venturing? How do existing corporations use a business plan to avoid failure and optimize success?

Scenario: Apple Inc.

In the late 2000s, Apple was considered one of the most innovative companies in the world. Its innovative success came following a near collapse after Apple produced no profits in the 1990s. How did such an innovative company create an astounding turnaround?

The Apple Computer Company was founded in April 1976 by Steve Wozniak, Steve Jobs, and Ron Wayne with $1,300 as a startup in the garage of the Jobs family in Palo Alto, California. The initial 50 orders for the Apple I occurred the next month. By August, investors were lined up; Mike Markkula, an angel investor and later the second CEO of Apple, invested $92,000 in the company. The company progressively grew in the number of employees, the quantity of computers sold, and the cost at which it was selling them. In May 1980, the Apple II was released and sold for up to $7,800. On December 12 of that year, Apple Computer went public; the company's share price rose by 32 percent that day, making the 40 current employees millionaires.

Apple reached $1 billion in sales during 1982 and became the highest earning firm in personal computers. In May 1983, Apple's success continued as it became a member of the Fortune 500, and in December, Apple released the Apple III+, which sold for $2,995. In 1985, the same year Steve Jobs was removed from his position, the company sold 500,000 Macintoshes.

By the early 1990s, Apple's products faced significant competition from Microsoft, IBM, Motorola, and NeXT (Steve Jobs's new company). In 1993, Apple began losing money and did not see profitability again until 1998.

In 1996, the year of Apple's twentieth anniversary, the company bought Steve Jobs's NeXT for $340 million, and by early 1997, Jobs was back at Apple. Later that year, the Mac Operating System 8 was released, and 1.25 million copies were sold in less than two weeks. This made OS8 the bestselling software of the time.

Apple was once again profitable in 1998 with $47 million in profits in the first quarter alone. The iMac and PowerBook G3 models were introduced and seen by many as the most innovative machines in the world. In addition, Jobs refocused Apple's business plan by targeting personal and business consumers who desired portable or desktop computers. Second quarter profits in 1998 were $101 million.

Also in 1998, Apple started creating products not totally associated with computers: iMovie and Final Cut Pro were released, serving the digital video editing market. A few months later, music productivity applications were released, namely Emagic and GarageBand.

The company really took off in 2001 when the first Apple Retail Store opened in Virginia and later that year when Apple introduced the iPod. In 2003, the iTunes Store was created, allowing users to download songs to their iPods for approximately 99 cents per song. By mid-2008, customers had downloaded over 5 billion songs.

In 2007, Apple officially changed its name from Apple Computers to Apple Inc. and began producing the iPhone as well as Apple TV. Once App Stores were opened in July 2008, the company was selling roughly $1 million a day and a few months later had become ranked as the third largest supplier of mobile handsets.

There is not much doubt that Steve Jobs's leadership and highly skilled engineers played a significant role in Apple's comeback, but it took more than programming talent and a good CEO to create such spectacular success. It was the company's focus on innovation and a unique company culture that encouraged such a leap in product innovation (iPhone, Apple TV, iPods), putting Apple ahead of the curve and, in some instances, ahead of its time.

Several key aspects made Apple particularly successful in its endeavor to greatness. Apple uses what it calls "Network Innovation." This process has the ability to tie together ideas from the outside with Apple's own twists and charm. The iPod, for example, was envisioned by a consultant. The product simply combined already existing external, off-the-shelf technologies and added a unique, elegant, and stylish design. By admitting that not all great ideas are born within the company, Apple was able to avoid the "not invented here" syndrome where in-house ideas and creations are valued more than those from outside the company.

Internal innovation also calls for a strategy that includes using a business plan approach. According to Steve Jobs, it requires more than just discipline, processes, and procedures to invent and create great products. It requires a laid back, horizontal culture where employees know each other and meet in the hallway or feel comfortable calling each other at 10:30 p.m. to discuss a new idea about an ongoing project. The company has created a culture where employees are not afraid to speak up and call an ad hoc meeting among six colleagues to receive feedback on a brand new idea. According to Jobs, it takes a thousand good ideas to come up with a great one.

While many companies focus on the demands of technology, Apple structured itself internally to have the ability to understand and focus on the needs of users. Rather than making yet another digital music player that required the skills of an engineer in order to use it, Apple focused on the desires and needs of the nonengineer users. When technology firms, including Apple's competitors, strove for developing the more complex, Apple distinguished itself, its innovation strategies, and its products by appealing to a mass audience through straightforward, easy-to-use products.

Contrary to the usual market beliefs, Apple ensured its incredible comeback by *not* listening to the market. Ironically, had Apple engaged in "user-centric innovation" (adapting product designs to customer feedback), it may have never produced the iPod. The iPod was so innovative with such a unique development that upon its launch in 2001, it was considered ludicrous.

Just as a culture of innovation is important to corporate venturing, so is the ability to fail wisely. Rather than stigmatizing failure, Apple has created an environment where failure is both tolerated and seen as a companywide learning and enrichment experience.

www.apple.com/about/
www.apple-history.com/?page=history&section=h1

Introduction

Every successful and innovative company follows its own path to success. The strategies used by Apple may not work for every organization attempting to be innovative; Apple followed its own rules and created its own culture. Having a culture that emphasizes and supports innovation with creative out-of-the-box thinking is essential for establishing a successful corporate venturing program. An equally important aspect is the evaluation of the idea created through the creation of a business plan, the focus of this chapter.

This chapter starts by giving an overview of the important aspects of a business plan followed by a discussion of its scope and value. Following the informational needs for the plan is a thorough description of each aspect of the plan. The chapter concludes by presenting the uses and implementation of the business plan and why they often fail.

Importance of a Business Plan

In any organization, there are a variety of plans—financial plans, marketing plans, production and operation plans, sales plans, and staffing plans. A plan can be strategic or operational and focus on the short or long term. Regardless of its scope, each plan has the purpose to provide guidance and structure for success in a rapidly changing, hypercompetitive global market.

A corporate venture business plan is a document describing all relevant external and internal elements involved in launching the corporate entrepreneurial venture. It is often an integration of various functional plans that addresses both short- and long-term decisions for usually the first three years of operation of the corporate entrepreneurial venture highlighting the time it will take to break even and begin producing profits.

As a game plan or road map, the business plan is as important as planning a trip from Phoenix, Arizona, to Vienna, Austria. Since there are a number of possible routes and airlines available, each having its own time frame and costs, the traveler, like the corporate entrepreneur, needs to gather external information and make the most appropriate decision determined by the availability of time and money. Like the traveler, the corporate entrepreneur needs to prepare the business plan for the corporate entrepreneurial activity using any resources available in the organization.

Scope and Value of the Business Plan

The individuals creating the corporate business plan need to be prepared to address issues, needs, and concerns of each constituency in the organization. While these individuals will definitely include management of the organization and/or the internal venture fund's evaluation team, they could also include consultants, customers, employees, suppliers, or even outside funders.

Corporate entrepreneurs need to put themselves in the position of the potential buyer. Apple's tremendous turnaround in 1998 (with its focus on desktop and portable computers) and continued success in 2009 (with the simple-to-use iPod) was a direct result of considering the product from the end user's point of view.

The business plan is valuable to the corporate entrepreneur as it: (1) establishes the objectives and goals of the proposed corporate entrepreneurial venture; (2) provides guidance to the corporate entrepreneur about the needs and planning necessary for implementing the corporate entrepreneurial venture; (3) helps determine the viability of the corporate entrepreneurial venture in the organization; and (4) provides the information necessary to obtain management approval and funding.

The original plan frequently needs to be revised. This often focuses on such questions as: Does the idea really have value? Who is the customer, and will the customer purchase it? Who are the competitors, and is there any protection against competitive threats? Can I really manage the corporate entrepreneurial venture? Do I really want to do this?

The Corporate Business Plan

Most corporate business plans are tailored to the needs of the organization particularly reflecting its goals, products or services offered, and industry. While the plans are indeed organizationally specific, just about all contain most of the aspects indicated in Figure 9.1. In general, corporate business plans start with an executive summary

Executive Summary
Product or Service Analysis
- Purpose of the product or service
- Stage of development
- Product limitation
- Proprietary rights
- Government approvals
- Product liability
- Related services and spin-offs
- Production

Corporate Fit
- Product fit into corporate goals
- Customer base
- Utilization of assets
- Staff needs
- Distribution fit

Market Analysis
- Current market size
- Growth potential of the market
- Industry trends
- Competition profile
- Customer profile
- Customer benefits
- Market segment(s)
- Target market(s)

Marketing Plan
- Product
- Price
- Supply chain (distribution channels)
- Promotion

Profitability
- Pro forma income statements
- Capital expenditures

Plan for Further Action
- Problems
- Benefits
- Corporate management and staff needed

FIGURE 9.1   Elements of a Corporate Business Plan

followed by specific details of the plan, such as the product or service analysis, corporate fit, market analysis, marketing plan, profitability, and plan for future actions, each of which will be discussed in turn.

Executive Summary

The executive summary is written following the completion of the plan. It is usually no more than two to three pages in length, although some companies want only one page. As the name implies, it summarizes the entire plan by highlighting in a concise, convincing manner the major parts of the corporate business plan. Of particular importance to the corporate readers are a brief description of the unique value proposition of the product or service, the degree of corporate fit, and the market size, trends, and growth rate.

Product or Service Analysis

This section focuses on the various aspects of the product or service idea. This requires a detailed description of the product or service idea and how it fulfills the market need. Where appropriate, a prototype or detailed design helps ensure a complete understanding of the concept. Regardless of what is included, it is necessary to clearly and thoroughly delineate the specific aspects of the idea. Any product limitations should also be discussed as well as the type and extent of product liability. The analysis should also cite any specific government approvals needed and the obtainment process.

One aspect to consider is product differentiation focusing on the aspects of a product that make it different and unique. Each product can be placed somewhere on a commodity-specialty continuum with commodity products having few, if any, perceived differences (mainly competing on price) and specialty products having many differences to the point of being unique and capturing a price premium. For a commodity product, profitability will depend on a company's ability to offer a price lower than the competition's. In order to achieve this, the company needs to be highly skilled in machine design and able to reduce labor costs. The opposite talents are needed for a specialty product whose profitability depends on the knowledge and application of marketing, an approach centered on the determination and execution of a unique selling proposition.

To build an image of uniqueness, there needs to be an individualized name supported by advertisements and an innovative sales message. Two companies that have done this successfully are General Foods with Minute Rice and Quaker Oats with oatmeal. General Foods made its long-grain rice a specialty product when there were more than 20 products competing on price. Likewise, in 2009, Quaker Oats integrated the "supergrain" aspect and the heart healthy benefit of eating this product.

One way of converting a commodity product into a more specialty item is to process a product in a unique way that adds increased value for the customer. A second way of converting a commodity product to a more specialty item is to add something to the actual product that is desired by the consumer and differentiates the product from others in that commodity category. Miller, in heavy competition with many other companies making similar beers, eliminated calories in its Lite Beer.

Miller's strategy makes an interesting comparison to the successful product differentiation of one of its competitors, Dos Equis. The "Most Interesting Man in the World" campaign increased market share, especially in markets outside its home country of Mexico, such as the United States. This campaign further strengthened the competitive advantage of Dos Equis by using social media in addition to traditional television commercials.

A third method of changing a commodity product into a specialty one is by "being the firstest with the mostest." This establishes the first mover advantage. In this strategy, the company determines something unique about its commodity product that is beneficial to the consumer and has not been previously available. Even though competitive products can have the same qualities in their product, by being first and consistent in advertising, a company can establish that its product really possesses these qualities.

A good example of this is Wonder Bread. When the company started its advertisement—"Helps build strong bodies 12 ways"—indicating the combination of 12 minerals and vitamins, any competitor could have claimed the same attributes. Yet by being first, Wonder Bread uniquely positioned itself as the trendsetter and original builder of strong bodies in the bread category.

A fourth way of changing a commodity product into a specialty one is through packaging, or a combination of package and brand name. Even though the components of salt are the same throughout the industry, Morton's patented spout (the patent rights have now run out), combined with informing the consumer about the uniqueness of "When it rains, it pours," moved the company's salt from its commodity category to a specialty position.

An example of combining package and brand name is Janitor in a Drum. The drum, made to look like an industrial drum, combined with the name implies that this floor detergent is stronger than others. It was marketed as an intensive cleaner that takes some of the work away from the consumer, as if an actual janitor had cleaned the area.

A final method of converting a commodity product into a specialty item is by structuring the product differently. This occurred for a quinine-flavored soda pop that was restructured into Schweppes Tonic Water, a product used to mix alcoholic beverages. A similar tactic was used by Warner-Lambert upon acquiring Hall's Candy Company. Hall's was making 40 commodity candy items, none doing well, and was losing money. One of these commodity candy items was restructured as a cough drop with the slogan, "It helps you breathe easier." The item was successfully introduced as Hall's Mentho-Lyptus in the United States.

There are several other things to consider in describing the product or service idea—brand name, trademark, logo, and patents. A manufacturer's brand is when the registered name is owned by the company making the product. This name may be an umbrella name, a category name, or a specific product name. A family brand name—also referred to as a corporate name, umbrella, or family brand—is a brand name placed on all products sold by a firm. Borden is a firm that utilizes a family brand name to cover its many diversified commodity products, from pastas to soups to adhesives.

A category brand name is a brand name used on a common category of products. Firms that use a category name usually have several category brand names. An example is Sears, with Kenmore products for household appliances. A specific product name is a brand name used on one and only one product. When specific product names are assigned to a second product, it is frequently the start of a category name.

A trademark gives the firm the exclusive right of ownership on all goods associated with the trademark. The name Kodak, awarded to Eastman Kodak, belongs to the company and cannot be used by anyone else on similar products. Kleenex is another trademark example that has worked its way into everyday language to describe a tissue rather than the brand.

A logo is a letter, symbol, or sign used to represent the entire word or words of the trademark. These can also be registered with the federal government and used on an exclusive basis. While the picture of Aunt Jemima on a syrup bottle is a logo, the words Aunt Jemima are a trademark. Visual symbols are a valuable way to translate the company's message and brand across language barriers.

While patents are not granted on brand names, they are granted on: (1) unique ideas that contribute something new to the state of the art; or (2) new materials or ingredients that have not been used before but that can be used as a substitute for the original material or ingredient established in the art. Patents can also be held on the machinery used in the actual production of the product itself. For example, the spout on Morton Salt was patented.

In selecting a meaningful brand name, the company needs to avoid geographic words. Many companies have regretted taking the name of a city, a country, a river, or a valley as they found out later that others also have a right to this name. One classic example of this is the original Smithfield Hams, a name based on the town of its location, Smithfield, Virginia. At one time, there were three Smithfield Hams made by different companies because the original Smithfield Hams could not be solely used.

Another category of brand names that the organization needs to avoid is generic terms. A generic category is one that identifies homogeneous products concerning composition and/or use. For example, sodium acetylsalicylic acid is the generic term for aspirin tablets. When a name becomes generic, anyone can use that name.

It is also risky to use a word whose pronunciation is similar to that of a word used to describe products in a particular category. Miller beer made this mistake with the name "Lite," which is pronounced like *light*, a word commonly used to describe beers. Any beer manufacturer has the right to use the same term, which is exactly the strategy used by Anheuser-Busch and Amstel.

Even though Coca-Cola fought for years to maintain its name, the courts forced the company to relinquish half of its name, "cola," feeling it was a generic beverage name, allowing others to have similar rights. This made a wide variety of colas available, such as Pepsi-Cola.

Often a new product can be effectively linked to a proven brand name, thereby decreasing the odds of failure. By using the recognizable asset of a proven name, many companies have successfully entered new markets and introduced new products. Examples of this include the Bic Roller pen, Levi's skirts and shoes, Del Monte Mexican foods, Easy-Off window cleaner, and Vaseline Intensive Care skin lotion, bath oil, and baby powder. However, this does not necessarily guarantee success. Such failures as Arm & Hammer antiperspirant, Certs gum, and Listerine household cleaner illustrate that a strong name in one category does not necessarily guarantee success in another.

While there are many criteria that can be used in selecting and establishing a brand name, the most important ones are pronunciation, connotation, and memorability.

A brand name should be easily pronounced and in only one way in a given market. This aspect can be tested by printing the proposed name in one- to two-inch type on white cardboard and presenting the name for pronunciation to a sample in the market. It is important to keep this pronunciation and name as consistent as possible when entering new markets with different cultures and languages. In 2009, Pepsi-Cola changed its longtime name Pepsi to Pecsi to better accommodate the pronunciation of its brand in Argentina.

A name that is easily remembered is most desirable because it needs to stick in the minds of consumers. This can be determined by selecting the 30 best names and telling a sample of consumers that the 30 names are to be used on a "name category of a product" (such as a grocery item, pharmaceutical product, or a hardware product). Each name is then presented on a card and pronounced for the consumer sample. Each person is asked to write down the most remembered names with the name recalled most frequently in each product category being the most memorable.

A final area to consider in the product or service idea is the packaging. The product's final packaging mix represents decisions in a variety of areas. A good packaging mix is one that creates consistency for the product's brand message, protects the product, adapts to production line speeds, promotes or sells the product, increases the product density, facilitates the use of the product, provides reusable value to the consumer, satisfies legal requirements, is eco-friendly, and keeps the packaging costs as low as possible.

The consumer package is the package that is purchased and taken home by the consumer. At times, the consumer package is made so that it can be put on display for the consumer at the retail level.

The shipping case is the container in which the product is shipped and stored in the warehouse. It is packed either with display boxes, as in the case of Alka-Seltzer retail boxes; with consumer packages, such as Pillsbury cake mix boxes; or with bulk products such as kegs of nails.

The first requisite of a good packaging design is that it protect the product. The proper packaging must protect according to the needs of each product. If the product is perishable, the manufacturer must have temperature and humidity charts for each marketed area of the product.

Packaging can also be used simultaneously to achieve product uniqueness as well as product protection. The Morton Salt pour spout, which was a convenience to the consumer, also protected the salt from moisture by sealing the package after usage. Frequently, the packaging innovations are developed by the packing material manufacturers. Procter & Gamble, working with Container Corporation of America, introduced the protective composite can used today for so many snack items, such as Pringles and Cheetos.

A packaging innovation sold to the wine industry is the Mega-Cask, a bag-in-a-box container. The special container saves money for restaurants, hotels, and clubs by preserving the quality of wine while allowing faster serving in a more efficient manner.

The final task of the package is to sell the product to the consumer. Four general merchandising principles are important: apparent size, attention-drawing power, impression of quality, and brand name readability.

When a product is displayed among a myriad of competing products, a package should have the inherent ability to capture and hold the attention of the targeted consumer. What gives a package this power? The package design—that combination of elements that together produces attractiveness, purity, appetite appeal, and high quality. Breakfast cereals for children have two target markets, children and parents. The children are the end consumers but the mothers purchase the cereal, often accompanied by the children at the grocery store. Companies such as Kellogg's consider this by making sure to include on its packaging the colorful, fun images sought out by children and the nutritional value desired by parents.

Whenever appropriate (such as in the case of food products), a picture of the product should be displayed on the front panel in an appetizing manner. Nothing attracts and holds interest like pictures of a food product.

A package should convey the feeling of quality. One way to test that a package does not denote poor quality is to evaluate the finished package on a scale of several good and bad product qualities. The company should always make sure that the package printing does not appear washed-out or faded as this gives an impression of an older product with poor quality. Printing should be bright but not gaudy.

The brand name on a package should be easily readable. Readability is especially important in the case of packages that are distributed mainly through large self-service outlets since these packages must compete with numerous items in the same product class in relatively restricted shelf areas. To achieve readability, it is important to make the letters as large as possible using the same print used in large daily paper headlines.

If the new idea is a manufacturing operation, there is a need for an initial production plan. This plan should describe the complete manufacturing process. If some or all of the manufacturing process is to be subcontracted, the plan should describe the subcontractor(s), including location, reasons for selection, costs, and any completed contracts.

Corporate Fit

An important aspect of the product or service idea is that it support the mission statement, direction, and focus of the company. This part of the corporate business plan clearly differentiates it from an entrepreneurial start-up business plan. The better the idea fulfills the corporate goals and utilizes the assets of the company, the more likely it will receive favorable attention. Other fits that make the idea more attractive include selling to the same customer base, using the same distribution system, and applying present employee expertise in making, delivering, and marketing the idea. The more the synergy, the better the idea fits.

Market Analysis

This section of the corporate business plan can be the most difficult to prepare, particularly for individuals from the technical side of the organization. Some companies, such as American Greeting Cards and Xerox Ventures, help reduce this problem by providing a workshop on market analysis, information sources, and the marketing plan. This workshop not only provides a better understanding for writing an effective corporate business plan, but it also brings awareness of the importance of market analysis.

The market analysis should focus on the market need for the idea. The identified market should address size, trends (the last three years), growth rate, and characteristics. In addition, this section needs to focus on identifying all products or services and the companies that presently serve this need.

The various sources of information—such as general information, industry and market information, competitive company and product information, search engines, and trade associations and publications—are found in Chapter 4, "Identifying, Evaluating, and Selecting the Opportunity."

Market Segmentation

This market information provides the basis for doing significant market segmentation for the new product or service idea. Table 9.1 lists the six overall segmentation criteria that can be used along with their specific applications in each of the three major markets: business-to-consumer (B2C), business-to-business (B2B), or business-to-government (B2G). The two most commonly used segmentation techniques are demographic and geographic, which also have the most published secondary data available, the sources of which were discussed previously. The most widely used consumer demographic variables are income, gender, and age, while the most widely used industrial variables are type of product lines and sales. These can be used on any defined geographic region.

Other less used techniques include psychological benefits, volume of use, and controllable marketing elements. Of these, the segmentation variable producing the most effective results is benefit segmentation. While in Table 9.1 generic benefits are listed as durability, dependability, reliability, economy, status from ownership, and efficiency in operation for use in the business-to-consumer and

TABLE 9.1   Market Segmentation by Type of Market

Segmentation Criteria	Basis for Type of Market		
	Business-to-Consumer	Business-to-Business	Business-to-Government
Demographic	education level, income, nationality, occupation, age, race, gender	number of employees, size of sales, size of profit, type of product lines	type of agency, size of budget, amount of autonomy
Geographic	region of country, city, country	country, region of country	federal, state, local
Psychological	personality traits, motives, lifestyle	degree of industrial leadership	degree of forward thinking
Benefits	durability, dependability, economy, esteem enhancement, status from ownership, handiness	dependability, reliability of seller and support service, efficiency in operation or use, enhancement of firm's earning, durability	dependability, reliability of seller and support services
Volume of Use	heavy, medium, light	heavy, medium, light	heavy, medium, light
Controllable Marketing Elements	sales promotion, price, advertising, guarantee, warranty, product attributes, reputation of seller	price, service, warranty, reputation of seller	price, reputation of seller

business-to-business categories, the organization should determine the exact benefits the customer wants through market research. When these benefits match the unique selling propositions of the product or service being considered, there is an even better chance of a successful launch.

Marketing Plan

The marketing plan needs to be based on the market analysis and market segmentation for the idea. This fourth area of the corporate business plan needs to be developed in terms of four major areas: product or service mix, price mix, distribution mix, and promotion mix as indicated in Figure 9.2. Each element has its own mix to fill the market need and achieve customer satisfaction. These elements need to be aimed at the satisfaction of the target group of customers, which requires that the customer be the hub and focal point of all the firm's activities. Customer wants and needs should be analyzed, enabling the company's offering to match these—the essence of the marketing concept.

The product or service area includes all the aspects that make up the physical product or service. Decisions need to be made on quality, assortment, breadth and depth of line, warranty, guarantee, service, and packaging. All these characteristics make the final product or service more (or less) appealing to the target market.

Closely related to the product and its mix is the price. While probably the least understood of the elements, the price of the product greatly influences the image of the product as well as the product's purchase potential. The established price needs to take into consideration the three Cs—cost, competition, and consumer.

An illustration of the effect of price on channel of distribution members is indicated in Figure 9.3. As shown, every time a channel member is added, the percentage margin increases the final selling price for the consumer. While the cheapest price is obtained by not using any channel members—as in the case of direct, mail order, or Web-based sales—often channel members are needed for

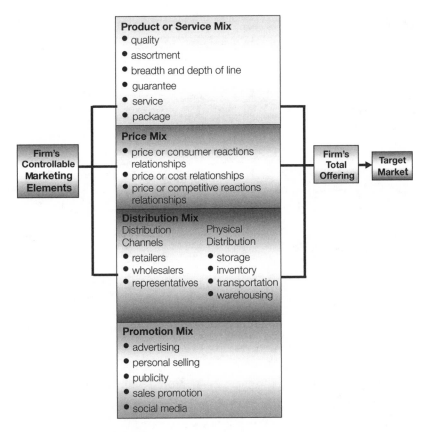

FIGURE 9.2   Marketing Plan

successful sales. Channel members often have better access to the targeted market segment and can facilitate relations with the end customer.

The third basic element of the marketing mix—distribution— covers two different areas. The first area—channels of distribution— deals with the institutions such as wholesalers and retailers that deliver the product from the firm into the hands of the consumer. Physical distribution, the second area, deals with the aspects of physically moving the product from the firm to the consumer. This includes such things as warehouse, inventory, and transportation. This part of the marketing plan is often not required in a corporate

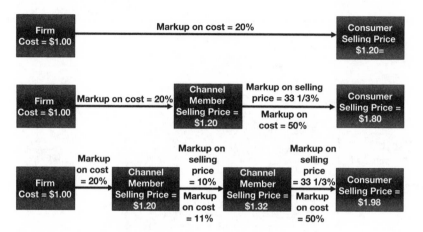

FIGURE 9.3   Channel Members and the Price

business plan, particularly if the company's present channel and system will be used.

The final element—promotion—involves policies and procedures related to five areas:

1. **Personal selling.** Emphasis on personal selling and the methods employed in the manufacturer's organization and in the trade often used in businesses such as car dealerships, pharmaceuticals, and residential construction.
2. **Advertising.** Policies and procedures relating to budget, message, and media such as television, radio, print ads, and so on.
3. **Promotions.** Policies and procedures relating to budget, types of consumer deals, trade promotions, and in-store displays.
4. **Publicity.** Policies and procedures relating to a comprehensive program for effective media coverage and a strong company image.
5. **Social media.** The media such as Facebook, Twitter, banner ads, viral commercials, and others that can be used to successfully relate the value and benefits of the new product or service to the targeted consumers.

Again, for similar reasons as distribution, this is often not required, at least in the initial corporate business plan.

Profitability

The profitability section of the corporate business plan focuses on the pro forma income statement shown in Figure 9.4 and any capital expenditures on equipment that are needed in developing and launching the new product or service. While not all the categories need to be estimated, the most important ones—such as total revenue, cost of goods sold, and gross profit (margin)—should be estimated as closely as possible for at least the first year. An example

	Three-Year Summary		
	Year 1	Year 2	Year 3
TOTAL REVENUE[1]			
Less: COST OF GOODS SOLD[2]			
GROSS PROFIT (Margin)			
OPERATING EXPENSES:			
Management Salaries			
Fringe Benefits			
Other Salaries			
Other Fringe Benefits			
Consultant			
Advertising & Promotion			
Delivery			
Bad Debts			
General Administration Expense			
Legal Expenses			
Rent			
Utilities			
Insurance			
Taxes and Licensing			
Interest			
Outsource Accounting and Payroll			
Depreciation			
Miscellaneous			
TOTAL OPERATING EXPENSES			
PROFIT (LOSS) PRETAX			
TAXES			
NET PROFIT (LOSS)			

[1] The calculation for the Total Revenue should be shown with reference to the marketing plan.
[2] The Cost of Goods Sold should be broken down into its components on a separate table.

FIGURE 9.4 Pro Forma Income Statement

ASSUMING:	1) 1,400 units sold	
	2) Price = $40	
	3) Cost = $10	
TOTAL REVENUE:	Units × Price	
	1,400 × 40	$56,000.00
Less: Cost of Goods Sold	Units × Cost	
	1,400 × 10	$14,000.00
GROSS PROFIT (Margin)		$42,000.00
OPERATING EXPENSES:		
Salary		$60,000.00
Fringe Benefit (25%)		$15,000.00
Rent & Shared Office Answering Service ($300/ month)		$3,600.00
Electricity ($70/month)		$840.00
Gas ($20/month)		$240.00
Legal (start-up expenses)		$4,000.00
Manufacturer's Representative	(5% of sales price to retail $40)	
	(1,400 × 40 × 5%)	$2,800.00
Advertising (from advertising budget)		$40,000.00
Telephone (unlimited cell phone) ($100/month)		$1,200.00
Consultant ($3,000/month)		$36,000.00
Outsourcing Accounting & Payroll ($75/month)		$900.00
TOTAL OPERATING EXPENSES		$164,580.00
NET PROFIT (Loss)		($122,580.00)
TAXES		$0.00
NET PROFIT (Loss)		($122,580.00)

FIGURE 9.5   Example of Pro Forma Income Statement

of these and other calculations of a pro forma income statement are shown in Figure 9.5.

Plan for Further Action

The corporate business plan should end with a brief section called the "Plan for Further Action." This section addresses any potential problems in developing and marketing the idea as well as the expected benefits for the organization. This section concludes with a general discussion about the size and type of corporate management and staff needed to develop and successfully launch the idea. This final part usually is not very specific.

Summary

This chapter focuses on the corporate business plan. While the format and requirements of the business usually are company specific, some areas usually occurring in most corporate business plans are discussed. The major aspects of a corporate business plan—executive summary, product or service analysis, corporate fit, market analysis, market segmentation, marketing plan, profitability, and plan for further action—were covered along with their importance and use.

10

Selecting, Evaluating, and Compensating Corporate Entrepreneurs

What are the most important factors in recruiting and selecting a corporate entrepreneurial team? What must the corporate entrepreneur do to successfully develop the corporate entrepreneurial idea? What is the most effective way to evaluate the performance of corporate entrepreneurship? What form of compensation and incentives should be used to reward success?

Scenario: Nokia

Nokia is a world leader in mobility, driving the transformation and growth of the converging Internet and communications industries. It is the world's largest manufacturer of mobile telephones. In 2010, the average number of employees was over 123,000 in 120 countries, and net sales were €29,795 million. Nokia produces mobile devices for major market segments and protocols including Global System for Mobile communication (GSM), Code Division Multiple Access (CDMA), Wideband Code Division Multiple Access (W-CDMA), and Universal Mobile Telecommunications System (UMTS). Through its Ovi platform, Nokia offers Internet services such as applications, games, music, maps, media, and messaging. Nokia Siemens Networks, a subsidiary of Nokia, produces telecommunications network equipment, solutions, and services.

Nokia was founded in 1865 when Fredrik Idestam, a mining engineer, built a wood pulp mill on the banks of the Tammerkoski rapids in southern Finland. In 1871, Idestam named his company Nokia Ab. Eduard Polón founded Finnish Rubber Works in 1898, which later became Nokia's rubber business. Arvid Wickström started Finnish Cable Works in 1912, which was the foundation of Nokia's cable and electronics businesses. Nokia Ab, Finnish Rubber Works, and Finnish Cable Works formally merged in 1967 to create Nokia Corporation. The present Nokia Corporation has five businesses: rubber, cable, forestry, electronics, and power generation.

From 1968 to 1991, the newly formed Nokia Corporation was ideally positioned in the evolution of mobile communications. With the deregulation of the European telecommunications markets, Nokia led the way with some iconic products. In 1979, radio telephone company Mobira Oy was started as a joint venture between Nokia and a leading Finnish television maker, Salora. In 1981, the first international mobile phone network, Nordic Mobile Telephone (NMT), was built. In 1982, the company's first digital telephone switch, the Nokia DX200, became operational. The Mobira Talkman, the world's first portable NMT car telephone, was launched in 1984. In 1987, the classic Mobira Cityman, the first handheld NMT phone, was introduced by the company.

From 1992 to 1999, the mobile revolution, Nokia made one of the most important strategic decisions in its history by deciding to focus on its telecommunications business. In 1992, Nokia launched its first GSM handset, the Nokia 1011. Nokia became the world leader in mobile phones in 1998. In 1999, the company launched the world's first WAP (Wireless Application Protocol) handset, the Nokia 7110, with access to mobile Internet services such as banking, e-mail, and news.

The story of Nokia continues with 3G, mobile multiplayer gaming, multimedia devices, and a look to the future. In 2002, Nokia launched its first 3G phone, the Nokia 6650, as well as the first phone with a built-in camera, the Nokia 7650, and its first video capture phone, the Nokia 3650. In 2003, mobile gaming went multiplayer with the N-Gage. Nokia launched the first mobile phones to include energy saving alerts encouraging people to unplug the charger once the battery is full. This could save enough electricity to power 85,000 homes a year.

One of Nokia's success factors is its high investment in research and development (R&D). In 2009, 17,196 people were employed in research and development with an R&D budget of €5.909 billion, 14.4 percent of Nokia's net sales that year. The research aims to disrupt the present by focusing on different sciences. Researchers are encouraged to generate ideas for new business development. The company participates in R&D projects in cooperation with universities, research institutes, and other companies.

Nokia's Research Center is actively engaging in what it calls "Open Innovation" through selective and deep research alliances with world-leading institutions resulting in global business opportunities in collaboration with the world's best experts. Through the sharing of resources, leveraging ideas, and utilizing knowledge and expertise, Nokia is able to create vibrant, innovation ecosystems, multiply efforts, enhance innovation speed and efficiency, and derive more value for the organization and customers.

Nokia Corporate Business Development manages Nokia's strategic growth areas and searches for breakthrough ideas that are "industry shakers"—innovative business concepts and technologies—that integrate with and expand beyond the core business of Nokia. When new opportunities are validated, they are then developed as new business programs within Nokia or collaboratively with other companies to establish licensing deals, joint ventures, acquisitions, or partnership agreements. With its strategy to become

> the leading provider of mobile solutions, Nokia will continue its
> innovation into the future.
>
> www.nokia.com
> www.nokiagrowthpartners.com

Introduction

The challenge facing many business ventures today is how to develop a successful business approach that will contribute to corporate venture success. This requires selection and recruitment of
individuals with entrepreneurial competencies, evaluation of their
performance, and providing equitable compensation and rewards
that generate motivation.

The role of the corporate entrepreneur needs to be diverse. He
or she must identify entrepreneurial opportunities and transform
them into action. Corporate entrepreneurs need to constantly
seek new venture opportunities. The corporate entrepreneur can
monitor change and compete in a dynamic environment by using
a corporate management checklist for evaluating the potential of
creating a successful new corporate venture within the existing
organization (see Table 10.1). This chapter discusses the selection,
evaluation, and compensation of the corporate entrepreneur.

Selecting a Corporate Entrepreneur
and a Team

The single most important factor in determining the success of a
corporate entrepreneurial activity is having a leader and a team
with the ability and passion to transform ideas into reality. While
selecting and retaining the right talent can be difficult, with the
right incentives, this can be accomplished. Jack Welch, former
CEO of General Electric (GE), spent the last years of his tenure
developing policies and practices that would enable GE to recruit,

(continues on page 239)

TABLE 10.1 Corporate Checklist for Evaluating the Potential of Creating a Successful Corporate Entrepreneurial Activity within the Existing Organization

Evaluation Criteria

Evaluate the Venture Potential in Relation to the Following Criteria:	No	Uncertain	Yes
1. Has a business plan been developed?			
2. Is the business idea or concept feasible?			
3. Have financial statements and projections been prepared and discussed with the financial manager?			
4. Are there adequate financial resources available?			
5. Is the time required to reach positive cash flow realistic?			
6. Are the required human resources with the necessary skills and abilities available?			
7. Do the financial needs for the new venture match the capacity of the existing organization?			

Market Viability

Evaluate the Market Viability in Relation to the Following Criteria:	Inadequate	Similar to Competitors	Better Than Competitors	Excellent	Uncertain
1. Evaluate the potential of a viable and credible market opportunity.					
2. Assess the market approach including strategies for: • managing customers • suppliers • competitors • other external factors					
3. Evaluate the ability to create a successful business, while at the same time protecting the parent organization.					

(Continued)

TABLE 10.1 Continued

Venture Management Criteria

Evaluate the Venture Management Potential in Relation to the Following Criteria:

	No	Uncertain	Yes
1. Is there at least one member of the venture management team qualified to lead the team to undertake the necessary work?			
2. Is there an appropriate management team to undertake the work that has to be done?			
3. Is there an opportunity to bring in additional management either from the parent organization or outside?			
4. Is there an appropriate group of professionals in the existing organization or outside advisors?			
5. Does the venture management team have the ability and expertise to leverage scarce resources?			

Technological Viability

Evaluate the Technological Viability in Relation to the Following Criteria:

	Inadequate	Similar to Competitors	Better Than Competitors	Excellent	Uncertain
1. Assess the feasibility and viability of technological development and achieving the specified goals and objectives.					
2. Compare the proposed development program with existing technologies (or with possible competing and future technologies).					
3. Evaluate the organization's existing technological achievements.					

Resources

Evaluate Resources in Relation to the Following Criteria:	Inadequate	Similar to Competitors	Better Than Competitors	Excellent	Uncertain
1. Evaluate the adequacy of the organization's budget in the context of the potential new venture.					
2. Evaluate the possibility of raising additional funds to carry out the project, as well as the potential sources of funding available for the new venture.					
3. Evaluate the adequacy of the facilities required in relation to the availability of space for the new venture.					

Commercialization

Evaluate the Commercialization in Relation to the Following Criteria:	Inadequate	Similar to Competitors	Better Than Competitors	Excellent	Uncertain
1. Evaluate the proposed commercialization schedule in relation to:					
1.1 R&D					
1.2 Proprietary protection					
1.3 Human resources					
1.4 Marketing					

(Continued)

TABLE 10.1 Continued

Commercialization (Continued)

Evaluate the Commercialization in Relation to the Following Criteria:	Inadequate	Similar to Competitors	Better Than Competitors	Excellent	Uncertain
1.5 Manufacturing					
1.6 Potential regulatory requirements					
2. Assess the organization's ability to successfully compete in the market.					
3. Assess the organization's channels of distribution.					
4. Assess the organization's customer service philosophy.					
5. Assess the organization's capabilities in terms of: • financial control • management • strategic planning					
6. Assess the feasibility of the organization's commercialization.					

select, and retain entrepreneurial individuals and develop the entrepreneurial potential needed among existing employees. Since usually no single individual possesses the wide variety of skills necessary to develop a corporate venture, the composition of the right team is needed. At Xerox New Enterprises, a division that commercializes novel technologies, the head corporate entrepreneur of each new company is recruited externally.

The corporate entrepreneurial activity needs individuals who give unbiased advice and are relatively unconcerned about the parent company's internal politics. Finding such people is a challenge in most organizations. The secret to engaging the right people is to determine the skills and knowledge needed for corporate entrepreneurship. To attract this talent requires appropriate incentives and compensation.

Corporate entrepreneurial activities often use outside advisors. These individuals are separate from the more formal board of advisors. Advisors should be assessed or interviewed just as if they were being hired for a permanent position, with references checked.

When building a corporate entrepreneurial team, the parent company can be reluctant to establish it as an independent new entity with different rules and policies. As a result, some of the parent company's recruitment, selection, evaluation, and compensation strategies are adopted. This can be a particular problem in determining compensation levels that often need to be different from the standard compensation package offered. Issues can emerge if the parent company has corporate managers hold the most senior roles in the corporate venture and lead the venture in the usual manner of the corporate culture and control. Realizing that a new culture and environment may be needed can be the first challenge to the parent company's culture and organization.

Companies like Walmart, General Mills, Intel, and United Parcel Service have invested millions of dollars in their venturing projects. One challenge is how to make early-stage financing decisions in corporate entrepreneurial ventures. If organizations like Cisco Systems, Genentech, and Yahoo! were evaluated in their infancies on the basis of near-term earnings of large corporations, they could never have become the businesses they are today.[1] A corporate entrepreneur recognizes the potential impact on the parent company's core business, has the drive and ability to influence any actions needed, and creates, establishes, and meets realistic milestones. The corporate entrepreneur needs to be an innovator with concern for the long-term viability of the new venture.

The best managers in an existing business are not necessarily the best for a new corporate entrepreneurial venture. These managers often are more committed to preserving corporate traditions than willing to challenge them. They often do not have the experience and ability needed for a new venture.

There may be, however, more corporate entrepreneurial individuals in the parent company than the management team realizes. Organizations can undertake the challenge of developing their internal executives and fostering an entrepreneurial culture. Companies such as Chevron Corporation, United Airlines, Ford Motors, and Xerox selected their corporate entrepreneurial leaders from internal ranks. It is important that any internal talent transferred to the new corporate entrepreneurial venture does not leave a void of missing talent for the parent company. A corporate entrepreneur needs to identify a core group of people who understand the business and the demands of start-up by asking the following questions:

- Do we have a corporate entrepreneur who has the competencies and ability to lead the new venture?
- Do the existing advisors or board members have the expertise and knowledge to bring the corporate entrepreneurial venture to the next stage of its life cycle?

- Do we have a team of people who have the drive, motivation, and experience to be part of this new corporate entrepreneurial venture?
- Is there evidence to suggest that the corporate entrepreneur and his or her team can effectively work together to achieve "synergy"?

Some corporate venture units recruit external individuals with the skills and experience relevant to the corporate entrepreneurial venture. The newly hired corporate entrepreneur needs to be a dynamic leader who is a manager, leader, spokesperson, networker, decision maker, and coordinator. The new corporate entrepreneurial team needs to work creatively and innovatively together, united by a common purpose and vision. The team needs to be tightly integrated with open communication, constantly updating one another and providing feedback. Different skills are required (for example, marketing, financing, technology) throughout the life cycle of a corporate entrepreneurial venture project.

Corporate Entrepreneurial Team Roles

One important factor is that the corporate entrepreneurial venture team can make decisions quickly. Corporate entrepreneurship takes many roles:

- **Venture CEO.** The corporate entrepreneur who is responsible for the overall development and advancement of the project.
- **Technical innovator.** The individual who is responsible for the major technical innovation, such as Art Fry, who developed 3M's Post-it Note.
- **Product or service champion.** All individuals who contribute to the project by promoting its development and advancement through all the key stages up to its implementation.
- **Resource allocator.** The individual who helps the venture obtain the necessary human and nonhuman resources.

Key Characteristics of the Corporate Entrepreneurial Leader

The corporate entrepreneurial leader needs to have the following characteristics:

- High level of energy, drive, and enthusiasm
- Ability to attract, select, and motivate the right people
- Charisma to lead the venture and the team internally and externally
- Resourcefulness
- Excellent communication skills
- Ability to sell the project internally and externally

The leader needs to manage the expectations of:

- Senior members of the parent company
- New corporate entrepreneurial venture managers and their team
- Members of the organization at large
- All members associated with the new corporate entrepreneurial venture

The corporate entrepreneur leading the new venture needs to:

- Support and protect the team
- Tolerate mistakes
- Lead and advise management and the team
- Take moderate risks
- Share the vision
- Delegate to those closest to the problem
- Tolerate internal competition
- Stimulate innovation and creativity
- Actively search for ideas

- Tolerate disorder
- Encourage experimentation and tests
- Trust management and the team
- Tolerate ambiguity
- Drive and motivate the team

The corporate entrepreneur needs to obtain appropriate support and collaboration, and utilize resources, while acting in the best interest of both the new corporate entrepreneurial venture and the overall organization. The team must have an entrepreneurial mindset, with each individual's activities properly integrated to achieve the goals and objectives.

Survival Guidelines for Corporate Entrepreneurs

Here are some guidelines that have been followed by successful corporate entrepreneurs:

- Only pursue ideas where the potential reward justifies the potential risk.
- Request feedback at each stage of development.
- Identify an executive champion and other key alliances.
- Become your most objective and rigorous critic.
- Recognize your core competencies and utilize them to compensate for potential weaknesses.
- Avoid unnecessary publicity from the internal organization and the external media.
- Recognize and adapt to the life cycle stage of the corporate entrepreneurial venture.
- Ensure that new venture policies and procedures are developed and supported by the CEO.
- Lead by example, providing the leadership and the management for the venture.

Venture Life Cycle and Selection of the Corporate Entrepreneurial Team

At each stage of the corporate entrepreneurial venture's life cycle, there may be a need to change the team and even the corporate entrepreneur leading the team. Some team members will want to develop the corporate entrepreneurial venture through the main stages; others will see it as an opportunity for promotion within the parent organization; others will want to start additional new corporate entrepreneurial ventures; and others will want to go back to their previous position. Each stage of the process requires different skills and experience.

- **Conception and development.** At this stage, the corporate entrepreneur needs to demonstrate drive, motivation, perseverance, resourcefulness, charisma, and the ability to communicate the opportunity to the team. This leader needs to be innovative, focused, and believe in the idea and the opportunities it can create and have the needed energy to complete the task.
- **Commercialization.** The corporate entrepreneur needs to demonstrate enthusiasm, desire, and competence and be action-orientated.
- **Growth and development.** Innovation and creativity are needed by the corporate entrepreneur to ensure further growth and development of the new venture.
- **Performance.** Since the corporate entrepreneurial venture has been launched and has maintained its position in the market, the corporate entrepreneur needs to develop the innovation to maintain its market position.

Companies such as Intel and Boeing invest millions in their corporate entrepreneurship group, with the goal of increasing their investment over time.

The corporate entrepreneur should lead the team by:

- Developing effective problem-solving techniques
- Piloting the methods (i.e., identifying what needs to be changed)
- Doing what it takes (i.e., dedication and commitment)
- Demonstrating clarity about what needs to be done
- Encouraging participative decision making
- Knowing the venture project
- Keeping focused on the vision
- Fostering teamwork

Evaluating the Corporate Entrepreneurial Team's Performance

Evaluating performance focuses on how close the corporate entrepreneurial team achieves its goals and objectives. While the corporate entrepreneurial venture starts with clearly defined goals and objectives, it needs to be flexible to fit reality. Cisco followed an unconventional form of corporate entrepreneurial venturing known as "external R&D." The company developed a tight formula for evaluating, acquiring, and integrating start-ups and growing technology firms, acquiring more than 65 start-ups in the last decade. The performance of a single venture cannot inhibit the parent organization as the new corporate entrepreneurial venture directly influences the cash flow and profit of the parent organization.

Evaluation Criteria for the Corporate Entrepreneurial Team

It is not appropriate to evaluate a new corporate entrepreneurial venture using the traditional performance criteria of the parent company. Evaluation criteria need to be focused on timely completion of events at a reasonable cost, with quality standards being maintained. There also needs to be evidence of teamwork, collaboration, and commitment.

The following is an approach to establish appropriate evaluation criteria:

- **Identify what to evaluate.** All evaluations need to be undertaken with a clear, objective, and consistent approach. All key aspects need to establish an appropriate and consistent evaluation strategy so comparisons can be accurately made.
- **Clearly define the desired standards of performance.** These need to be realistic and clearly communicated to all involved. Standards can be measured at intervals as well as on completion to ensure that events have been completed within a reasonable time frame and at a reasonable cost.
- **Assess and evaluate actual standards of performance.** Assessment needs to be carried out within a time frame based on the quality of conclusions and alternative courses of action.
- **Compare the desired standard of performance with the actual standard of performance.** If there are acceptable differences between the actual and the desired performance, then the evaluation and control process does not have to rectify any deviations beyond this point.
- **Appropriate courses of action need to be undertaken if any deviations were identified.** If deviations are unacceptable, then action must be undertaken quickly.

While an effective control system does not guarantee organizational success, it does contribute toward it. Corporate entrepreneurship needs a control system that is developed and implemented based on the long-term goals and objectives of the organization. Each venture control:

1. Should be easy to understand and apply to the new venture
2. Should assess and evaluate all important venture activities
3. Should be undertaken within an appropriate time frame
4. Should be short term, medium term, and long term
5. Should quickly and comprehensively identify any deviations
6. Should be adapted to help the new venture excel

The control system needs to be flexible while evaluating the performance of the corporate entrepreneurs and their venture.

Compensating Corporate Entrepreneurs

Corporate entrepreneur compensation and incentive practices vary greatly. At Nokia, there are no financial incentives. At DCA Food Industries Inc., 20 percent of profits go to the corporate venture management team. Tektronix offers salary-related milestone awards. At 3M, all individuals involved in the new corporate entrepreneurial venture will have changes in their employment and compensation as a function of the product sales growth achieved. Because new product sponsorship is the responsibility of management, 3M has special compensation incentives for those managers.

The compensation program of the corporate entrepreneur leading the venture needs to have an incentive to motivate individuals to achieve desirable performance and be related to the returns to the organization. The financial incentive package can help attract and retain the appropriate team. The following are aspects that need to be considered in developing an appropriate compensation plan:

- Emphasize long-term performance
- Customize specifically for the new venture

- Tailor to individuals achieving and excelling in performance outcomes
- Emphasize individual performance with incentives for teamwork
- Merit and incentive based
- Significant financial reward over a certain time frame
- Based on external equity

Compensation plans are important to retain innovative and creative people; these incentives need to be motivational. Individual incentives need to be balanced with group incentives to encourage individuals to work on their own initiative as well as being part of a team. While it is more challenging to link compensation to collective performance of a corporate entrepreneurial venture, this is possible by basing salary increases on the attainment of milestones or giving corporate entrepreneurs a share in the ownership or performance of the corporate venture. These can take the form of large bonuses or stock options that vest over a period of time.

The compensation package is especially important in attracting individuals under the following circumstances:

- If an internal person is being encouraged to leave a major project to join the new corporate entrepreneurial team.
- If an external person is being encouraged to leave an existing high-profile position to join the new corporate entrepreneurial team.
- If financial incentives are a major motivating factor for the internal or external individual to take the position in the corporate entrepreneurial venture.
- In terms of balancing the risk and reward factors associated with leaving a more secure position to take a position in the corporate entrepreneurial venture.
- As a demonstration of appreciation for the hard work and commitment of the corporate entrepreneurial team.

If the corporate entrepreneur and the team are not adequately compensated, the parent company is essentially encouraging them to leave the organization. If the company develops a compensation plan that is weighted toward unrealistic targets, it will frustrate employees. While it is easy to reward success, according to Xerox, it is more important to reward failure. Xerox does not judge people by results, but by the quality of their efforts.

While Hewlett-Packard and Microsoft compete for software engineers, each company demonstrates a different corporate culture, which is reinforced in its compensation systems.[2] This also applies to Toyota and Toshiba, which have the same national culture but different organizational cultures and different compensation and reward systems. From a strategic perspective, organizations need to structure compensation and reward systems that develop a corporate entrepreneurial culture.

Components of a Compensation and Incentive System

The following compensation and incentive components can help develop a compensation plan that can attract and retain corporate entrepreneurs who will successfully contribute to the development of the new venture:

- **Equity.** Part ownership interest in the new corporate entrepreneurial venture or parent company in the form of common stock or preferred stock.
- **Bonuses.** Money linked to individual or group performance achievements such as sales, profits, and return on investments. These amounts can be fixed, variable, or discretionary.
- **Salary increases.** Applied in the same way to a new corporate entrepreneurial venture as the existing corporation.
- **Career progression and advancement.** As opportunities emerge, those who make the greatest contribution to the new

corporate entrepreneurial venture should be recognized and given the chance to apply for a more advanced position.

- **Recognition and rewards.** Nonfinancial incentives can be as valuable to many corporate entrepreneurs as financial incentives. Individuals recognized for their contribution through recognition ceremonies and awards (which can be financial, such as at DuPont), peer recognition, employee of the month, or sponsorship of sabbaticals. These incentives need to be consistent with the organizational culture and equitable to all who make certain achievements and contributions to the new venture.

Compensation and Incentive Components for New Success

Table 10.2 identifies some compensation and incentives that can contribute to the success of the corporate entrepreneurial venture.

Some creative approaches to compensating and rewarding corporate entrepreneurial behavior include:

- Employees put a percentage of their salary at risk and then can either lose it, double it, or triple it based on team performance.
- Personalized "innovator" jackets, shirts, and leather folders are given to employees who make entrepreneurial contributions.
- When a new idea is accepted by the company, the CEO awards shares of stock to the employee.
- Employees are given $500 to spend on an innovative idea that relates to their job.
- A company rents out a major sports stadium, fills the stands with employees, families, and friends, and then has innovation champions run onto the field as their name and achievement appears on the scoreboard.

- A company sets a target, and then 30 percent of incremental earnings above that target are placed into a bonus pool that is paid out based on each employee's performance rating.
- Small cash awards are given to employees who try something new and fail—and the best failure of the quarter receives a larger sum.
- Some companies have point systems where employees receive differing numbers of points for different categories of innovation contributions. Points are redeemable for computers, merchandise, free day care, tuition reimbursement, and other types of rewards.
- A parking spot is reserved for the "innovator of the month."
- Team members working on a major innovation are awarded shares of zero value at project outset, and as milestones are achieved (on time), predetermined values are added to the shares. Milestones not achieved lead to a decline in share value.
- Another company ties cash awards for employees to a portfolio of innovation activities produced over time, including ideas generated, patents applied for, prototypes developed, and so forth.
- Employees receive recognition for innovative suggestions, and then a drawing is held at the end of the year for all accepted suggestions, with the winner receiving a sizable financial reward.
- One company has a "frequent innovator" program that works like an airline frequent flier program.
- "Hero biographies" are written about an employee, her background, and an innovation that she has championed. The stories are full of praise and a little humor.
- One company provides gift certificates within a day of an employee idea being implemented, and another takes employees

TABLE 10.2 Compensation and Incentives Factors for Corporate Entrepreneurship

Corporate Entrepreneurship Success Factors	Compensation and Incentive Factors That Influence Satisfaction
Satisfaction with the compensation and incentives offered	• **Purchasing power:** based on standard of living • **Fairness:** a personalized evaluation of what is seen as appropriate commensurate with ability, contribution, and effort • **Equitable:** in terms of internal and external comparisons • **Expectation and value:** where the rewards meet expectations as to their value and are commensurate with the effort and skill needed to achieve them • **Balanced:** between intrinsic and extrinsic rewards • **Total package:** depends on the overall mix of compensation and incentives offered
Drive, motivation, and commitment among CEO, venture management, and the team	• Competitive earning opportunities • Transparency and equity in compensation and incentives • Equitable and competitive plan in relation to parent company and external organizations • Individual compensation and incentive plans • Financial and nonfinancial incentives offered
Effective teamwork and synergy	• Teamwork incentive plans • Equity and fairness for all team members and their contributions • Effective composition of team members • Team recognition

TABLE 10.2 Continued

Corporate Entrepreneurship Success Factors	Compensation and Incentive Factors That Influence Satisfaction
Corporate and new venture support	• Parent company support for the new venture and recognition and respect for the differences between them • Providing a balance between the risks taken and rewards offered
Recognizing the importance of the external environment	• Team flexibility and adaptability to external environmental factors • Individual and group autonomy to achieve desirable results in light of change

to a "treasure box" where they can choose from among a number of gifts.

- A company gives 15 percent of out-of-pocket savings achieved by the innovator's ideas in the first two years of use and, if the idea is for a product, 3 percent of first-year sales.
- The top-performing team in terms of innovation is sent to a resort for a week.
- A company gives a savings bond to the employee who raises the most challenging question in management meetings.
- One organization has $500 on-the-spot awards for anyone showing special initiative.
- Some companies have their own Olympics, rodeos, competitions, game shows, hit parades, and murder mysteries in an attempt to recognize initiative and excellence.
- Others have praise and recognition boards, threshold performance clubs, and atta-person awards, and some allow innovators to appear in company advertisements.

There are some key lessons for corporations and their new ventures:

- The corporate venture needs to create an environment that the corporate culture supports and facilitates.
- New venture goals and objectives are different from corporate goals and objectives.
- New ventures can learn valuable lessons from the corporate venture as a way of identifying innovative opportunities for growth and development.
- Having the right people in the right place at the right time is critical to new venture success.
- It takes time, commitment, and energy for the new venture to develop. It must be monitored and evaluated to measure its progress and recognize the need for changes or termination.
- Compensation and incentive practices should be fair and equitable in the context of the new venture's goals and objectives, culture and needs of management, and the team.

Summary

This chapter focused on a fundamental component of corporate entrepreneurial venturing—attracting, recruiting, selecting, evaluating, and compensating the corporate entrepreneur and the team. The corporate entrepreneurial activity needs to attract talent and establish relationships with potential partners, advisors, consultants, and customers. A corporate entrepreneur needs to be committed and enthusiastic and effectively manage, lead, and integrate. The selection of a board of advisors adds support. Proper recruitment and selection procedures need to be established to ensure that potential internal and/or external innovative candidates are recruited and selected.

The corporate entrepreneurial activity needs to be monitored and evaluated by milestones that are based on the completion of tasks and whether desirable results are achieved. Continual evaluations are needed so that corrective action can be quickly taken. Appropriate compensation and incentive plans need to be in place. There should be both financial and nonfinancial compensation and incentive plans including equity, bonuses, salary increases, career progression and advancement, and recognition and rewards.

11

Funding the Venture

How should corporate entrepreneurship be funded? What should the amount of funding be and what type should be used? What funding process does Unilever use?

Scenario: Unilever

Like many companies, Unilever values innovation, research, and development and new, unique products. The company regularly spends around €1 billion on research and development to support its 400 brands that span 14 industries. Many new research projects had been given to universities to explore and develop, but Unilever executives began to notice that university development ideas were increasingly being taken to venture capital firms. The company realized it was passing up excellent expansion opportunities. Unilever was also finding it difficult to test whether internally generated ideas would effectively work as a business. Rather than creating an entrepreneurial atmosphere internally, Unilever executives decided to drive innovation and corporate entrepreneurial venturing with a business strategy—through external resources. The corporate entrepreneurial venture program eventually received support from top management, and in 2002, Unilever Technology Ventures (UTV) was established in California, and Unilever Ventures was established in London, both as independent entities from Unilever.

UTV and Unilever Ventures were governed under three main elements. First, management built the corporate entrepreneurial venture programs to resemble a venture capital model as closely as possible. Second, management split the corporate entrepreneurial venture into different roles and areas of investment focus (start-ups, later stage development, and buyouts). Third, in order to ensure that vested projects were managed as unique businesses, Unilever Ventures executives decided to involve other venture capital and private equity partners in the funding process.

The corporate entrepreneurial venture program had three main objectives. The first was concerned with creating growth options for Unilever by creating new businesses or by taking stakes in companies that showed potential to grow and be profitable; the goal was to take the Unilever brand into new areas. The second objective involved ensuring that Unilever was putting money into technology start-ups to access new and emerging technologies. Third, new businesses were to be created for spin-outs through making use of Unilever's intellectual property. The purpose of Unilever's Ventures program was to help Unilever make money. Because the businesses sponsored by the fund have access to Unilever's large technological base and intellectual property, the idea was to build two or three businesses over the course of five to eight years that Unilever might have interest in buying. The businesses would contribute to the bottom line by extending Unilever's brand with new and innovative products and services. Also, Unilever executives thought it was important for the company to get a glimpse into what other corporations were doing, and funding external start-ups was an ideal way to do so.

Unilever Technology Ventures was formed to focus on providing funds to companies in the technology space. Founded in 2002,

UTV centered on investing in start-ups in the life sciences and materials space and by 2009 had expanded to include companies in other business areas such as new technologies (e.g., neurophysics and brain research); choice and behavioral science product designs, nanotechnology, and process technology (including miniaturization, optimization, robotics, sensors, physics, and chemistry in food and home); and personal care (such as designing functionalities, modeling, fabrication technology, safety, self assembly, measurement science, and new water purification methods). The life sciences investments included biotechnology, genetics, food and nutrition, devices for drug delivery, pharmaceuticals, systems biology, novel chemistry, diagnostics, and devices for cosmetic use. Because it is in Unilever's best interest to focus on such profound science and technology innovation, Unilever, as the parent company, found that investment into such technology start-ups and early-stage companies helped promote the continuation of Unilever's cutting-edge and innovative products.

The ideal investment companies employ fewer than 100 people and are valued between $5 million and $20 million. If possible, UTV prefers to take a minority stake in each company and remain an observer with regard to the investment allocation. In keeping with the venture strategy, UTV provides vital strategic operational and financial advice, along with an extensive network of relationships, knowledge of global supply chains, and experience of research and development in various industries. UTV selects companies that are building a unique, advanced, and proprietary product or technology that would be difficult to quickly replicate by competitors. Ideally, the company should also have a large target market, an attractive market opportunity, an excellent management team that has advanced scientific and technical abilities, and an operating record that has past proven success.

The second branch of Unilever Ventures (UV) is based in central London and focuses on European expansion. Industry focus includes consumer products and services, health care, leisure, retail, media, and environmental services. UV looks to invest in businesses that fit into and are able to embrace an already existing Unilever brand, technology, expertise, or Unilever know-how. Though initially formed to invest in start-up and early-stage businesses that were looking for successful growth, Unilever Ventures now looks at funding firms in their later stages of development and also considers buyouts. Later-stage development companies use UV's venture proceeds to accelerate growth by financing increased production and product development as well as additional working capital. Management buyouts are considered with an enterprise value of up to €50 million. Buyout criteria consist of being a stand-alone investment or a strategic addition to Unilever's existing portfolio.

Between 2002 and 2009, Unilever Ventures invested in roughly 20 businesses. One such business that Unilever Ventures established jointly with another venture company, Vectura Group, in May 2006 was PharmaKodex. PharmaKodex's purpose was to create a pipeline of consumer health and pharmaceutical prescriptions; it was focused on creating improved medicine products, repurposing existing drugs, and developing new administration routes. By making use of Unilever's and Vectura's intellectual property and established technologies, PharmaKodex had an excellent chance at success. In another investment in April 2008, Unilever Ventures (along with Porton Capital, Ploughshare Innovations, and the Rainbow Seed Fund) invested in P2i Ltd., a business providing ion-mask, a super liquid-repellant. Having long ago realized that true technical innovation tends to be rare, Unilever invested in and helped roll out what it thought to be a revolutionary invention. Other Unilever Venture investments are in such services as Brain-Juicer. The business provides quantitative online research using innovative software to produce better quality marketing data.

Today, Unilever employs about 174,000 people, has senior managers of 20 nationalities, and operates in 100 countries. The company continues to innovate through a unique funding process.

www.thedeal.com/corporatedealmaker/2008/03/unilevers_
    unique_model.php
www.ariadnecapital.com/journal/v2e6/comment_last_corp_
    venturers.htm
www.h-i.com/downloads/casestudy_unilever.pdf
www.unileverventures.com

Introduction

This chapter focuses on funding the corporate entrepreneurial activity by first looking at the need for financing and presenting an overview of the venture capital industry. Following a discussion of the evaluation process, the chapter concludes by discussing several venture valuation techniques.

Need for Financing

Innovative ideas and concepts require financing at various stages of development, and internal financing in an organization requires financial justification and returns of some sort, whether these are monetary or nonmonetary. The expected returns can take the form of profitability, turnover, sales, volume increases, cost reductions, employment, evaluation, line extensions, or some other benefit. Boards of directors (advisors), presidents, vice presidents, and intracapital investment committees invest money in a corporate entrepreneurial venture only if there is evidence that the potential for a return on the investment is equal to or greater than returns on alternative investment opportunities. In any organization, funds are limited, and any support for a corporate entrepreneurial idea requires detailed financial projects, extensive research, and a contingency plan in case the projections (usually sales and profits) are overestimated. Corporate entrepreneurs, regardless of the level of their passion for their idea, need to be adept at financial projections and calculations or else have someone on the corporate entrepreneurial team who has these skills and is able to develop the numbers portion of the venture business plan (see Chapter 9). Numerous corporate entrepreneurs have indicated that they were turned down for funding due to the lack of believable sales, financial projections, and profit margins.

This difficulty in obtaining resources is particularly a problem in the initial stages of development of a new corporate entrepreneurial idea. This difficulty in obtaining such resources as financial, people, materials, and/or use of the organization's production and service systems can severely constrain the corporate entrepreneur. It is particularly problematic when the idea is significantly new—a discontinuous innovation to the organization—and thus the corporate fit in terms of the organization's goals, assets, customer base, and/or distribution system is low, as discussed in Chapter 9, "Developing the Business Plan." As would be expected given the overall resources of the organization, the corporate entrepreneur is attempting to take resources from some other aspect of or person in the organization.

Overview of the Venture Capital Industry

Venture capital is not a very well understood area.[1] Overall, venture capital is best viewed as a professionally managed pool of equity capital. Frequently, the equity pool is formed from the resources of limited partners. Other principal investors in venture capital limited partnerships are pension funds, endowment funds, and other institutions, including foreign investors. The pool is managed by a general partner—that is, the venture capital firm—in exchange for a percentage of the gain realized on the investment and a fee. The investments are in early-stage deals as well as second- and third-stage deals and leveraged buyouts. In fact, venture capital can best be characterized as a long-term investment discipline, usually occurring over a five- to seven-year period for the creation of early-stage companies, the expansion and revitalization of existing businesses, and the financing of leveraged buyouts of existing divisions of major corporations or privately owned businesses. In each investment, the venture capitalist takes equity participation through stock, warrants, and/or convertible securities and perhaps a debt position and has an active involvement in the monitoring of each portfolio company, bringing investment, financing planning, and business skills to the firm.

Although the role of venture capital was instrumental throughout the industrialization of the United States, it did not become institutionalized until after World War II. The first step toward institutionalizing the venture capital industry took place in 1946 with the formation of the American Research and Development Corporation (ARD) in Boston. The ARD was a small pool of capital from individuals and institutions put together by General Georges Doriot to make active investments in selected emerging businesses.

The next major development, the Small Business Investment Act of 1958, combined private capital with government funds to be used by professionally managed small-business investment companies (SBIC firms) to infuse capital into start-ups and growing small businesses. With their tax advantages, government funds for leverage, and status as private capital companies, SBICs were the start of the now formal venture capital industry. The 1960s saw a significant expansion of SBICs with the approval of approximately 585 SBIC licenses that involved more than $205 million in private capital. There are approximately 360 SBICs operating today, of which 130 are minority small-business investment companies (MESBICs) funding minority enterprises.

During the late 1960s, small private venture capital firms emerged. These were usually formed as limited partnerships, with the venture capital company acting as the general partner that received a management fee and a percentage of the profits earned on a deal. The limited partners, who supplied the funding, were frequently institutional investors such as insurance companies, endowment funds, bank trust departments, pension funds, and wealthy individuals and families. There are over 900 of this type of venture capital establishments in the United States.

Another type of venture capital firm was also developed during this time: the venture capital divisions of major corporations. These firms, of which there are approximately 100, are usually associated with banks and insurance companies, although such companies as 3M, Monsanto, Xerox, Intel, and Unilever have such firms as well, as was discussed in the opening scenario. Corporate venture capital firms are prone to invest in windows on technology or new market acquisitions that fit into their corporate mission.

In response to the need for economic development, a fourth type of venture capital firm has emerged in the form of the state-sponsored venture capital fund. These state-sponsored funds have a variety of formats. While the size and investment focus and industry orientation vary from state to state, each fund typically is required to invest a certain percentage of its capital in the particular state. Generally, the funds that are professionally managed by the private sector, outside the state's bureaucracy and political processes, have performed better.

An overview of the types of venture capital firms is indicated in Figure 11.1. Besides the four types previously discussed, there are

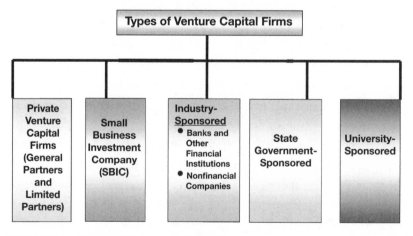

FIGURE 11.1   Types of Venture Capital Firms

now emerging university-sponsored venture capital funds. These funds, usually managed as separate entities, invest in the technology of the particular university. At such schools as Stanford, Columbia, and MIT, students can assist professors and other students in creating business plans for funding as well as assisting the fund manager in his or her due diligence, thereby learning more about the venture-funding process. For successful investments, an experienced fund manager is needed.

Corporate Venture Capital Units

Corporate entrepreneurial venturing involves corporate entrepreneurial efforts in which established business organizations invest in and/or create new businesses. When the new business is created within the parent company's organizational domain, this is sometimes called internal corporate venturing. External corporate venturing involves investments that facilitate the founding and/or growth of external businesses, companies outside the company's organizational domain as was discussed in the scenario of this chapter. Joint corporate venturing is a form of external corporate venturing in which the company invests with another established organization(s) in the creation of a new external business. All three approaches to corporate entrepreneurial venturing are important means for corporations to respond to the need for innovation. Unilever, Google, Intel, 3M, GE, Motorola, Procter & Gamble, and Microsoft all have successfully used corporate entrepreneurial venturing initiatives as key components of their innovation strategies.

Many corporate venture capital units are charged with the responsibility of investing in outside companies with product or service ideas that are in line with the mission of the company in addition to internally generated corporate entrepreneurship ideas. The venture capital unit of Dow Chemical would be interested in investing only in companies that are in the area of chemicals and related products. These investments usually take the form of a minority interest in the common and/or convertible preferred stock in return for use of the technology in the investing company's operation or product. Medtronic uses this as a strategy for technology development on a regular basis in the medical technology field. This is, in a sense, a type of off-balance sheet financing of research and development for the company. An investment by the venture capital unit of a well-established, recognized company improves the public legitimacy of the young, unknown venture. This "certification" can in turn help the invested firm attract new commercial firms and customers. In addition, the young venture can receive help in technology development, sales, supply chain and distribution, and overall industry from the more established investing company.

The other responsibility of the corporate venture capital unit is to invest in internal ventures created within the company. This provides the capital needed for the successful implementation of a corporate entrepreneurship program. Each internal venture invested in goes through the following evaluation process.

The Evaluation Process

First, the new product or service idea usually needs to align with the company's mission statement and direction in terms of the product line and market area presently being served. Companies like to use their present institutional knowledge to help ensure that the launch of something new will be successful and that synergies will occur. This institutional fit is a criterion used unless the company is trying to reinvent itself, which regularly occurs in the life cycle of any organization.

Second, if the product or service idea needs to be technologically feasible within some time frame, since the venture capital units are usually not the source of funds for research and development, the development costs and time frame must be clearly understood through commercialization.

Third, the market needs to be large enough and accessible to the company. This criterion, particularly for large organizations, which require high sales and return levels, often mitigates certain ideas from receiving funding. And for successful proposals and corporate entrepreneurship to occur, this is usually the area needing the most assistance, particularly for technology-based companies. The methods for obtaining market data were discussed in Chapter 4, "Identifying, Evaluating, and Selecting the Opportunity," but often this is an area where a company needs to provide training and assistance if it is really interested in having a vibrant corporate entrepreneurship program. Similar assistance is needed in developing the corporate business plan discussed in Chapter 9, "Developing the Business Plan."

Fourth, a champion for the idea must be present. While this is usually the originator of the idea, often a small team of individuals is needed to show that the capabilities are present along with the desire to make sure the idea is successfully launched. The capabilities, background, education, and work experience of the corporate entrepreneur submitting the idea and any corporate entrepreneurial team members need to be carefully discussed.

Fifth, some indication of the revenues and costs should be indicated. Example pro forma statements are shown in Tables 11.1 through 11.4. Table 11.1 can be used as a guide for determining the revenue potential for the product or service idea. While training and/or assistance can greatly increase the accuracy, even without these, the corporate entrepreneur submitting the proposal needs to be conscious of pricing and possible sales. In many companies, only the first year sales are required. Table 11.2 assists in the determination of the cost of the product or service or the cost of goods sold. This is best accomplished by thinking of the various items that make up the unit cost, which is then multiplied by the number to be sold from Table 11.1 and gives the total cost

TABLE 11.1   Revenue Potential

First Year	
1. What is the selling price?	
2. How many can you sell?	
Revenue: Multiply line 1 by line 2	$
Second Year	
1. What is the selling price?	
2. How many can you sell?	
Revenue: Multiply line 1 by line 2	$
Third Year	
1. What is the selling price?	
2. How many can you sell?	
Revenue: Multiply line 1 by line 2	$

of goods sold per year. The number of years is company-specific. Table 11.3 indicates some of the items that might be included in one-time and ongoing monthly expenses. Again, this item needs to be tailored to the specific company situation from the general

TABLE 11.2   Cost of Goods Sold

Each Part		Cost	
Total Unit Cost		$	

Yearly Costs	Year 1	Year 2	Year 3
Units Sold			
Total Unit Cost			
Cost of Goods	$	$	$

list of items in the table. Finally, the results in Tables 11.1, 11.2, and 11.3 are summarized in Table 11.4 to give the profit potential for the new product or service idea. While the details desired in each of these tables vary from company to company, it is highly

TABLE 11.3 Expenses Estimates

	Year 1	Year 2	Year 3
One-time			
Accounting Fees			
Computer Hardware			
Computer Software			
Equipment			
Furniture			
Incorporation			
Legal Fees			
Market Research			
Product Certification			
Product Prototype			
Product Testing			
Packaging			
Promotions			
Telephones			
Miscellaneous			
Total One-time	$	$	$
Monthly			
Labor			
Office Rent			
Lease Payments			
Loan Payments			
Office Supplies			
Miscellaneous			
Total Monthly	$	$	$

TABLE 11.4 Profit Potential

	Year 1	Year 2	Year 3
Revenue			
Units Sold			
Selling Price			
Total Revenue	$	$	$
Cost of Goods			
Gross Profit	$	$	$
Expenses			
One-time			
Monthly × 12			
Total Expenses	$	$	$
Net Profit	$	$	$

recommended that each table be a part of the corporate entrepreneurial venture proposal as it helps the corporate entrepreneur be much more market and profit focused.

Valuing the Idea

A problem confronting the venture capital unit is determining the value of the idea. This valuation is at the core of determining how much the idea is really worth and whether funding should be provided. This is determined by considering several factors in valuation.

Factors in Valuation

There are several factors that, although they vary by situation, are involved in valuing the idea. The first factor, and the starting point in any valuation, is the nature and history of the idea. The characteristics of the idea and the industry in which it operates are fundamental to every evaluation process as are the risks involved and the company's ability to withstand any adverse conditions.

The valuation process must also consider the outlook of the economy in general as well as the outlook for the particular industry. This second factor involves an examination of the financial data of the industry in the national and global economies. Management's capability now and in the future is assessed, as well as the future markets for the idea and whether these markets grow, decline, or stabilize, and in what economic conditions need to be addressed.

Ratio Analysis

Since venture capital units construct pro forma balance sheets and income statements, some ratio analysis is usually done. Calculations of financial ratios are extremely valuable as an analytical and control mechanism to test the financials of a new corporate entrepreneurial venture. These ratios serve as a measure of the financial strengths and weaknesses of the proposed corporate entrepreneurial venture, but they should be used with caution since they are only one control measure for interpreting its financial success. There is no single set of ratios that must be used, nor are there standard definitions for all ratios. There are industry rules of thumb that the corporate entrepreneur can use to help create the financial data. While ratio analysis is typically used on actual financial results, it can also provide some sense of where problems exist in the pro forma statements. There are four categories of ratios that will be discussed: liquidity, activity, leverage, and profitability.

Liquidity Ratios

Liquidity ratios indicate the organization's ability to pay its short-term debts as they fall due. Liquidity is a measure of how quickly an asset can be converted into cash. Highly liquid organizations can convert assets into cash when needed to repay loans. Less liquid organizations have difficulty meeting their obligations or obtaining loans at lower interest rates. The two most common liquidity ratios are the current ratio and the acid test ratio.

Current Ratio

This ratio is commonly used to measure the short-term solvency of the corporate entrepreneurial venture or its ability to meet its short-term debts. The current liabilities must be covered from cash or its equivalent; otherwise, the corporate entrepreneur will need to borrow money to meet these obligations. The formula and calculation of this ratio when current assets are \$108,050 and current liabilities are \$40,500 is:

$$\frac{\text{Current assets}}{\text{Current liabilities}} = \frac{108,050}{40,500} = 2.67 \text{ times}$$

While a ratio of 2:1 is generally considered favorable, the corporate entrepreneur should also compare this ratio with any industry standards. One interpretation of this result is that for every dollar of current debt, the company has \$2.67 of current assets to cover it. This ratio indicates that our hypothetical company, MPP Plastics, is liquid and can likely meet any of its obligations even if there were a sudden emergency that would drain existing cash.

Acid Test Ratio

This is a more rigorous test of the short-term liquidity of the venture because it eliminates inventory, which is the least liquid current asset. The formula given the same current assets and liabilities and inventory of \$10,450 is:

$$\frac{\text{Current assets} - \text{inventory}}{\text{Current liabilities}} = \frac{108,050 - 10,450}{40,500} = 2.40 \text{ times}$$

The result from this ratio suggests that the venture is very liquid since it has assets convertible to cash of $2.40 for every dollar of short-term obligations. Usually a 1:1 ratio would be considered favorable in most industries.

Activity Ratios

Activity ratios indicate how effectively an *organization* is using its resources.

Accounts receivable turnover ratio measures the number of times that an organization's inventory has been sold during the year. It is the organization's cost of goods sold and current inventory.

Average Collection Period

This ratio indicates the average number of days it takes to convert accounts receivable into cash. This ratio helps the corporate entrepreneur to gauge the liquidity of accounts receivable or the ability of the corporate entrepreneurial venture to collect from its customer. Using the formula with accounts receivable of $46,400 and sales of $995,000 results in:

$$\frac{\text{Accounts receivable}}{\text{Average daily sale}} = \frac{46,000}{995,000 \div 360} = 17 \text{ days}$$

This particular result needs to be compared with industry standards since collection will vary considerably. However, if the invoices indicate a 20-day payment required, then one could conclude that most customers pay on time.

Inventory Turnover

This ratio measures the efficiency of the corporate entrepreneurial venture in managing and selling its inventory. A high turnover is a favorable sign indicating that the corporate entrepreneurial venture is able to sell its inventory quickly. There could be a danger with a very high turnover that the corporate entrepreneurial venture is understocked, which could result in lost orders. Managing inventory is very important to the cash flow and profitability of a new corporate entrepreneurial venture. The calculation of this ratio when the cost of goods sold is \$645,000 and the inventory is \$10,450 is:

$$\frac{\text{Cost of goods sold}}{\text{Inventory}} = \frac{645,000}{10,500} = 61.4 \text{ times}$$

This would appear to be an excellent turnover as long as the corporate entrepreneur feels that he or she is not losing sales because of understocking inventory.

Leverage Ratios

Leverage ratios show the relative amount of funds in the business supplied by creditors and shareholders. Two common leverage ratios are debt-to-equity ratio and times-interest-earned ratio.

Debt Ratio

Many new corporate entrepreneurial ventures will incur debt as a means of financing the start-up. The debt ratio helps the corporate entrepreneur to assess the firm's ability to meet all its obligations (short and long term). It is also a measure of risk because debt also consists of a fixed commitment in the form of interest and principal repayments. With total liabilities of \$249,700 and total assets of \$308,450, the debt ratio is calculated as:

$$\frac{\text{Total liabilities}}{\text{Total assets}} = \frac{249,700}{308,450} = 81\%$$

This result indicates that the venture has financed about 81 percent of its assets with debt. On paper, this looks very reasonable, but it would also need to be compared with industry data.

Debt-to-Equity Ratio

This ratio assesses the company's capital structure. It provides a measure of risk to creditors by considering the funds invested by creditors (debt) and investors (equity). The higher the percentage of debt, the greater the degree of risk to any of the creditors. The calculation of this ratio using the same total liabilities, with stockholders' equity being $58,750, is:

$$\frac{\text{Total liabilities}}{\text{Stockholders' equity}} = \frac{249,700}{58,750} = 4.25 \text{ times}$$

This result indicates that this corporate entrepreneurial venture has been financed mostly from debt. The actual investment of the corporate entrepreneurs or the equity base is about one-fourth of what is owed. Thus, the equity portion represents a cushion to the creditors. For MPP Plastics, this is not a serious problem because of its short-term cash position.

Profitability Ratios

Profitability ratios indicate the organization's ability to generate a financial return on sales or investment as compared with earnings. Over time, these ratios indicate how successfully or unsuccessfully management operates the business. Two common profitability ratios are return on equity and return on sales.

Net Profit Margin

This ratio represents the corporate entrepreneurial venture's ability to translate sales into profits. You can also use gross profit instead of net profit to provide another measure of profitability. In either case, it is important to know what is reasonable in your industry as well as to measure these ratios over time. The ratio and calculation when net profit is $8,750 and net sales are $995,000 is:

$$\frac{\text{Net profit}}{\text{Net sales}} = \frac{8,750}{995,000} = 0.88\%$$

The net profit margin for MPP Plastics, although low for an established firm, would not be of great concern for a new corporate entrepreneurial venture. Many new corporate entrepreneurial ventures do not incur profits until the second or third year. In this case, we have a favorable profit situation.

Return on Investment

The return on investment measures the ability of the corporate entrepreneurial venture to manage its total investment in assets. You can also calculate a return on equity, which substitutes stockholders' equity for total assets in the formula below and indicates the ability of the corporate entrepreneurial venture in generating a return to the stockholders. The formula and calculation of the return on investment when total assets are $200,400 and net profit is $8,750 is:

$$\frac{\text{Net profit}}{\text{Net sales}} = \frac{8,750}{200,400} = 4.4\%$$

The result of this calculation will also need to be compared with industry data. However, the positive conclusion is that the company has earned a profit in its first year and has returned 4.4 percent on its asset investment.

Nonfinancial Factors

There are many nonfinancial factors that also need to be evaluated. These include uniqueness of idea, its contribution to the product line, the synergies of the idea with the company's capabilities, the length of time of development, the amount of investment involved versus alternative investments available, the strength of the management team, the size of the market, and the possibility for more products or services in the area.

Summary

This chapter was devoted to the topic of funding the idea and the corporate entrepreneurial venture. An overview of the venture capital industry was presented, putting into perspective the venture capital unit of a nonfinancial company wanting to be active in corporate entrepreneurship. This venture capital unit is often charged with funding any ideas or ventures outside the company as well as funding internally generated ideas and any corporate entrepreneurial process established.

General factors used in evaluating an idea include: the alignment of the new idea with the company's mission and strategy; the technological feasibility of the idea within the resources of the company; a market large enough and important enough and able to be reached usually by the company's present capabilities; a champion and team that can move the idea along to fruition; and the idea's ability to generate sufficient sales or profits, whether on its own or by stimulating the revenues or reducing the costs of other operations of the company.

Similarly, financial value is determined using pro forma financial statements and ratio analysis.

12

Implementing Corporate Venturing in Your Organization

How does an organization implement corporate venturing? How can the results be evaluated? What are some good measurements and benchmarks that can be used?

Scenario: Johnson & Johnson

Not until the late 1800s was it discovered that infections were, in large part, caused by airborne germs from operating rooms. The discovery inspired Robert Wood Johnson to join forces with his brothers Edward Mead Johnson and James Wood Johnson to begin producing sterile sutures, dressings, and bandages for treating patients and their wounds. The idea was widely accepted by doctors and hospitals as they had been looking for a solution to decrease the number of infections and deaths. By 1886, 14 employees were working in the Johnson & Johnson factory—an old wallpaper factory. The process for bandage creation improved from year to year, and by 1910, the company was growing rapidly. In 1919, a Canadian office was opened, and in 1923, Johnson & Johnson expanded globally.

The company slowly moved into additional health-care segments including pharmaceuticals, hygiene products, and textiles. It began producing and selling products such as sanitary napkins and birth control, and by 1968, annual sales were at $700 million. Additionally, Robert Johnson, who served as CEO for several years in the 1900s, was a "champion of social issues." He rallied support to increase the minimum wage and stressed the important role businesses play within a community. Johnson & Johnson formally outlined its principles and responsibilities, stating that its first responsibility was to its customers and second to its employees. The community was third on the list, and shareholders were fourth.

In 1966, Johnson & Johnson became concerned about a possible slowdown in its professional product division and focused on searching for other profit-generating consumer products. James Burke, the marketing manager who led Johnson & Johnson to its future success, took charge and focused on television and magazine marketing campaigns. For example, aggressive campaigns for sanitary napkins were launched, and within 12 years, Johnson & Johnson had half the feminine hygiene market. Burke also led Tylenol to overtake all other pain relievers with the same ingredients by significantly lowering the cost of the product.

In 1982, there was a sudden tragedy to Johnson & Johnson and the victims of the Tylenol tampering ordeal; seven Tylenol customers died after taking capsules covered in cyanide. Upon hearing the news, Johnson & Johnson not only stopped all advertising but also removed all Tylenol products from store shelves, costing millions of dollars and decreasing its share price by 18 percent in one single day. Once the tampering was found to have occurred at the retail level and not manufacturing, the company ran a well-managed PR campaign and added not one but two additional tamper-resistant layers of protection to its containers, bringing the protection layer count to three.

Due to its long history of dedication to social responsibility, Johnson & Johnson withstood the criticism of rising health-care costs in the United States. By 2009, Johnson & Johnson was considered one of the most admired companies in the country. Operational business units in 2010 consisted of: (1) pharmaceuticals (39 percent of revenues), (2) professional (36 percent of revenues), and (3) consumer (25 percent of revenues). Half of revenues were from outside the United States; the company had a network of 190 operating companies spread among 51 countries and sold its products in over 175 nations around the world.

The importance of constant innovation is not a new idea to Johnson & Johnson executives. Innovation and corporate entrepreneurship have been a factor in the company's success, and Johnson & Johnson is enriched with corporate entrepreneurship spirit in nearly every layer of its corporate structure.

Jeff Murphy, an executive director at the company, focuses on finding ways to improve methodologies and further innovation. Murphy uses several criteria to promote and encourage corporate entrepreneurship. He believes innovation should be made an absolute business priority through:

- Encouraging cross-functional collaboration on innovation
- Incorporating innovation in performance reviews
- Publicly recognizing and rewarding innovation
- Accepting failures as a learning opportunity
- Emphasizing questions rather than emphasizing demands
- Hiring employees with diverse thinking styles, experience, perspectives, and expertise
- Implementing an idea management system
- Establishing seed funds for early innovation developments

One form of formally promoting innovation and corporate entrepreneurship is through the Johnson & Johnson venture capital subsidiary, the Johnson & Johnson Development Corporation. This area consists of many health-care and technology experts who focus on identifying early market indicators, uncovering health-care trends, and finding strategic investment opportunities. The company focuses less on financial returns and more on finding long-term strategic options for company growth. The development corporation is integrated within the corporate development of the company as a whole, playing a crucial role in promoting new revenue opportunities. The goal is to provide appropriate funds for investments focused on products or services in emerging health-care segments. Life science and technology within medical devices, consumer products, diagnostics, and pharmaceuticals are the primary focuses.

Another form of promoting and supporting corporate entrepreneurship comes from employee initiatives, such as the Web site jnjbtw.com. Marc Monseau, a Johnson & Johnson employee in media relations, created a site in 2007 for Johnson & Johnson employees to interact informally about their company. Whether it is to promote new ideas, make corrections, or discuss what the company is doing and why, the opportunity to discuss things among colleagues from around the world is available. The site even raises the issue of ways to attain corporate funds to support new ideas and inventions.

Some of the resulting innovations would not have been possible without the Johnson & Johnson corporate entrepreneurship structure and accessibility to funds:

- **1893.** Baby powder introduced and created a completely new business segment for Johnson & Johnson.
- **1889.** Dental floss, originally invented and made with leftover suture silk, introduced.
- **1921.** Band-Aid brand ready-made adhesive introduced.
- **1928.** Acuvue, disposable contact lenses, introduced.
- **1931.** Ortho-Gynol, first prescription contraceptive jelly, introduced.
- **1960s.** Johnson & Johnson's operating company, Cordis Corporation, introduced coronary stents.

What innovative product or service is next for Johnson & Johnson? With the proper setup and funding structure, there is no doubt a new breakthrough is soon on its way into consumer hands.

www.stefanlindegaard.com/2009/06/22/johnson/
www.jnj.com/connect/about-jnj/company-history/healthcare-
    innovations/?&pageNo=1
www.fundinguniverse.com/company-histories/Johnson-amp;-
    Johnson-Company-History.html
www.jjdevcorp.com/
http://medicalinnovationsummit.clevelandclinic.org/2009/10/
    corporate-venturing-in-time-of.html

Introduction

This chapter addresses these and other questions by first looking at different models of corporate entrepreneurship that can be implemented. Then some specific examples of the process already operationalized are discussed. The chapter closes with some ways to benchmark and evaluate the results.

Models of Corporate Entrepreneurship

Corporate entrepreneurship is one strategy for improving corporate performance. Internal corporate entrepreneurship occurs when the new process or new business is created within the parent company's organizational domain. External corporate venturing involves strategic investments outside the company's organizational domain. Joint corporate venturing is a form of external corporate venturing that involves a co-investment with another parent organization that results in the creation of a new organization with both parent organizations continuing to exist.

There are five overall general business models of corporate entrepreneurship.

Model 1

Model 1, according to Andrew Campbell, highlights four different types of corporate entrepreneurial business ventures: (1) ecosystem venturing, (2) innovation venturing, (3) harvest venturing, and (4) private equity venturing.[1] Ecosystem venturing refers to promoting the vivacity of the business network (customers, suppliers, distributors, and franchisees). Ecosystem venturing supports entrepreneurs in the specific business community through venture capital to improve prospects of existing businesses.[2] Value is created through the minority stakes in the invested firms.

The second type of venturing, innovation venturing, is the implementation of venture capital methods into existing functions such as research and development. This model is used to help stimulate activity by rewarding people based on the value created within an existing function.

The third type of business model is harvest venturing. This model seeks to generate cash from excess corporate resources through licensing or the sale of assets. Often, new businesses are created to fully utilize the excess resources.

Corporate private equity venturing, the fourth type, relates to company units that function as independent private equity groups to obtain financial returns.

Model 2

Model 2 identifies five types of linkages between corporate venturing (CV) and business strategy (BS) to explain how companies are venturing in ways to strategically benefit the existing company: (1) CV and BS are poorly linked or unrelated, (2) BS drives CV, (3) CV drives BS, (4) CV and BS are interdependent, and (5) CV as the BS.[3] Corporate venturing can be an internal CV whereby a new business is created within the domain of the existing company. A second type is external CV where the company is involved in creating a new business or growing a business outside of the parent company's domain. Joint CV is the third category and refers to an external CV established by the existing business and another parent organization.

Model 3

Garud and Van de Ven's model for internal corporate entrepreneurship is trial-and-error learning.[4] This model is based on the observation that the internal corporate entrepreneurial process is filled with uncertainty and ambiguity. Uncertainty is defined as the incomplete information of the underlying relationship between means and ends. The assumption is that corporate entrepreneurs will continue with the plan when the associated outcomes are positive, and when the outcomes are negative, they will stop or change their course of action. This model argues that when the level of ambiguity is high and excess resources are available, corporate entrepreneurs are more likely to persist with a course of action despite negative consequences.

Innovative companies are less likely to penalize entrepreneurs in the early stages of the development process due to the high level of uncertainty. It is more beneficial for the company to provide support through a trial-and-error process whereby the entrepreneur makes decisions based on what he believes will yield successful outcomes.

Ambiguity, on the other hand, implies incomplete information about which outcomes to pursue. When ambiguity comes into play and excess resources are available, entrepreneurs are likely to continue with a course of action despite facing negative outcomes.

Model 4

Since a company's foundation is its current business activities, corporate entrepreneurship is the introduction of a business model that is new to the company.[5]

In the company's operating core, where profits are generated in existing business activities, there is lower risk. In the business extension for growth, there is low to medium risk. Here, the company introduces new products or moves into new markets. Core ventures for renewal involve existing business activities but risk increases slightly from low to medium. As newness increases, so does risk; therefore, the noncore venturing quadrant carries the most risk.

Based on the strategic pair analysis, the business activity and the business model, from a strategic standpoint, businesses should maintain core entrepreneurial capabilities as a defense against disruptive change. Instead of noncore ventures, it is important and practical for companies to focus on corporate entrepreneurship inside the existing business structure.

Model 5

Robert A. Burgelman lays out a process model for internal corporate venturing (ICV) in major diversified firms.[6] In the process model for ICV, there are three main elements: (1) definition and impetus, (2) strategic and structural context, and (3) managerial activities. As the core processes of ICV, definition and impetus are the first step in the model process. The definition process includes the conceptualization and preventure stages of the development process. Moreover, the model involves expressing the technical and economic qualities of an ICV project so that a project develops into an embryonic business organization. The linking processes are important to demonstrating that the newly developed concept is coupled with a market need. Product championing takes the linking process further and pushes it to the impetus process.

Support within the organization is then obtained through the impetus process because market interest is created and resources are mobilized. In the impetus process, a project transforms from a venture idea into its own business. Strategic forcing is the commercialization of the new product, which needs to be combined with efforts from strategic building. In this way, both a broader strategy and an implementation of the strategy are developed for the new business.

The second element of the ICV process encompasses strategic context and structural context. Strategic context determination is the political process whereby managers of the corporate entrepreneurial business persuade corporate managers to alter the existing concept of strategy to include the new venture. The goal is to gain support from upper corporate management by showing them how the corporate entrepreneurial activity fits into current strategy and has strategic benefits. Delineation is also an important factor that helps outline the new arenas into which the business development will lead the existing company. Structural context refers to the internal selection environment in which corporate managers exert control over the ICV process.

The third element of the ICV process addresses the vital role middle-level management plays. The process is a bottom-up approach, and managers must foster support and secure resources for new venturing strategically. Management championing the new corporate entrepreneurial activity must be adept at linking the new business venture with the corporate strategy.

Specific Examples of Corporate Entrepreneurship

To better understand the way corporate entrepreneurship can work in an organization, four examples—3M, Grameen Bank, Xerox, and Google—are discussed below.

3M

Creativity, risk, innovation, and the spirit of entrepreneurship are words strongly associated with 3M (formerly Minnesota Mining and Manufacturing). Its products are ubiquitous; while some are widely well known, such as Post-it Notes and sandpaper products, others are found in medical equipment, dog food, and the Apple iPhones. In fact, to date, there are over 55,000 3M products in the market.[7] The company's secret to improving its existing products and bringing new products to market is its culture of innovation and corporate entrepreneurship. A few of its cultural characteristics are described below:

- **Fifteen percent rule.** 3M gives the right to its researchers to spend up to 15 percent of their work time pursuing whatever research idea interests them. The employees can use the time to travel to other labs and conferences, research and brainstorm, or tinker in the lab. According to Bill Coyne, 3M's head of research and development, the purpose of the 15 percent rule is that the "system has some slack in it. If you have a good idea, and the commitment to squirrel away time to work on it, and the raw nerve to skirt your lab manager's expressed desires, then go for it."[8]

- **Communication.** The company encourages researchers to seek advice from outside their own labs. To encourage the flow of ideas within the company and foster a sense of community, managers try to bring people together through such semistructured events as meetings, conferences, cross-functional teams, computer software, and databases.

- **Genesis Grants.** This is a grant awarded to company scientists by their peers for research projects that might not otherwise receive funding in part due to the particular idea not fitting in with the division's business plans. The award is up to $100,000.[9]

- **Pacing Plus.** This is a system that fast-tracks projects that have high potential to win in the market. The criteria and characteristics for the Pacing Plus program are to "change the basis of competition in new or existing markets; offer large sales and profit potential, with attractive returns on investment; receive priority access to 3M resources; operate in an accelerated time frame; and employ the best available product commercialization processes."[10] The Pacing Plus program is considered to be one of the most effective management tools used at 3M to encourage a project with high potential.

- **Goal.** 3M has instituted a corporate goal to generate 30 percent of revenue from new products introduced in the past five years. Referred to as a stretch target, this 30 percent goal helped spark creativity within the entire company.

A final factor in 3M's success with corporate entrepreneurship is management's tolerance and acceptance of high risk. The company views failure as a learning opportunity, encouraging those who want to prove the practicality or impracticality of an idea.

Grameen Bank

The implementation of corporate entrepreneurship has at its core a dire need for resources and often in its most basic form. A bamboo stool-maker in Jobra, India, by the name of Sufia Khatun was a struggling entrepreneur under the pressing restraints of high interest loans caught in a cycle of servitude to the local moneylender. In exchange for the loan, the lender required her to sell the stools back to the organization at such a low price that she made only two cents profit per day as compared to her potential earnings of $1.25. This was a common occurrence in the city of Jobra, contributing to its debilitating poverty, and was noticed by an economics professor named Muhammad Yunus in 1974.

Further investigation revealed that 47 local entrepreneurs like Khatun, who were caught in this cycle, had the potential to make considerably higher profits if relieved of the high interest debt. Yunus discovered that these entrepreneurs needed only $27 to pay off the loans and found a group of informal backers willing to invest this money at more reasonable interest rates. All 47 loans were repaid and the entrepreneurs were able to earn higher profit margins and climb above the poverty level. This was the beginning of the Grameen Bank headquartered in Bangladesh, India, and the start of the microfinance and microcredit industry.

Muhammad Yunus, the founder of the microcredit Grameen Bank, which was officially recognized by the Indian government in

1983, was the recipient of the Nobel Peace Prize. His objectives are to reach the poorest families and empower those entrepreneurs with the potential to earn wealth rather than distributing loans to those who have previously accumulated money. This allows poverty-stricken families and less developed nations to create a higher level of living without the valuable monetary resources that are so crucial as the springboard for thriving entrepreneurial activity.

The microcredit business model as practiced by the Grameen Bank is based on a conjoint goal combining economic results with social initiatives. It focuses on providing financial loans to create entrepreneurs in the poorest sectors and particularly with women living in rural areas. Yunus and Grameen Bank believe that obtaining loans at reasonable, repayable rates should be a basic right, accessible to those who need it the most. The loans are given in small increments (micro) with repayment schedules based on weekly amounts. There are no official documents protecting the repayment of the loans as they are based on the honor system (social responsibility of the group), with pay periods being extended if the recipients experience financial troubles. The loan recipients must be part of a five-person entrepreneurial group so that collectively they support one another in financial matters and in social values.

Unlike conventional loans, these are based on simple interest rather than quarterly compounded interest rates, and any excess profits (after costs are covered) are put back into the bank or are used for local initiatives such as education for children and women in these rural areas; nutritional yogurt for the malnourished; bed nets to protect villagers from malaria spread by mosquitoes; and information technology to leapfrog the rural areas into the twenty-first century. Due to its business practices, microcredit requires investors willing to earn small monetary but large social returns. Yunus and the Grameen Bank have attracted large global firms like Danone, Intel, and BASF as well as nongovernment organizations and outside governments like Norway, Sweden, and Germany as investors in backing these loans to provide entrepreneurial support in less developed areas.

Astounding positive results have occurred from its microcredit activities. Benefits include a 99 percent repayment rate with 58 percent of the borrowing families moving out of poverty. Grameen Bank has given $5.7 billion in loans since its inception to over 6.6 million people, 97 percent of whom are women. The bank now has 2,226 branches serving over 71,000 villages. As shown by the results, these entrepreneurs did indeed have enormous potential when the needed resources were available.

As of December 2010, Yunus and the Grameen Bank have been under close scrutiny by the Norwegian government and the Bangladeshi prime minister, Sheikh Hasina, for placing $100 million worth of aid funds into a spinoff organization of the bank called Grameen Kalyan. While this movement of money was explained as a way to decrease tax payments on the donations, the paper trail has not been transparent, and consequently, Grameen Bank and Yunus are experiencing negative attention for its microcredit activities. This has also called into question the unintended, destructive results of microcredit increasing suicides among those who cannot repay loans due to social pressures.

Despite this recent backlash, the goal of microcredit continues to be increasing entrepreneurial practices at the most fundamental level for the lowest economic sector. This, in turn, raises the overall wealth of a nation, enhances education and business experience for women, and ultimately increases the lifestyle of the individuals and their families. Promoting entrepreneurship is closely linked to allowing those individuals to gain control of their lives, increase independence, fulfill market niche needs of rural areas, and achieve higher standards of living.

Xerox

Xerox traces its history back to 1906, when the Haloid Company was incorporated to make and sell photographic paper. After decades of innovative distinction in the market, Xerox's competitive edge began eroding; the company faced losing $273 million in 2001.[11] As a result, Anne Mulcahy, then COO, was appointed as the new CEO and led Xerox's return to the market with a competitive fervor. Contributing to Xerox's competitive edge are its acquisitions of companies with new technologies and access to customers that fit into the Xerox corporate strategy. Another way Xerox maintains its innovative edge is through its renowned research and development program.

Acquisitions play a major role in Xerox's corporate entrepreneurship model. The strategy gives Xerox access to both new customers and technology. As an example, Xerox spent $1.2 billion to acquire Global Imaging, an office equipment distributor. From the deal, Xerox gained access to 200,000 more customers. In early 2010, Affiliated Computer Services Inc. (ACS) was acquired, giving Xerox access to new business and government clients, technologies related to business process outsourcing, and information technology services. In November 2010, Xerox acquired Spur Information Solutions, a company with software for parking enforcement.

Xerox's research and development program has long been the engine of growth for the company. R&D is so important to the company's long-term growth that in the face of enormous debt, Mulcahy and Ursula Burns (then COO and now current CEO) cut costs elsewhere in the company rather than subject its coveted R&D to shrinking budgets. The annual R&D budget at Xerox is around $1.5 billion. The Xerox Innovation Group comprises four research facilities. The facility in Toronto, Canada, works with materials; the facility in Grenoble, France, deals completely with intelligent documents; the facility in Rochester, New York, researches next generation systems; and the most well-known research facility, the Palo Alto Research Center (PARC), is located near Stanford University in California. This research structure has three roles. The first is the explorer role that involves fostering and pushing creativity to formulate innovative ideas. The second role is as incubator, where the ideas are analyzed in the labs to see whether they are appropriate for further company investments to bring to market. This essential role underscores the company's intrapreneurial spirit. The third role is that of the partnership role, whereby business group engineers have the challenge of formulating the idea into an actual service or product.

PARC plays a vital role in Xerox's innovative success; it is estimated that 95 percent of Xerox's products can be attributed to PARC. Researchers at PARC are given credit for inventing the personal computer, laser printing, and the Ethernet. Some of the researchers are referred to as "work-practice specialists" who observe real life office operations and note where efficiencies can be made and new technologies introduced. The eclectic group of scholars includes scientists, engineers, anthropologists, physicists, artists, and psychologists. Guiding Xerox's research function is what are referred to as the Six Ss: simpler, speedier, smaller, smarter, more secure, and socially responsible.

Open face-to-face discussions on ideas are encouraged, and the researchers are also heavily involved in blogging and contributing to an intercompany wiki. Xerox strongly believes in creating the most conducive environment for creative thinking; the belief embedded within the company culture is that the best ideas and strategies do not come from top-down but from within. The culture encourages creative thinking, corporate entrepreneurship where employees are challenged to consider how the idea fits into the entire value chain, and loyalty and long-term vision for Xerox.

Google

Google is a good example of a company engaged in corporate entrepreneurship. Google has long invested in start-up companies. In March 2009, Google announced that despite the economic downturn, it was creating a $100 million venture fund to invest in exceptional start-ups in consumer Internet software, biotechnology, and health care. The company also invests millions of dollars in other projects that involve driverless cars, wind turbines, and lunar robots. Google often invests in projects that do not seem connected to the company's core competencies in order to innovate in the industry's rapidly changing environment.

Google's corporate entrepreneurship spirit is rooted in innovation. Among the notable ways in which Google fosters the most conducive environment for creativity are:

- **Culture**. Google goes to great lengths to hire people who are the best fit for the company culture. It rewards those who are the most capable and offer the best ideas. Risk taking, creativity, and innovativeness are among the characteristics that help employees fit in at Google. The layout of the offices is designed to foster more communication among the employees. Google conducts Friday meetings where all employees meet over beer and are encouraged to speak candidly.
- **Budgeted time for innovation**. Technical employees are encouraged to spend 20 percent of their time on self-selected independent projects.[12] Even managers have time allotted to spend on special innovative projects. Managers spend 70 percent of their time on the core business, 20 percent to related but different projects, and 10 percent to new businesses and ideas.
- **Qualification process**. Ideas are modeled, piloted, and tested in controlled experiments before becoming authorized projects. The amount of time for an idea to become an authorized project is not long.
- **Crowd sourcing**. Google lets its users decide which products are best among a set of product offerings. The company strategy is to note the most useful ones and give them more development.
- **Tolerance for risk, failure, and chaos**. In order to introduce innovative products, Google encourages risk taking. The company has a high tolerance for failure and chaos, and it hopes

that Google employees learn quickly from mistakes and move forward with creating the next innovative products.

The keystones of the company's strategy are innovation, passion, and risk taking. Indeed Google is a good model of corporate entrepreneurship.

Implementing and Evaluating a Corporate Entrepreneurship Program

Implementing a corporate entrepreneurship program as well as evaluating the results varies significantly by company, depending on the organization's objectives. Some of the major issues include: determining the most appropriate corporate entrepreneurship model; committing the entire organization to the concept of corporate entrepreneurship for at least a three-year period; "thawing" any "frozen" obstacles (permafrost) in the organization that would inhibit corporate entrepreneurship; identifying corporate entrepreneurs; and developing an appropriate compensation scheme.

Implementing

As has been indicated in the examples in this chapter as well as in each of the chapter scenarios, there are many ways to implement and operationalize a corporate entrepreneurship program. A general approach, which can be tailored to the specific objectives of an organization, is indicated below.

Developing a Corporate Entrepreneurship Program

- Develop the vision and objectives of the program with key members of the management team.
- Develop example(s) of the proposal to be submitted; establish the evaluation criteria; and determine the amount of money available.
- Select members of the evaluation committee.

- Announce the start of a program with proposal submissions due in four to six weeks.
- Select winning proposals.
- Form venture teams.
- Communicate results and provide information on the program internally throughout the company on a regular basis.
- Implement and structure corporate entrepreneurial activity and climate.

Vision Statement

The first step in the process is for the CEO and key members of the management team to develop the vision (mission) of the program. It is extremely important to avoid the syndrome, "Without a detailed map, many roads will get you there." Aspects of vision statements of several companies are indicated in Table 12.1. Some common elements in these mission statements are customer focus; quality product or service; employees are important; innovative activity; consistent quality delivery of product or service; and ethics and social responsibility.

Elements of Program

Once the vision for the corporate entrepreneurship program has been established, several examples of a submission for support of a corporate entrepreneurial idea should be written. Ideally, these would be examples of the submission itself but at least should contain the elements needed. Having these examples has significantly increased the number of corporate entrepreneurship proposals received in companies being assisted by one of the authors. Also, the proposal evaluation criteria and the amount of money available should be determined.

Evaluation Committee

A committee that will be evaluating the proposals needs to then be established. This committee needs to include an individual from

TABLE 12.1 Core of Mission Statements of Selected U.S. Companies

3M	Innovation "Thou shalt not kill a new product idea" Absolute integrity Respect for individual initiative and personal growth Tolerance for honest mistakes; Product quality and reliability
American Express	Heroic customer service Worldwide reliability of services Encouragement of individual initiative
Ford	People as the source of our strength Products as the "end result of our efforts" (we care about cars) Profits as a necessary means and measure for our success Basic honesty and integrity
General Electric	Improving the quality of life through technology and innovation Interdependent balance between responsibility to customers, employees, society, and shareholders (no clear hierarchy) Individual responsibility and opportunity Honesty and integrity
Merck	"We are in the business of preserving and improving human life. All of our actions must be measured by our success in achieving this goal." Honesty and integrity Corporate social responsibility Science-based innovation, not imitation Unequivocal excellence in all aspects of the company Profit, but profit from work that benefits humanity
Nordstrom	Service to the customer above all else Hard work and productivity Continuous improvement, never being satisfied Excellence in reputation, being part of something special
Procter & Gamble	Product excellence Continuous self-improvement Honesty and fairness Respect and concern for the individual
Walmart	"We exist to provide to our customers"—to make their lives better via lower prices and greater selection; all else is secondary Swim upstream, buck conventional wisdom Be in partnership with employees Work with passion, commitment, and enthusiasm Run lean Pursue ever-higher goals

each important functional area and should reflect some diversity in terms of position in the company. The CEO or head of the division should not be a member of the selection committee. Being a member of the committee compromises the ability of the CEO or division head to champion the entire program.

Program Announcement

The next step is to announce the program throughout the company about four to six weeks before the proposal submission deadline. The announcement should include examples or elements of the submission required, the amount of money available, the evaluation criteria, and the members of the evaluation committee. The proposal announcement should come from the highest-level position in the group involved such as the CEO or division head and should include an enthusiastic message encouraging every employee to participate. This support will significantly increase the degree of participation and the number of proposals submitted.

Proposal Selection

At the same time the winning proposals are selected and announced, carefully crafted letters indicating why other proposals were not accepted, along with encouragement to submit a proposal in the next round of proposals, should be sent to the individuals submitting proposals that were not funded. Complete transparency is needed in the selection process in order to establish an environment that is very positive for the corporate entrepreneurship activities.

Venture Team Formation

Where needed, the individuals with the winning proposals should be helped in their selection of a venture team. While assistance should be available, the corporate entrepreneur should make the final decision and ask whoever he or she feels would be a good team member. Alternative individuals should be identified, as usually some of the individuals asked will not want to participate. It is extremely important that no employee be forced to participate as companies have experienced problems when this occurs.

Communicate Results

In order for the corporate entrepreneurship process to become an integral part of the corporate culture, information on the activities of the funded venture proposals should be distributed regularly throughout the company. An internal company newsletter or at least e-mail blasts are two means to accomplish this. Periodically, the CEO or division head should show support through the same medium. Successes should be celebrated.

Implement Program

The second date for proposals should be announced at least four weeks before the due date; ideally, it would be announced along with the selection of the winning proposals of the first round. This enhances the acceptance of the program and makes it a regular activity of the company and part of the corporate culture. One of the authors has had good success in implementing corporate entrepreneurship programs in both large and medium-sized companies using this approach. The actual corporate entrepreneurship program differed significantly by company, reflecting its vision and objectives.

Benefits of a Corporate Entrepreneurship Program

The benefits of establishing and implementing a corporate entrepreneurship program will be discussed in terms of benefits to the company and benefits to the employees.

Benefits to Company

The principal benefits of corporate entrepreneurship to the company are indicated below. One of the most important benefits is the increase in morale through the establishment of a new corporate culture. Employees will "own their jobs" and want to make their positions operate in the best possible, most efficient ways. The new culture will make it fun for employees to come to work.

Benefits of Corporate Entrepreneurship to the Company
- Establishing a new culture, better morale
- Reduction in employee turnover
- Motivated workforce
- New business concepts
- New ways of doing things
- More flexible organizational structure
- Organizational learning
- Positive impact on revenues and profits

Employees liking what they do results in a reduction in employee turnover. Given the high cost of recruiting, hiring, and training a new employee, higher retention rates result in substantial savings as well as retaining trained, experienced employees.

Employees are motivated to make sure the company does as well as possible. Can you imagine the quality of output and performance that result from an experienced, motivated team? These highly motivated employees will contribute to increase in revenues, reduction of costs, and increase in profits.

Corporate entrepreneurship provides new business concepts. These can include new products or services, better systems, and new ways of doing things. These new ways of doing things will be the norm as employees are encouraged to try new things for the best performance of their positions. Failure will be allowed and experimentation encouraged.

This will result in the company evolving into a more flexible organizational structure. There will be little or no turf protection, and teams can be easily formed to carry a project from start to finish. New products or services and new customers will occur and present customers will be more satisfied.

With flexibility and newness constantly occurring, organizational learning will be an integral part of the company's operation. Learning results in employees being able to do multiple jobs, grow in their own competencies, and increase the productivity of the company.

All these benefits will result in increased revenues and profits. New products or services, new customers, and more efficient operations will reduce operational costs, increase revenues, and increase profits.

Benefits to Employees

The major benefits of corporate entrepreneurship to the employees are shown below. With a flexible organizational structure and corporate entrepreneurial culture, employees will feel self-actualized. Experiencing self-achievement will in turn enhance loyalty, efficiency, and performance.

Benefits of Corporate Entrepreneurship to the Employee

- Feeling of self-achievement
- More job satisfaction
- Increased skills
- Financial and nonfinancial rewards
- Excited to come to work
- Able to be creative

Increased job satisfaction is a common result of corporate entrepreneurship. With a culture of trial-and-error and try-and-experiment, employees actively make sure their jobs are done in the best possible way to the extent of being excited to come to work. This is perhaps the greatest benefit of corporate entrepreneurship for employees. Employees who are happy with their jobs and the company will make sure everything possible is done for the company to grow and prosper.

With a learning organization operating, employees will increase their skills. And of course employees with increased skills feel better about themselves and their ability to perform better and more efficiently.

Financial and nonfinancial rewards will be given to employees involved. Performance-based pay rewards will regularly occur, as will nonfinancial rewards. Successful activities will be heralded, rewarded, and made known throughout the organization. The trial-and-error culture will allow employees to be more creative and open to change the way their jobs are done, to invent new processes, and to develop new products and services.

Evaluating the Results

A company implementing corporate entrepreneurship needs to establish a system to evaluate the results. One of the authors has had good success in establishing two overall evaluation procedures: benchmarking and measurements of output.

Benchmarking

In order to understand the impact of corporate entrepreneurship on the overall company culture, benchmarking should be done before the program starts, then every six months for the first two years, and once a year starting in the third year. An overall good benchmarking tool is indicated in Table 12.2. This table is composed of pairs of words or phrases that each person involved in the program should rate on a scale of one through seven. One of the authors has tried variations of this scale, such as one through five and one through nine. One through five ratings do not give enough dispersion in the data, as individuals have the habit of avoiding the extremes, and one through nine causes some confusion because of the nine points on the scale. A one through seven scale provides a midpoint—four—where there is no opinion on the direction of the variable.

Table 12.2 shows some general pairs of variables aimed at determining the impact of the corporate venturing program. These

TABLE 12.2   Benchmarking Cultural Values and Norms

Traditional Organizational Culture	→	Corporate Entrepreneurial Culture	Rating 1 through 7
Fragmentation	→	Wholeness	
Instruction	→	Vision	
Controlled	→	Freedom to act	
Dislike coming to work	→	Like coming to work	
Having no responsibility	→	Having responsibility	
Nonmotivated	→	Enthusiasm and motivation	
Defined limits	→	Few barriers	
Limiting people	→	Growing people	

include such benchmarking variables as: instruction–vision; dislike coming to work–like coming to work; distrust–trust; and limiting people–growing people. Some, if not all, of these should be used along with any specific pairs of variables the company wants to use to measure any changes in the corporate culture. Launching and implementing a solid corporate entrepreneurship program causes a shift in the company from a traditional organizational culture to an entrepreneurial culture. The most significant change will occur in the first two years and should be measured twice a year.

Output Measurements

A corporate entrepreneurship program should impact the operations of a company in addition to changing the culture. The following six measurements should be taken at the same time each year for the first two years, and once a year starting in the third year:

- Amount of cost reduction achieved (currency)
- Amount of increased revenue achieved (currency)
- Employee turnover (actual number and percentage of workforce)

- Customer turnover (actual number and percentage of customers)
- Percent of total company sales from products or services introduced in last five years
- Percent of total company sales from new customers obtained in the last three years

A company with a sound corporate entrepreneurship program should experience a decrease in costs, an increase in revenues, less employee turnover, less customer turnover, a higher percentage of sales coming from new products or services introduced in the last five years, and a higher percentage of sales from new customers obtained in the last three years.

These benefits should start occurring in the second year of the program if not before. Some companies one of the authors worked with achieved positive results in the first year.

Summary

This chapter focused on implementing a corporate entrepreneurship program. Following the introduction of five general models, some in-depth case histories of companies were discussed. A general implementation procedure was presented that can be modified for any company desiring to implement a corporate entrepreneurship program. The benefits to both the company and the employees were discussed. The chapter concludes with a discussion of a benchmarking instrument and six measurements of output. Each of these should be administered to individuals participating in the corporate entrepreneurship program before the program starts and on a regular basis thereafter.

Notes

Chapter 1

1. John Stuart Mill, *Principles of Political Economy with Some of Their Applications to Social Philosophy*, London: Longman, 1848, 45–60.
2. Robert D. Hisrich, Michael P. Peters, and Dean A. Shepherd, *Entrepreneurship* (8th ed.), Chicago: McGraw-Hill/Irwin, 2010, 6–10.
3. William D. Guth and Ari Ginsberg, "Corporate Entrepreneurship," *Strategic Management Journal* (special issue) 11 (4), 1990, 5–15.

Chapter 2

1. P. F. Drucker, *Innovation and Entrepreneurship: Practice and Principles*, London: Butterworth-Heinemann, 1985, 43.
2. R. M. Kanter, "When a Thousand Flowers Bloom: Structural, Collective and Social Conditions for Innovation in Organizations," *Research in Organizational Behavior* 10, 1988, 169–211.
3. D. C. McClelland, "Achievement Motivation Can Be Developed," *Harvard Business Review* 43 (6), November/December 1965, 6–25.
4. D. C. McClelland, *The Achieving Society*, Princeton, New Jersey: D. Van Nostrand, 1961, 67 and 205.
5. P. A. Abetti, "The Birth and Growth of Toshiba's Laptop and Notebook Computers: A Case Study in Japanese Corporate Venturing," *Journal of Business Venturing* 12 (6), 1997, 507–529.

Chapter 3

1. John P. Kotter, "Leading Change: Why Transformation Efforts Fail," *Harvard Business Review*, March–April 1995, 50–62.

Chapter 4

1. For an in-depth presentation on focus group interviews in general and quantitative applications, see "Conference Focuses on Focus Groups: Guidelines, Reports, and 'The Magic Plaque,'" *Marketing News*, May 21, 1976, 8; Keith K. Cox, James B. Higginbotham, and John Burton, "Application of Focus Group Interviews in Marketing," *Journal of Marketing*, 40, no. 1, January 1976, 77–80; and Robert D. Hisrich and Michael P. Peters, "Focus Groups: An Innovative Marketing Research Technique," *Hospital and Health Service Administration*, 27, no. 4, July–August 1982, 8–21.
2. Jena McGregor, "The World's Most Innovative Companies," *Business-Week*, April 24, 2006, www.businessweek.com/magazine/content/06_17/b3981401.htm.

Chapter 5

Chapter 6

1. H. Chesbrough, "Designing Corporate Ventures in the Shadow of Private Venture Capital," *California Management Review* 42 (3), 2000, 31–50.
2. Gregory G. Dess, Abdul M. Rasheed, Kevin J. McLaughlin, and Richard L. Priem, "The New Corporate Architecture," *Academy of Management Executive* 9 (3), 1995, 7–20.
3. Daniel A. Levinthal and James G. March, "The Myopia of Learning," *Strategic Management Journal* 14 (S2), 1993, 95–112.
4. Zi-Lin He and Poh-Kam Wong, "Exploration vs. Exploitation: An Empirical Test of the Ambidexterity Hypothesis," *Organization Science* 15 (4), 2004, 481–494.
5. Arie Y. Lewin, Chris P. Long, and Timothy N. Carroll, "The Co-evolution of New Organizational Forms," *Organization Science* 10 (5), 1999, 535–550.
6. Rita Gunther McGrath, "Exploratory Learning, Innovative Capacity, and Managerial Oversight," *Academy of Management Journal* 44 (1) 2001, 118–131.

Chapter 7

1. Michael H. Morris, Donald F. Kuratko, and Jeffrey G. Covin, *Corporate Entrepreneurship and Innovation*, Mason, Ohio: Thomson/South-Western, Chapter 14, 2008, 375–377.

2. Michael H. Morris, Jeffrey Allen, Minet Schindehutte, and Ramon Avila, "Balanced Management Control Systems as a Mechanism for Achieving Corporate Entrepreneurship," *Journal of Management Inquiry* 18 (4), 2006, 468–493.

Chapter 8

1. D. A. Buchanan, "You Stab My Back, I'll Stab Yours: Management Experience and Perceptions of Organization Political Behavior," *British Journal of Management* 19, 2008, 49–64.

Chapter 9

Chapter 10

1. James Clayton, Bradley Gambill, and Douglas Harned, "The Curse of Too Much Capital: Building New Businesses in Large Corporations," *The McKinsey Quarterly* 3, 1999, 48–59.
2. Michael Beer, Rakesh Khurana, and James Weber, Harvard Business School Case: Hewlett-Packard: Culture in Changing Times, February 5, 2004.

Chapter 11

1. This material was adapted from Robert D. Hisrich, Michael P. Peters, and Dean A. Shepherd, *Entrepreneurship,* eighth edition, New York: McGraw-Hill/Irwin, 2010. 341–344.

Chapter 12

1. Andrew Campbell, Julian Bradshaw, Andy Morrison, and Robert van Basten Batenburg, "The Future of Corporate Venturing," *MIT Sloan Management Review* 45 (1), 2003, 30, ABI/INFORM Global, ProQuest Web, September 30, 2010.
2. Robert Park and Andrew Campbell, *The Growth Gamble*, London: Nicholas Brealey International, 2005, 10–32.
3. Jeffrey G. Covin and Morgan P. Miles, "Strategic Use of Corporate Venturing," *Entrepreneurship: Theory & Practice*, March 2007, 183–207, ABI/INFORM Global, ProQuest Web, September 30, 2010.
4. Raghu Garud and Andrew H. Van de Ven, "An Empirical Evaluation of the Internal Corporate Venturing Process," *Strategic Management*

Journal, Summer 1992, 93, ABI/INFORM Global, ProQuest Web, September 30, 2010.

5. William Buckland, "Defining What Corporate Venturing Actually Is and What Firms Should Do about It," *Strategic Direction* 19 (9), September 2003, ABI/INFORM Global, ProQuest Web, September 30, 2010.

6. Robert A Burgelman, "A Process Model of Internal Corporate Venturing in the Diversified Major Firm," *Administrative Quarterly* 28, 1983, ProQuest Web, September 30, 2010.

7. Marc Gunther, Marilyn Adamo, and Betsy Feldman, "3M's Innovation Revival," *Fortune* 162 (5), 2010, 73–76, EBSCO Host Web, October 5, 2010.

8. Ernest Gundling, *The 3M Way to Innovation*, Tokyo: Kodansha International, 2000, 45.

9. Marc Gunther, Marilyn Adamo, and Betsy Feldman, "3M's Innovation Revival," *Fortune* 162 (5), 2010, 73–76, EBSCO Host Web, October 5, 2010.

10. Ernest Gundling, *The 3M Way to Innovation*, Tokyo: Kodansha International, 2000, 46.

11. J. P. Donlon, "The X Factor," *Chief Executive*, June 2008, 234, ABI/INFORM Global, 26–31.

12. Bala Iyer and Thomas H. Davenport, "Reverse Engineering Google's Innovation Machine," *Harvard Business Review*, April 2008, 59–68, EBSCO Host Web, November 28 2010.

Suggested Readings

Chapter 1

Barringer, Bruce R., and Allen C. Bluedorn, "The Relationship between Corporate Entrepreneurship and Strategic Management," *Strategic Management Journal* 20 (5), 1999, 421–444.

> *In this article, the authors examine the relationship between corporate entrepreneurship intensity and five specific strategic management practices. The five strategic management practices include scanning intensity, planning flexibility, planning horizon, locus of planning, and control attributes. The results of their study indicated a positive relationship between corporate entrepreneurship intensity and scanning intensity, planning flexibility, locus of planning, and strategic controls.*

Burgelman, Robert A., "Managing the Internal Corporate Entrepreneurship Process," *Sloan Management Review* 25 (2), 1984, 33–48.

> *The author conceptualizes the internal corporate entrepreneurship process in this article, which suggests that vicious circles and managerial dilemmas typically emerge in the development of new ventures. This article presents four major recommendations for improving the effectiveness of a firm's internal corporate entrepreneurship strategy.*

Busenitz, Lowell, and Jay Barney, "Differences between Entrepreneurs and Managers in Large Organizations: Biases and Heuristics in Strategic Decision Making," *Journal of Business Venturing* 12 (1), 1997, 9–30.

> *In this article, the authors explore the differences in the decision-making processes between entrepreneurs and managers in large organizations. In particular, they focus on a number of biases,*

such as the overconfidence bias, but also point out some benefits from the use of biases and heuristics.

Doyle, Corner Patricia, and Marcus Ho, "How Opportunities Develop in Social Entrepreneurship," *Entrepreneurship, Theory and Practice* 34 (4), 2010, 635–659.

In this article, the authors' purpose is to extend existing research on opportunity identification in the social entrepreneurship literature through empirically examining this phenomenon. In particular, they ask the following research question: How are opportunities to create social value identified and exploited?

Haynie, J. Michael, Dean Shepherd, Elaine Mosakowski, and P. Christopher Earley, "A Situated Metacognitive Model of the Entrepreneurial Mindset," *Journal of Business Venturing* 25 (2), 2010, 217–229.

In this article, the authors develop a framework to investigate the foundations of an "entrepreneurial mindset," described by scholars as the ability to sense, act, and mobilize under uncertain conditions. The authors focus on metacognitive processes that enable the entrepreneur to think beyond or reorganize existing knowledge structures and heuristics, promoting adaptable cognitions in the face of novel and uncertain decision contexts.

Parker, Simon C., "Intrapreneurship or Entrepreneurship?" *Journal of Business Venturing* 26 (1), 2011, 19–34.

In this article, the author explores the factors that determine whether new business opportunities are exploited by starting a new venture for an employer (nascent intrapreneurship) or independently (nascent entrepreneurship). The author develops theoretical arguments and tests hypotheses about the factors promoting nascent intrapreneurship relative to nascent entrepreneurship.

Chapter 2

Baron, A. Robert, and Tang Jintong, "The Role of Entrepreneurs in Firm-Level Innovation: Joint Effects of Positive Affect, Creativity, and Environmental Dynamism," *Journal of Business Venturing* 26 (1), 2011, 49–60.

In this article, the authors investigate the joint effects on firm level innovation of two variables pertaining to entrepreneurs (their positive effect and creativity) and a key environmental variable (environmental dynamism). Findings of the research indicate that positive effect among founding entrepreneurs is significantly related to their creativity and that creativity, in turn, is positively related to firm-level innovation. Both of these relationships are moderated by environmental dynamism, being stronger in highly dynamic than stable environments.

Brundin, Ethel, Patzelt Holger, and Dean A. Shepherd, "Managers' Emotional Displays and Employees' Willingness to Act Entrepreneurially," *Journal of Business Venturing* 23 (2), 2008, 221–243.

In this article, the authors analyze how and why emotional displays of managers influence the willingness of employees to act entrepreneurially. Their findings show that managers' displays of confidence and satisfaction about entrepreneurial projects enhance employees' willingness to act entrepreneurially, whereas displays of frustration, worry, and bewilderment diminish employees' willingness.

Burgelman, A. Robert, "A Process Model of Internal Corporate Venturing in the Diversified Major Firm," *Administrative Science Quarterly* 28 (2), 1983, 223–244.

The author in this article reports findings of the internal corporate venturing (ICV) process in a diversified major firm. It presents a grounded process model of the interlocking activities of managers at different levels in the organization, which constitutes the strategic process by which new ventures take shape. Successful ICV efforts are shown to depend on the availability of autonomous entrepreneurial activity on the part of operational level participants, the ability of middle-level managers to conceptualize the strategic implications of these initiatives in more general system terms, and the capacity of top management to allow viable entrepreneurial initiatives to change the corporate strategy.

Gumusluoglu, Lale, and Arzu Ilsev, "Transformational Leadership and Organizational Innovation: The Roles of Internal and External Support for Innovation," *Journal of Product Innovation Management* 26 (3), 2009, 264–277.

In this article, the authors investigate the impact of transformational leadership on organizational innovation and endeavor to determine whether internal and external support for innovation as contextual conditions influence this effect. Their results provide support for the positive influence of transformational leadership on organizational innovation.

Ireland, R. Duane, Jeffrey G. Covin, and Donald F. Kuratko, "Conceptualizing Corporate Entrepreneurship Strategy," *Entrepreneurship Theory and Practice* 31 (1), 2009, 19–46.

In this article, the authors conceptualize the components of corporate entrepreneurship (CE) to include: (1) the antecedents of CE strategy (i.e., individual entrepreneurial cognitions of the organization's members and external environmental conditions that invite entrepreneurial activity), (2) the elements of CE strategy (i.e., top management's entrepreneurial strategic vision for the firm, organizational architectures that encourage entrepreneurial processes and behavior, and the generic forms of entrepreneurial process that are reflected in entrepreneurial behavior), and (3) the outcomes of CE strategy (i.e., organizational outcomes resulting from entrepreneurial actions, including the development of competitive capability and strategic repositioning).

Kelley, J. Donna, and Hyunsuk Lee, "Managing Innovation Champions: The Impact of Project Characteristics on the Direct Manager Role," *Journal of Product Innovation Management* 27 (7), 2010, 1007–1019.

The authors investigate when to lend direct managerial support, and how much support, to those championing entrepreneurial projects. Their research provides insights into the connection between project characteristics and the type and frequency of direct manager involvement. Overall, the article suggests that both empowerment and manager roles are relevant to the management of innovation.

Chapter 3

Burgelman, Robert A., and Liisa Välikangas, "Managing Internal Corporate Venturing Cycles," *MIT Sloan Management Review* 46 (4), Summer 2005, 26–34.

Internal corporate venturing (ICV) is believed to be cyclical in nature: firms invest in ICV, which eventually gets closed down, but eventually invest in ICV again, which continues the cyclical process. ICV is somewhat dependent on financial resources that may not be entirely committed to the venture and on the growth of the firm's primary business. ICV cyclicality factors are analyzed and discussed in this article. The most optimal venturing results are obtained when firm executives understand the importance of ICV to their business model.

Chakravarth, Bala and Peter Lorange, "Driving Renewal: The Entrepreneur–Manager," *Journal of Business Strategy* 29 (2), 2008, 14–21.

Business renewal strategies help ensure a company's continuity by extending and protecting the business. However, the effectiveness of a firm's renewal strategies are dependent on the ability of top managers to affirm the firm's broad vision and establish the pace and scope of the renewal strategies. Additionally, success depends on the ability to promote the renewal agenda among the company units.

Ernst, Holger, Peter Witt, and German Brachtendorf, "Corporate Venture Capital as a Strategy for External Innovation: An Exploratory Empirical Study," *R&D Management* 35 (3), 2005, 233–242.

Studies reveal that large corporations that encompass a corporate venture capital unit tend to pursue external innovation endeavors. This study of 21 German companies with corporate venture units analyzes whether or not the ventures follow the traditionally accepted CVC management strategies. CVCs that incorporate mixed objectives, such as short-term financial planning, and lack effective management and/or corporate organization perform poorly and are often unable to attain long-term benefits from their venture programs.

Maine, Elicia, "Radical Innovation through Internal Corporate Venturing: Degussa's Commercialization of Nanomaterials," *R&D Management* 38 (4), September 2008, 359–371.

Internal corporate entrepreneurship in well-established companies must be strategically designed and managed in order to ensure that radical innovation, rather than incremental innovation, is maintained. Companies need to take advantage of their current capabilities and their complementary assets to ensure such radical innovation. Evnoik Degussa, a chemical firm, serves as an example of a company making the most of its advantages and overcoming its managerial and organizational challenges to promote the desired innovative culture.

Vanhaverbeke, Wim, Vareska Van de Vrande, and Henry Chesbrough, "Understanding the Advantages of Open Innovation Practices in Corporate Venturing in Terms of Real Options," *Creativity and Innovation Management* 17 (4), 2008, 251–258.

Companies that plan to be innovative must create a culture within the organization that promotes open innovation. Corporate entrepreneurship, often a high-risk pursuit, benefits from open innovation in several ways: new business opportunities or technologies are discovered early on; committing significant financial resources is often unnecessary until the venture has proven to be a probable success; a venture has the capability to exit the market without significant losses; and in the case that a venture becomes spun off from the parent company, its exit is typically delayed.

Chapter 4

Hayton, James C., and Donna J. Kelley, "A Competency-Based Framework for Promoting Corporate Entrepreneurship," *Human Resource Management* 45 (3), Fall 2006, 407–427.

Competitive advantage is often attained through a company's ability to innovate and engage in corporate entrepreneurship. This report discusses the diverse activities involved in corporate entrepreneurship, such as developing internal and external ventures and developing a variety of business models.

Husted, Kenneth, and Christian Vintergaard, "Stimulating Innovation through Corporate Venture Bases," *Journal of World Business* 39 (3), August 2004, 296–306.

The process of corporate entrepreneurship takes specific planning by management. This paper focuses on the initial steps that must be taken by venture management to promote the development of original and innovative ideas, which can lead to a venture base.

O'Leary-Collins, Michael, "A Powerful Business Model for Capturing Innovation," *Management Services* 49 (2), Summer 2005, 37–39.

> *It is no secret that companies face risk when attempting to increase their business potential. A study is performed on ways to minimize this risk through efficiently connecting technologies, funding, and ambition, while carefully selecting start-up companies to invest in. As a general rule, diversification of project investments is a safe strategy, as only some innovations will result in high profits.*

Rohrbeck, René, Mario Döhler, and Heinrich Arnold, "Creating Growth with Externalization of R&D Results—the Spin-Along Approach," *Global Business and Organizational Excellence* 28 (4), May 2009, 44.

> *In recent years, businesses have trended toward outsourcing and restructuring and are now looking for new growth and business opportunities. Growth is limited in most companies with such an organizational structure, which creates the desire to search for expansion in new business areas through corporate venturing. Internal and external ventures are analyzed with the constraints of such business structures.*

Thornberry, Neal E., "Corporate Entrepreneurship: Teaching Managers to Be Entrepreneurs," *Journal of Management Development* 22 (4), 2003, 329–344.

> *Corporate entrepreneurship is necessary for companies to engage in during good and bad economic times. This article looks at whether corporate entrepreneurship needs strong entrepreneurial leadership and how large companies can train their management-level employees to become corporate entrepreneurs.*

Vintergaard, Christian, "Opportunities in Corporate Venturing—Actors Creating Passageways," *International Journal of Innovation Management* 9 (2), June 2005, 215–239.

> *This article presents a broad understanding of the players involved in corporate venturing through a report on Danish corporate entrepreneurship capitalists. Specifically, the paper presents the complexity of technological and market capabilities required to pursue new discoveries.*

Chapter 5

Burgers, J. Henri, Justin J. P. Jansen, Frans A. J. Van den Bosch, and Henk W. Volberda, "Structural Differentiation and Corporate Venturing: The Moderating Role of Formal and Informal Integration Mechanisms," *Journal of Business Venturing* 24 (3), 2009, 206–220.

> *The existence of corporate entrepreneurship within an organization to promote positive strategic renewal and company existence is undoubted. The way an organization should be structured to maximize the corporate entrepreneurship results, however, is still under debate. This report explains the positive results when a firm has structural differentiation and employees share a vision, though socially assimilated senior managers tend to be ineffective concerning venturing.*

Callaway, Stephen K., and Robert D. Hamilton, "Exploring Disruptive Technology: The Structure and Control of Internal Corporate Ventures," *International Journal of Organizational Analysis* 14 (2), 2006, 87–106.

> *Internal corporate entrepreneurship is affected not only by internal company disruptions but also by disruptions caused by the uncertainty of the environment the company is in. The resource dependence theory and institutional theory are examined to develop a proposed relationship between the external factors and internal organizational setup of organizations. The relationship is attributed to the organization and strategy of internal corporate ventures.*

Christensen, Karina Skovvang, "Enabling Intrapreneurship: The Case of a Knowledge-Intensive Industrial Company," *European Journal of Innovation Management* 8 (3), 2005, 305–322.

> *This study focuses on identifying the factors and management structure of successful entrepreneurship within a knowledge-intensive industrial firm. The results point to five factors that encourage intrapreneurship and identify several intrapreneurship inhibiting factors.*

Hayton, James C., and Donna J. Kelley, "A Competency-Based Framework for Promoting Corporate Entrepreneurship," *Human Resource Management* 45 (3), Fall 2006, 407–427.

> *The competitive advantage of a company is largely derived from corporate entrepreneurship. This advantage, however, requires a*

specific corporate environment that includes innovation in products and processes, the development of internal as well as external corporate ventures, and the creation of new business models. Additionally, the need for superior human capital competencies is vital in order to ensure a successful venture.

Leary, Myleen M., and Michael L. DeVaughn, "Entrepreneurial Team Characteristics That Influence the Successful Launch of a New Venture," *Management Research News* 32 (6), 2009, 567–579.

The characteristics that an organization should encompass in order to create a successful internal entrepreneurial team have often been debated. This study focuses on identifying the management structure of successful entrepreneurship within banks: CEOs should be involved in the venture process, equity per member should be limited to 10 percent, less industry experience is better than more experience, and a higher proportion of the team members should have prior founding experience.

Chapter 6

Dess, Gregory G., G. T. Lumpkin, and Jeffrey E. McGee, "Linking Corporate Entrepreneurship to Strategy, Structure, and Process: Suggested Research Directions," *Entrepreneurship: Theory & Practice* 23 (3), 1999, 85–102.

In this article, the authors discuss corporate entrepreneurship's unique relationship with strategy, structure, and process issues, and the difficulties of fostering corporate entrepreneurship in a traditional hierarchical organization.

Lumpkin, G. T., Claudia C. Cogliser, and Dawn R. Schneider, "Understanding and Measuring Autonomy: An Entrepreneurial Orientation Perspective," *Entrepreneurship Theory & Practice* 33 (1), 2009, 47–69.

The authors, in this article, address the theoretical relevance of autonomy as an element of firm-level entrepreneurial behavior. They first investigate autonomy from an EO perspective, exploring the role that autonomy plays in entrepreneurial value creation; second, they provide clarity, both theoretically and empirically, regarding the measurement of firm-level autonomy.

Miles, Morgan P., and Jeffrey G. Covin, "Exploring the Practice of Corporate Venturing: Some Common Forms and Their Organizational Implications," *Entrepreneurship, Theory and Practice* 26 (3), 2002, 21–40.

> *In this article, the authors explore the domain of corporate entrepreneurship using a theoretically grounded classification typology as an organizing scheme. The typology is applied in a field study of corporations that are active in entrepreneurship and based in the United Kingdom or the United States. The authors classify corporate entrepreneurship into four generic forms by the focus of entrepreneurship and the presence of investment intermediation: (1) direct-internal venturing, (2) direct-external venturing, (3) indirect-internal venturing, and (4) indirect-external venturing.*

Chapter 7

Goodale, John C., Donald, F. Kuratko, Jeffrey S. Hornsby, and Jeffrey G. Covin, "Operations Management and Corporate Entrepreneurship: The Moderating Effect of Operations Control on the Antecedents of Corporate Entrepreneurial Activity in Relation to Innovation Performance," *Journal of Operations Management* 29 (2), 2011, 116–127.

> *In this article, the authors investigate the effect on innovation performance of several commonly acknowledged antecedents of corporate entrepreneurship. The moderating effects of operational control variables—specifically risk control and process control formality—on the relationship between the antecedents of corporate entrepreneurship and innovation performance are examined.*

Morris, Michael H., Jeffrey Allen, Minet Schindehutte, and Ramon Avila, "Balanced Management Control Systems as a Mechanism for Achieving Corporate Entrepreneurship," *Journal of Management Issues* 18 (4), 2006, 468–493.

> *In this article, the authors assess the relationship between control and entrepreneurship in established organizations. Insights from the literature on the nature of control are reviewed, and underlying dimensions of a control system are identified.*

Patzelt, Holger, Dean A. Shepherd, David Deeds, and Steven W. Bradley, "Financial Slack and Venture Managers' Decisions to Seek a New Alliance," *Journal of Business Venturing* 23 (4), 2008, 465–481.

> *In this article, the authors examine two distinct perspectives to analyze the role of financial slack in the decisions of technology venture managers to seek strategic alliances. The findings support a combined capabilities perspective and resource dependent perspective demonstrating that managerial discretion in the form of financial slack moderates how internal capabilities and context encourage managers to seek alliances.*

Sykes, Hollister B., and Zenas Block, "Corporate Venturing Obstacles: Sources and Solutions," *Journal of Business Venturing* 4 (3), 1986, 159–167.

> *In this article, the authors examine the rationale for 10 "establishment" practices and the adverse effects they can have on new ventures. From this analysis, alternative "entrepreneurial" management practices are recommended.*

Chapter 8

Covin, Jeffrey G., and Morgan P. Miles, "Strategic Use of Corporate Venturing," *Entrepreneurship Theory and Practice* 31 (2), 2007, 183–207.

> *Based on a review of the corporate venturing (CV) literature and findings from a field study of 15 Swedish, U.K., and U.S. corporations, in this article the authors describe several models that depict the ways in which CV and business strategy coexist as organizational phenomena.*

Ensley, Michael D., Allison Pearson, and Craig L. Pearce, "Top Management Team Process, Shared Leadership, and New Venture Performance: A Theoretical Model and Research Agenda," *Human Resource Management Review* 13 (2), 2003, 329–346.

> *In this article, the authors articulate the process through which new venture performance may be explained. In so doing, they integrate concepts from entrepreneurship, top management teams (TMT), group process, and leadership research and propose an input–process–output model for examining new venture TMT (NVTMT) and new venture performance.*

Liu, Yongmei, Jun Liu, and Wu Longzeng, "Are You Willing and Able? Roles of Motivation, Power, and Politics in Career Growth," *Journal of Management* 36 (6), 2010, 1432–1460.

> Here, the authors test a comprehensive model of political behavior and its influence on career growth. Need for achievement and need for power were found to be positively related to political behavior, and perceptions of organizational politics strengthened the relationship between these personal needs and political behavior.

Chapter 9

Hisrich, Robert D., "The Business Plan," Chapter 16.3, *The Technology Management Handbook*, edited by Richard C. Dorf, Boca Raton: CRC Press, 1998, 16–25.

> This chapter succinctly describes the important aspects of a technology business plan. A detailed business plan outline is presented.

Hisrich, Robert D., Michael P. Peters, and Dean A. Shepherd, *Entrepreneurship*, eighth edition, New York: McGraw-Hill/Irwin, 2010, 186–221.

> All the essentials needed in a general business plan are described, such as the fundamentals of a business plan, scope and value of the business plan, evaluation of the business plan by potential investors, sources of data for the business plan, all the aspects of the business plan, and implementing and measuring the progress of the business plan.

Karlsson, Tomas, and Benson Honig, "Judging a Business by Its Cover: An Institutional Perspective on New Ventures and the Business Plan," *Journal of Business Venturing* 24 (1), 2009, 27–45.

> This article is based on a study of six companies over the last five years using interviews, observations, and archival data. The results indicate that the initial conformity of each company to the business plan gradually led to loose coupling. The business plans initially written were never updated and rarely referred to in the operations of the business venture.

Sellers, David, *Business Plan Project*, New York: Business Expert Press, 2009.

> *This book provides detailed instructions on how to write a comprehensive business plan. The book begins with brainstorming the idea, followed by opportunity analysis, organizational plan, marketing plan, and financial plan. It concludes with an overview of a business plan and its oral presentation.*

Chapter 10

Haas, Martine R., "The Double-Edged Swords of Autonomy and External Knowledge: Analyzing Team Effectiveness in a Multinational Organization," *Academy of Management Journal* 53 (5), 2010, 989–1008.

> *Extending the differentiation-integration view of organizational design to teams, the author proposes that self-managing teams engaged in knowledge-intensive work can perform more effectively by combining autonomy and external knowledge to capture the benefits of each while offsetting their risks.*

Hayton, James C., "Promoting Corporate Entrepreneurship through Human Resource Management Practices: A Review of Empirical Research," *Human Resource Management Review* 15 (1), 2005, 21–41.

> *In this article, the author reviews empirical research linking human resource management (HRM) practices with corporate entrepreneurship (CE). The author identifies two central themes that need to be addressed in seeking an explanation for this important relationship: individual risk acceptance and the encouragement of discretionary entrepreneurial contributions.*

Marvel, Matthew R., Abbie Griffin, John Hebda, and Bruce Vojak, "Examining the Technical Corporate Entrepreneurs' Motivation: Voices from the Field," *Entrepreneurship Theory and Practice* 31 (5), 2007, 753–768.

> *According to this article, previous research has proposed five conditions that support corporate entrepreneurship: rewards, management support, resources including time, organizational structures (at the macro level), and risk acceptance. In this article, the authors investigate the sufficiency of these conditions*

in motivating individual scientists or engineers who have created and commercialized multiple breakthrough innovations in mature corporations—or technical corporate entrepreneurs.

Santaló, Juan, and Carl Joachim Kock, "Division Director versus CEO Compensation: New Insights into the Determinants of Executive Pay," *Journal of Management* 35 (4), 2009, 1047–1077.

In this article, the authors highlight the importance of firm structure for the optimal compensation contracts of upper-management positions. Making use of task similarity between CEOs of undiversified firms and division directors within larger corporations, the authors analyze trade-offs between monitoring and incentive pay at below-CEO levels. Because division directors are subject to an additional layer of monitoring by upper management, they should receive less incentive pay and lower compensation than do CEOs of undiversified firms.

Yuan, Feirong, and Richard W. Woodman, "Innovative Behavior in the Workplace: The Role of Performance and Image Outcome Expectations," *Academy of Management Journal* 53 (2), 2010, 323–342.

The authors, in this article, examine how employees' innovative behavior is explained by expectations for such behavior to affect job performance (expected positive performance outcomes) and image inside their organizations (expected image risks and expected image gains). Significant effects of all three outcome expectations on innovative behavior were found.

Chapter 11

Buono, Anthony F., "Designing Matrix Organizations That Actually Work: How IBM, Procter & Gamble, and Others Design for Success," *Personnel Psychology*, October 1, 2009, http://www.allbusiness.com/company–activities–management/operations–quality–control/13120141–1.html.

This article underscores the need to implement a matrixlike structure to be successful in today's complex business environment. Problems found in this type of organization are explained by poor management decisions.

Guttman, Howard M., "Paradox of Risk," *Executive Excellence*, August 1, 2009, 13.

It is difficult to build a vibrant and successful organization on fear. Market opportunities will not be recognized and exploited when too much risk aversion is present. A leader is required, someone who can encourage people to look at the status quo, confront the outstanding issues, and take charge.

Staff reporter, "Expert Reveals Keys to Success," *Plus News Pakistan*, September 16, 2009.

This article explains Malcolm Gladwell's view regarding successful organizations. According to Gladwell, "Persistence, experimentation, collaboration, and the patience to nurture creativity are the keys to creating a successful organization." Success comes after hard work, preparation, experimentation, collaboration, and patience.

Chapter 12

Buckland, William, "Defining What Corporate Venturing Actually Is and What Firms Should Do about It," *Strategic Direction* 19 (9), September 2003, ABI/INFORM Global, ProQuest Web, September 30, 2010.

This article presents an overview of corporate entrepreneurship by describing the process and elements involved. It indicates how firms should be engaged in the process.

Campbell, Andrew, Julian Bradshaw, Andy Morrison, and Robert van Basten Batenburg, "The Future of Corporate Venturing," *MIT Sloan Management Review* 45 (1), 2003, 30, ABI/INFORM Global, ProQuest Web, September 30, 2010.

The focus of this article is the present stage and future direction of corporate entrepreneurship. Various phases of the activities and what lies ahead are explored.

Covin, Jeffrey G., and Morgan P. Miles, "Strategic Use of Corporate Venturing," *Entrepreneurship: Theory & Practice*, March 2007, 183–207, ABI/INFORM Global, ProQuest Web, 30 September 2010.

This article presents a discussion of the many uses of corporate entrepreneurship and its strategic implications. Research is cited that builds a foundation for its past and present use to further develop an organization.

Garud, Raghu, and Andrew H. Van de Ven, "An Empirical Evaluation of the Internal Corporate Venturing Process," *Strategic Management Journal*, Summer 1992, 93, ABI/INFORM Global, ProQuest Web, September 30, 2010.

The focus of this article is on the outcomes of the corporate entrepreneurship process. Both positive and negative outcomes are discussed based on industry examples.

Index

Ability, in creative process, 38
Accuracy, control system, 166
Acid test ratio, 272–273
Activity ratios, 273–274
Adams, Robert V., 67
Adobe, 142
Advertising, as promotion, 226
Alcatel-Lucent, 49
Alignment with company, new
    venture, 266
Alliances, political tactics, 196
Amazon, 169, 170, 198
American Express, 37, 119–122, 297
American Greetings Corporation,
    159–162, 221
American Research and Development
    Corporation (ARD), 263
Announcement of program,
    evaluation, 298
Apple Inc., 180–181, 207–210
Arm & Hammer, 149
AT&T, 77, 170, 172
Attitude, 46, 47–48
Attribute listing, 82
Autonomy, degree of, 150–153
Average collection period, 273

Bank of America, 198
Barnes & Noble, 170
Barrier-free philosophy, 150
Behavior, 31–55, 183–203
  corporate entrepreneur, 45–54
  creativity, 38–45
  entrepreneurial culture, defined, 52
  individual entrepreneur:
    creativity, 39–40
    need-achievement (nACH), 46–47
    organizational support for, 34–36
    personality attributes, 39–40,
      46–49
  innovation:
    as key element, 36–38

    organizational barriers to, 43–45
    organizational facilitation of,
      42–43, 49
    process of, 40–42
    internal political (*see* Political
      behavior, internal)
    personality attributes, 39–40,
      46–49
    risk management, 200
    risk taking, 17, 39, 46–49, 72
    scenario:
      Bord na Móna, 183–186
      Ericsson, 31–34
    talent shortage as organizational
      barrier, 123–124
Benchmarking, results evaluation,
    302–303
Benefits of corporate entrepreneurship
    program, 299–302
Bezos, Jeff, 41
Big-dream approach, 82
BMW, 115
Bonus, as compensation, 249
Bord na Móna, 183–186
Borden, 216
Boston Consulting Group, 73
Brainstorming, 40, 79, 95–96
Brainwriting, 40
Brand name, 218–219
Branson, Richard, 11, 46
Break-even analysis, 175–176
Breakthrough innovation, 37, 74, 75
Brin, Sergey, 57
Buchheit, Paul, 58–59
Budgetary control, 174–175
Bureaucracy, control systems, 168
Business plan, 207–229
  corporate, 212–229
  in entrepreneurial process, 22,
    62, 64
  importance of, 211
  scenario: Apple Inc., 207–210

Business plan (*continued*):
scope and value, 212
and types of entrepreneurships, 19–21
vs. opportunity analysis, 100
Business Times (magazine), 98
Business venturing, 68–69
Business-to-business (B2B) market,
222, 223, 224
Business-to-consumer (B2C) market,
222, 223
Business-to-government (B2G) market,
222, 223
Butterworth, Kenneth W., 5

Capital, venture, 262–266
Career advancement, as compensation,
249–250
Carnegie, Andrew, 9
Category brand name, 216–217
CEO, new venture design, 144–146
Champion, venture, 130–131, 141,
267
Change, as corporate entrepreneurship
aspect, 73, 83–86
Character, and types of
entrepreneurships, 17
Checklist method, 80–81
Chevron Corporation, 240
Chrysler Corporation, 152
Cisco Systems, 240, 245
Clean energy trends, 97
Climate indicators, program
development, 131–133
Coalition of supporters, leadership
characteristics, 124, 126
Coca-Cola, 218
Code Jam, 59–60
Collective notebook method, 81–82
Commitment of resources, managerial
vs. corporate entrepreneurship,
65–66
Commitment to opportunity,
managerial *vs.* corporate
entrepreneurship, 65–66
Committee for program evaluation,
296, 298

Commodity products conversion to
specialty products, 214–216
Communication, Web trends, 99
Company:
innovative strategies, 113–115
opportunity indicators, 112–113
(*See also specific corporate topics
and specific companies*)
Compensation, 126–127, 145
Competition:
competitive threat, program proposal
evaluation, 130, 131
competitiveness, 7
internal company indicators, 112
opportunity analysis, 100, 103
Computer industry trade shows, 112
Concept stage, opportunity evaluation
criteria, 105
Concurrent control, 173
Consumers, as new idea sources, 93
Container Corporation of America,
220
Control and control systems, 159–181
bureaucracy *vs.* corporate
entrepreneurship, 168
characteristics of effective, 166–168
control philosophy, 168–170
core management, 173–174
effective systems, 163
financial controls, 174–181
forms of control, 165
for innovation and creativity,
170–172
management control system, 164
measures and strategies, 165–166
methods of control, 174–179
nature of, 163–164
nonfinancial controls, 176–181
organizational control focus,
172–173
organizing corporate
entrepreneurship, 26
philosophy of, 168–170
political behavior, 197–201
of resources, managerial *vs.*
corporate entrepreneurship, 66

scenario: American Greetings
Corporation, 159–162
team evaluation, 245–247
Control and power, political behavior,
197–201
Cooperation, techniques for obtaining,
193
Core ideology and shared goals,
venture organization, 142–144
Core management control systems,
173–174
Core ventures model, 285–286
Corporate business plan, 212–229
corporate fit, 221
executive summary, 213–214
list of elements, 213
market analysis, 221–224
market segmentation, 222–224
marketing plan, 224–227
plan for further action, 228–229
product/service analysis, 214–221
profitability, 227–228
Corporate culture:
challenge of, 140–141
corporate entrepreneurship, 70–71,
140–142, 153–157
defined, 140
effective activities, 155–157
important features of, 141–142
influence on behavior, 35–36
managerial *vs.* corporate
entrepreneurship, 69–70
managing the entrepreneurship
process, 69–72
promoting entrepreneurial activity,
50–51
summary, 157
team development, 153–155
traditional *vs.* entrepreneurship,
69–71
Corporate entrepreneurial
environments, 75–76
Corporate entrepreneurs:
behavior, 31–55, 183–203
compensation and incentive
systems, 247–254

competencies for, 53, 54
entrepreneurial activities, 68–69
identification, evaluation and
selection, 231–255
need-achievement (nACH), 46–47
organizational support for, 34–36
personality attributes, 46–49
survival guidelines, 243
team leadership methods, 245
vs. managers, 14–15, 18
(*See also specific topics*)
Corporate entrepreneurship:
aspects of, 73–86
change, 73, 83–86
creativity, 73, 78–83
innovation, 73–75
ownership, 73, 75–78
corporate culture, 70–71
defined, 12–13, 67
entrepreneurial process, 20
framework for, 24–28
leadership characteristics, 124–127
managing (*see* Management of
corporate entrepreneurship)
operationalizing (*see* Operationalizing
corporate entrepreneurship)
organizing (*see* Organizing
corporate entrepreneurship)
vs. private and social
entrepreneurship, 12–13,
15–18
Corporate fit, business plan, 213, 221
Corporate venturing, 45, 284–285
(*See also* Corporate entrepreneurship)
Cost estimates, new venture, 267–268
Coyne, Bill, 288
Creativity:
behavioral aspects of corporate
entrepreneurship, 38–45
control systems, 170–172
as corporate entrepreneurship
aspect, 73, 78–83
inhibition, and ownership, 75–76
and innovation, 37–38
organizational barriers to, 43–45
organizational facilitation of, 42–43

Creativity (*continued*):
  problem-solving techniques, 78–83
  process of, 38–40
  techniques, 40
Culture (*see* Corporate culture)
Current ratio, 272

Data collection, 109–111, 166
DCA Food Industries Inc., 247
Debt ratio, 274
Debt-to-equity ratio, 274–275
Decision making, management,
    64–66, 72
Degree of autonomy, venture
    organization, 150–153
Dell (computer company), 140, 169,
    198
Dell, Michael, 11, 41, 46
Design of new corporate venture,
    144–146
Distribution mix, marketing plan,
    224–226
Dow Chemical, 265–266
Drive, in creative process, 38
Drucker, Peter, 41
DuPont, 24, 49, 51, 169, 180

Economic trends, 98
Economist view of entrepreneurship,
    11
Ecosystem venturing model, 284
Edison, Thomas, 9
Employees:
  control system acceptance, 166
  corporate entrepreneurship benefits
    to, 301–302
Entrepreneurial culture, 52
  (*See also* Corporate culture)
Entrepreneurial domain, managerial
    vs. corporate entrepreneurship,
    65
Entrepreneurial process, 15–21
  business plan development, 22, 62,
    64
  corporate context, 20
  defined, 11

private context, 19
social context, 21
Entrepreneurs (individual):
  creativity, 39–40
  need-achievement (nACH), 46–47
  organizational support for, 34–36
  personality attributes, 39–40, 46–49
  risk taking, 39
  (*See also* Corporate entrepreneurs)
Entrepreneurship, 3–29
  business plan development, 19–21,
    22
  corporate context, 12–13, 15–18,
    24–28
  defined, 8, 11
  entrepreneurial process, 15–21
  framework for corporate context,
    24–28
  opportunity identification,
    evaluation, and selection,
    18–22
  private, 8–17
  process management, 57–87
    change, 73, 83–86
    corporate aspects, 73–86
    corporate culture, 69–72
    creativity, 73, 78–83
    decision making, 64–66
    elements of process, 61–64
    innovation, 73–75
    interest in, 66–69
    managerial *vs.* corporate
      entrepreneurship, 64–66,
      69–72
    ownership, 73, 75–78
  resource requirements, 12, 19–21
  scenario:
    Google and Google Ventures,
      57–61
    Loctite Corporation, 3–7
  social, 13–18, 21
  starting and managing the
    enterprise, 19–21, 23
Environment, corporate culture, 141
Environmental understanding,
    leadership, 124

Equity in business, as compensation, 249
Ericsson, 31–34
Ericsson, Lars Magnus, 31
Estridge, Philip, 49
Evaluation criteria:
  for corporate venture design, 145
  for ideas, 99–102
  for opportunity, 102–107
  program, 295–299
  program proposals, 129–131
Executive management (*see* Top management)
Executive summary, business plan, 213–214
Existing products and services, as new idea source, 93–94
Expense estimates, new venture, 269
Experimentation and ownership, 75

Failure, traditional *vs.* corporate entrepreneur managers, 72
Family history, traditional *vs.* corporate entrepreneur managers, 72
Fast Company (magazine), 13
Feasibility, new venture, 266–267
Federal government as new idea source, 94
Feed forward control, 173
Feedback control, 173
Financial controls, 174–181
  audits, 177–178
  break-even analysis, 175–176
  budgetary control, 174–175
  goals and objectives, 179–181
  ratio analysis, 176
Financial ratio analysis, 271–276
  activity ratios, 273–274
  funding the venture, 271–276
  leverage ratios, 274–275
  liquidity ratios, 271–273
  profitability ratios, 275–276
Financing needs, 261–262
Flexibility:
  of control system, 167
  leadership characteristics, 124–125

Focus, and types of entrepreneurships, 16
Focus groups, 40, 95
Ford Motor Co., 198, 240, 297
Foreign market selection, 107, 109–112
Framework for corporate entrepreneurship, 24–28
Free association, 81
Frontiers of technology, 75
Fry, Art, 44, 89–92
Funding the venture, 257–277
  evaluation process, 266–270
  financial ratio analysis, 271–276
  financing need, 261–262
  nonfinancial factors, 276
  scenario: Unilever, 257–261
  valuation, 270–271
  venture capital industry, 262–265
  venture capital units within companies, 264, 265–266

Gantt charts, 177
Gates, Bill, 11, 46
Genentech, 129, 240
General Electric, 37, 48, 49, 51, 143, 146–147, 169, 234, 265, 297
General Foods, 96, 214
General Mills, 239
General Motors, 180, 198
Generating ideas, 95–96
Genesis Grants, 3M, 90, 114, 288
Gifts, games and hobbies sector trade shows, 112
Ginsberg, Ari, 12–13
Globus, 180
Gmail, 58–59
Goals and objectives:
  financial controls, 179–181
  political strategy, 194
  shared in venture organization, 142–144
  and types of entrepreneurships, 16
Goldman Sachs, 190
Google, 57–61, 67, 198, 265, 293–295

Google Ventures, 57–61, 67
Grameen Bank, 289–291
Green trends, 97
Griffing, Bruce, 48
Gross margin, 130, 131
Guth, William, 12–13

Harriman, Edward, 10
Harvest venturing model, 284
Hasina, Sheikh, 291
HB Associates, 110
Health trends, 99
Henkel, Fritz, 3, 6
Hewlett-Packard (HP), 12, 37, 49,
    51, 140, 143, 144, 172, 249
Hillenbrand Industries, 94–95
Historical view of entrepreneurship,
    8–10
House, Charles, 49

IBM, 12, 37, 51, 140, 169, 170, 198
ICU Global, 111
ICV (internal corporate venturing)
    model, 286–287
Ideas:
  evaluating, 99–102
  innovative company strategies,
    113–115
  methods for generating, 95–96
  opportunity evaluation stage,
    104–105, 106–107, 108
  sources of new, 93–95
Identity stage, creative process, 38
Idestam, Fredrik, 232
IKEA, 98, 171, 180
Implementing in your organization,
    279–304
  benefits of program, 299–301
  benefits to employees, 301–302
  creative process, 39
  evaluation of program, 295–299
  models, 283–287
  results evaluation, 302–304
  scenarios:
    Google, 293–295
    Grameen Bank, 289–291

Johnson & Johnson, 279–283
3M, 287–289
Xerox, 291–293
Incentive systems, 247–254
Incremental innovation, 37, 74, 75
Incubation stage, creative process,
    39
Indermil adhesive, 6
Indicators:
  choice of, and market selection,
    109
  of climate, program development,
    131–133
  internal company, 112–113
  weighting, and market selection,
    111
Individual entrepreneur:
  creativity, 39–40
  need-achievement (nACH), 46–47
  organizational support for, 34–36
  personality attributes, 39–40,
    46–49
  risk taking, 39
  (*See also* Corporate entrepreneurs)
Industry experience, program
    proposal evaluation, 130–131
Infosys Technologies Ltd., 114–115
Initial investment, program proposal
    evaluation, 130
Innovation:
  behavioral aspects of corporate
    entrepreneurship, 36–38,
    40–45, 49
  company strategies and ideas,
    113–115
  control systems, 170–172
  corporate culture, 141
  as corporate entrepreneurship
    aspect, 73–75
  as entrepreneurial behavior, 45–53
  as key element, 36–38
  organizational barriers to, 43–45
  organizational facilitation of,
    42–43, 49
  process of, 40–42
  and types of entrepreneurships, 17

Innovation venturing model, 284
Innovator, entrepreneurs as, 9–10
Intel, 142, 198, 199, 239, 265
Internal company indicators,
    opportunity identification,
    112–113
Internal corporate venturing (ICV)
    model, 286–287
Internal politics (*see* Political
    behavior, internal)
International market selection, 107,
    109–112
International reports, 110
Invacare, 133
Inventory control, 178
Inventory turnover, 273–274
iPods and iTunes, 208–210

Janitor in a Drum, 216
Jobs, Steve, 11, 46, 207, 208, 209
Johnson & Johnson, 144, 279–283

Kanter, Rosabeth Moss, 41–42
Kao Corporation, 148
Kelleher, Herb, 41
Key stakeholders, stinging, 189–190
Khatun, Sufia, 289
Kleenex, 217
Knowledge, in creative process, 38
Kodak, 217
Kotter, John P., 83
Kotter's approach to organizational
    transformation, 83–86
Krieble, Robert, 5

Law, John, 9
Leaders and leadership:
    characteristics of, 124–127,
    242–243
    political behavior, 200
    selection of, 234–241
Leads and past sales, 112
Legitimacy and political behavior,
    191–192
Leverage ratios, 274–275
LG-Ericsson, 33–34

Life cycle of venture, 244–245
LIOCC, 73
Liquidity ratios, 271–273
Loctite Corporation, 3–7
Logo, 217
Longevity Alliance, 98
Long-term orientation in corporate
    culture, 141
Lucent Technologies, 24, 49, 51, 140,
    142, 169, 172

Management:
    audits, as nonfinancial control,
    177–178
    control systems, 164
    of corporate entrepreneurship:
        behavioral aspects, 31–55
        entrepreneurship, 3–29
        entrepreneurship process, 57–87
        key elements in framework,
        25–27
        opportunity identification,
        evaluation, and selection,
        18–22, 89–116
    leadership characteristics, 129–131
    managing entrepreneurship process,
        64–66, 69–72
    opportunity analysis, 101
    political behavior, 187
    structure of, 66
    style of, 71–72
    (*See also* Top management)
Managers *vs.* entrepreneurs, 14–15,
    18
Manufacturer's brand, 216
Marco Polo, 8
Market analysis, 213, 221–224
Market availability, new venture, 267
Market opportunity evaluation,
    102–104
Market segmentation, 213, 222–224
Market selection model, 107,
    109–110
Marketing plan, 213, 224–227
Markkula, Mike, 207
McClelland, David, 46–47

McKenzie, Stephen, 111
McKinsey & Company, 143
McKnight, William L., 180
Measurement, corporate venture
    design, 145
    (*See also* Control and control
    systems)
Medtronic, 266
Merck, 143, 144, 297
Microsoft, 37, 45, 51, 140, 197, 249,
    265
Mill, John Stuart, 9
Miller Brewing, 215, 218
Mission statements, 297
Mistakes, 72, 141
Mixon, A. Malachi III, 133
Mobile apps, 99
Models for corporate entrepreneurship
    implementation, 283–287
Morgan, John Pierpont, 10
Morris, Michael H., 171
Morton salt, 215–216, 217, 219–220
Motivation, 39–40, 200
Motorola, 49, 144, 265
Mulcahy, Anne, 292
Multidisciplined team approach, 77
Murthy, N. R. Narayana, 114–115

National Trade Data Bank (NTDB),
    110
Nature of large organizations,
    as barrier, 123
Need-achievement (nACH), 46–47
Net profit margin, 275–276
Networks, political, 196, 201
New ideas, sources of, 93–95
New Venture Group (NVG), 142
New ventures:
    considerations, 266–269
    design of corporate, 144–146
    (*See also* Venture identification)
Nielson, Pete, 12
Nike, 143
Nokia, 24, 37, 49, 51, 113, 140,
    169, 180, 198, 231–234,
    247

Nonfinancial controls, 176–181
    inventory control, 178
    management audits, 177–178
    production control, 178
    project controls, 177
    quality control, 178–179
Nordstrom, 297
Norms, traditional *vs.* entrepreneurship
    corporate culture, 70
NTDB (National Trade Data Bank),
    110
NVG (New Venture Group), 142

O'Brien, William, 12
Obstacles, political behavior,
    190–193, 195
Official Gazette (USPTO), 94
Omidyar, Pierre, 41
Open discussion, leadership, 124,
    126
Operationalizing corporate
    entrepreneurship:
    business plan, 207–229
    entrepreneur identification,
        evaluation, and selection,
        231–255
    in framework diagram, 26
    funding the venture, 257–277
    implementing in your organization,
        279–304
    key elements in framework, 25,
        27–28
Opportunity:
    analysis of, 99–102
    assessment plan, 63
    commitment to, 65
    desire and motivation, 50–51, 53
    facilitation of, 50, 53
Opportunity identification,
    evaluation, and selection,
    89–116
    in entrepreneurial process,
        18–22
    evaluation criteria, 102–107
    foreign market selection, 107,
        109–111

ideas:
    evaluating, 99–102
    innovative company strategies,
        113–115
    methods for generating, 95–96
    sources of new, 93–95
    internal company indicators,
        112–113
    opportunity analysis, 99–102
    product planning and development
        process, 102
    scenario: 3M Post-it Notes, 89–92
    trends, 97–99
Ordinary innovation, 37, 74, 75
Organic orientation trends, 98
Organizational barriers, 43–45,
    123–127
Organizational competencies,
    entrepreneurial development,
    53, 54
Organizational facilitation, 42–43, 49
Organizational fit, 130
Organizational innovativeness, 68–69
Organizational structure (*see*
    Structure)
Organizational transformation,
    Kotter's approach to, 83–86
Organizing corporate entrepreneurship:
    control systems, 159–181
    in framework, 25, 26, 28
    internal politics, 183–203
    venture identification, 119–133
    venture organization, 135–158
Output measurement, 303–304
Ownership, as corporate
    entrepreneurship aspect, 73,
    75–78

Pacing Plus, 3M, 288
Packaging, 219–221
Page, Larry, 57
Palo Alto Research Center (PARC),
    292–293
Parameter analysis, 82–83
PARC (Palo Alto Research Center),
    292–293

Past sales and leads, 112
Patents, 217
Pepsi, 218
Permatex, 4–5
Persistence, leadership, 124, 126
Personal selling, as promotion, 226
Personality attributes, 39–40, 46–49
PERT (Program Evaluation Review
    Technique), 177
PharmaKodex, 260
Pillars, 3M seven core, 90–91
Pixazza, Inc., 60
Planning:
    corporate venture design, 145
    for further action, 213, 228–229
    product planning and development
        process, 102
    (*See also* Business plan)
Political behavior, internal, 183–203
    described, 189
    management, 187
    obstacles, 190–193, 195
    positive and negative consequences,
        189, 190
    power and control, 197–201
    resistance, 193, 194
    resource requirements, 192
    scenario: Bord na Móna, 183–186
    stinging, 189–190
    strategy, 193–196
    tactics and influence, 196, 201–202
    techniques for obtaining coopera-
        tion, 193
Post-it Notes, 89–92
Potential option identification,
    creative process, 39
Power and control, political behavior,
    197–201
Price mix, marketing plan, 224–226
Private entrepreneurship, 8–17
Private equity venturing model, 284
Pro forma income statement, 227–228
Proactiveness, 46, 69
Problem inventory analysis, 40, 96
Problem-solving techniques, creativity,
    78–83

Process (*see* Entrepreneurial process)
Process management (*see* Entrepreneurship process management)
Procter & Gamble, 144, 220, 265, 297
Product development stage, opportunity evaluation, 105–106
Product differentiation, 100
Product life cycle, 102
Product planning and development process, 102
Production control, 178
Product/service analysis, 213, 214–221
Product/service mix, marketing plan, 224–226
Profit potential, new venture, 269
Profitability, corporate business plan, 213, 227–228
Profitability ratios, 275–276
Program development, 128–133
climate indicators, 131–133
evaluation, 295–299
proposal evaluation, 129–131
Program Evaluation Review Technique (PERT), 177
Project controls, 177
Promotion mix, marketing plan, 224–226
Proposals, evaluation, 129–131, 298
Proprietary technology, 130, 131
Publicity, as promotion, 226

Quad Mark, 67
Quaker Oats, 214
Quality control, 178–179

Railroads, 10
Rate of return, evaluation criteria, 130, 131
Ratio analysis, 176
Raychem, 24
Readings, suggested, 309–324

Recognition, as compensation, 250
Recruitment, corporate venture design, 145
Relatedness, venture organization, 150–153
Relationships, traditional *vs.* corporate entrepreneur managers, 72
Research and development, for new ideas, 94–95
Resistance, political behavior, 193, 194
Resources:
accessibility of, 77, 141
commitment of, 65–66
control of, 66
control systems, 171–172
in entrepreneurial process, 12, 23, 62, 64
political behavior, 192, 201
and types of entrepreneurships, 19–21
Results communication evaluation, 299
Results evaluation, implementation, 302–304
Return on investment, 73–74, 103–104, 276
Revenue estimates, new venture, 267–268
Reverse brainstorming, 79–80
Reward system, 78, 126–127, 141, 145, 250
Risk management, 200
Risk taking, 17, 39, 46–49, 72
Roberts, Alan, 5
Roddick, Anita, 11

Salary increases, as compensation, 249
Sapirstein, Jacob, 159
Schulmeyer, Gerhard, 49
Schweppes Tonic Water, 216
Scope of business plan, 212
Sears, 198, 216–217

Selection of best option, creative
    process, 39
Self-renewal, 69
Senior management (*see* Top
    management)
Seven core pillars, 3M, 90–91
Sharp Corporation, 140
Short-run objective accomplishment,
    123
Siemens, 135–139
Siemens, Werner von, 135
Siemens Nixdorf, 24, 49, 137
Silver, Spencer, 91–92
Silver Spring Networks, 60
Skills, and types of entrepreneurships,
    17
Skunkworks, 77
Smith, Adam, 83
Smithfield Hams, 217
Social and social media trends, 98
Social entrepreneurship, 13–18, 21
Social media, as promotion, 226
Sony Corporation, 143, 144
Sony Ericsson, 33
Southwest Airlines, 113
Spirit of entrepreneurship, 78
Starbucks, 114
Starlight Telecommunications, 12
Starting the enterprise, 19–21, 23,
    62, 64
Status, traditional *vs.* corporate
    entrepreneur managers, 72
Stemmle, Dennis, 67
Stewart, Martha, 46
Stinging, political behavior, 189–190
Strategic orientation, managerial *vs.*
    corporate entrepreneurship, 65
Structure:
    managerial, 66
    organizational:
        corporate venture design, 145
        influence on corporate culture and
            behavior, 35–36
        promoting entrepreneurial activity,
            50–51

venture identification, 127–128
venture organization, 146–150
Suggested readings, 309–324
Sun Microsystems, 142
Super Glue, 4–7
Supply chain system, for new ideas, 94
Support, 124, 126, 141, 157
Survival guidelines, 243
Synergy with existing product line,
    opportunity evaluation, 103

Tactics and influence, political behavior,
    196, 201–202
Team:
    development of, 153–155
    evaluation of, 245–247
    leadership methods, 245
    roles of, 241
    selection of, 234–241, 244–245
    venture team formation evaluation,
        298–299
Teamwork, 124, 125, 141, 196
Techniques for obtaining cooperation,
    193
Technology:
    frontiers of, 75
    innovation, 37, 74, 75
    new venture feasibility, 266–267
    proprietary, 130, 131
    trends, opportunity identification,
        97–99
Tektronix, 247
Telecare Corporation, 144
Telecommunications (scenario),
    31–34
Test marketing stage, 107
Theory of Moral Sentiments (Smith),
    83
Thermo Electron Corporation,
    12, 24
3M, 12, 24, 37, 44, 45, 49, 51, 77,
    89–92, 114, 140, 143, 144,
    169, 172, 180, 198, 247, 265,
    287–289, 297
Time orientation, 72, 77

Timeline, opportunity analysis, 101–102
Timeliness of control system, 167
Top management:
 corporate culture, 141
 as entrepreneurial champions, 78
 need to support entrepreneurial activity, 35
 stinging, 189–190
Toshiba, 49, 51, 249
Total Quality Management (TQM), 178
Toyota Motor Corporation, 115, 249
Trade associations, 110–111
Trade shows, 112–113
Training and development, corporate venture design, 145
Transformation through strategic renewal, 13
Trends, opportunity identification, 97–99
Trial-and-error learning model, 285

Uncertainty, political behavior, 200
Unilever, 257–261, 265
Unilever Technology Ventures (UTV), 258–259
Unilever Ventures (UV), 259–260
Unique selling proposition, 100, 214–216
United Airlines, 240
United Parcel Service, 239
U.S. Department of Commerce, 110
U.S. Freedom of Information Act, 109
U.S. Patent and Trademark Office, 94

Valuation, funding the venture, 270–271
Value of business plan, 212
Values, traditional *vs.* entrepreneurship corporate culture, 70–71
Venture capital, 262–266
Venture champion, 130–131, 141, 267

Venture identification, 119–133
 climate indicators, 131–133
 evaluation criteria, 129–131
 organizational barriers, 123–127
 organizational structures for, 127–128
 program development, 128–133
 scenario: American Express, 119–122
Venture life cycle, 244–245
Venture organization, 135–158
 core ideology and shared goals, 142–144
 corporate culture, 140–142, 153–157
 design of new corporate venture, 144–146
 organizational structure, 146–150
 relatedness and degree of autonomy, 150–153
 scenario: Siemens, 135–139
 supporting systems, 157
 team development, 153–155
Venture team formation evaluation, 298–299
Vibrant Brains, 99
Vision statement, 295–296
Visionary leadership, 124–125
Volunteering, 78
von Siemens, Werner, 135

Wages and compensation, 126–127, 145
Walmart, 180, 239, 297
Walt Disney Company, 143, 144
Warner-Lambert, 216
Wayne, Ron, 207
Wealth creation, 11
Web communication trends, 99
Welch, Jack, 143, 146, 234
Whitman, Meg, 46
Whitney, Eli, 9
Whole Foods Market, 180
Wickstrom, Arvid, 232
Window of opportunity, 63
Wonder Bread, 215
Wozniak, Steve, 207

Xerox, 12, 67–68, 77, 142, 198, 221, 239, 240, 249, 291–293
Xeta Technology, 125
XTV (Xerox Technology Ventures), 67–68

Yahoo!, 240
Yunus, Muhammad, 289–291

Zennstrom, Niklas, 41
Zuckerberg, Mark, 41, 46

About the Authors

Robert D. Hisrich, Ph.D., is the Garvin Professor of Global Entrepreneurship and director of the Walker Center for Global Entrepreneurship at Thunderbird School of Global Management. He has authored or coauthored 26 books and more than 350 articles on entrepreneurship.

Claudine Kearney, Ph.D., is a visiting researcher in entrepreneurship at Thunderbird School of Global Management. She has extensive lecturing and research experience and has published numerous articles and book chapters on aspects of entrepreneurship, corporate entrepreneurship, and public-sector entrepreneurship.